The Mysteries of Miracles

HOW UNBELIEVABLE EVENTS SHAPE OUR LIVES

8
20
70
88
134
144
166
184
202

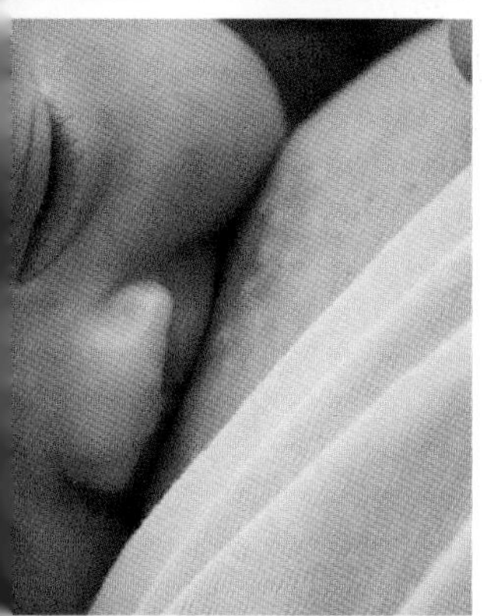

CONTENTS

Eighty percent of Americans believe in the miraculous and the afterlife.

introduction

In the human experience, miracles occupy the space beyond what we can easily explain. They are where our humanity lives, where we acknowledge the presence of something more powerful than any single man, woman, or child. They defy odds. They are an enduring source of inspiration. They guide faith, and bring hope.

In *The Mysteries of Miracles*, Time-Life editors seek to harness that spirit. Here we explore the powerful role the miraculous has played from pre-Biblical times, and how the inexplicable can bring joy into our daily lives.

This is not a book of definitive answers, but a testament to possibility that will resonate with believers and skeptics alike. The pages underscore astrophysicist Carl Sagan's observation that "The notion that science and spirituality are somehow mutually exclusive does a disservice to both."

We begin with the biggest miracle of all, the creation of man as recounted in the Bible, and revisit Old Testament and New Testament stories that have provided comfort for centuries. There are miracles essential to the world's major religions, such as Moses and the burning bush and Daniel surviving the lion's den; Jesus's birth and resurrection; Mohammed's encounter with the Angel Jibril; Buddha's transformation into fire and water.

We weave science into the picture as well, asking what role geology or meteorology or psychiatry might have played in these famous episodes. Did the burning bush grow above a volcanic vent that spewed flames? Did the Sea of Galilee freeze over in one night, creating the impression that Jesus could walk across water? Who can say for sure?

Miracles, of course, continue to awe in modern times—some religious, some medical, some feats of survival. Here uncovered are truly inspiring—and puzzling—events. We explore the recurring visions of the Virgin Mary around the world. We return to the stories of the German teen who fell 10,000 feet from an airplane over the Andes and survived, and the terminally-ill newborn whose leukemia disappeared after his parents brought him home to die. We marvel at the nun whose Parkinson's disease vanished after she prayed to Pope John Paul II. There are even tales of miracle animals—dogs who have saved human life by sniffing out cancer, a beluga whale that rescued a foundering diver, an elephant who carried an eight-year-old to safety during a tsunami.

In the pages of *The Mysteries of Miracles*, it is clear why 80 percent of Americans believe in the miraculous and the afterlife. Evidence of their existence, of individual strength, fortitude, reliance, and courage surrounds us every day.

Now, come ask questions and explore. Embrace the mysteries of life.

section 1

Miracles of Faith

The archangel Gabriel, detail from *The Annunciation*.
Flemish art (c. 16th century)

AVEGRA
APLENA

The Fall of Man (detail), by Hugo van der Goes (c. 1480)

CHAPTER 1

Foundational Miracles

According to scripture, these extraordinary moments in Judaism, Christianity, and Islam form the basis of everything that has happened since.

The Creation of Adam, by Michelangelo, on the ceiling of the Sistine Chapel (c. 1511)

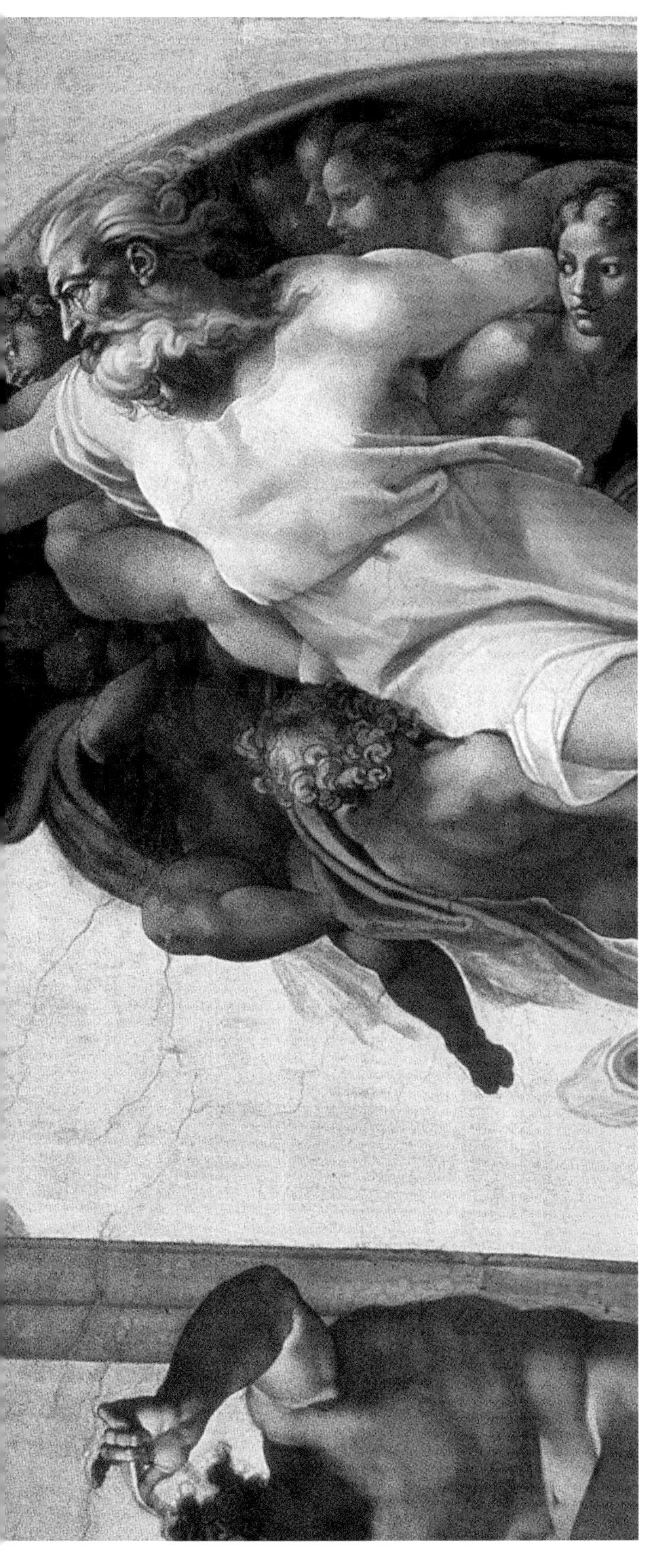

The Wonder That Began It All

THE CREATION OF THE HEAVENS, EARTH, AND HUMANKIND IS THE BASIS FOR EVERY OTHER MIRACULOUS OCCURRENCE IN THE TORAH AND BIBLE.

It starts with nothing. There is darkness and a vast, watery void. And then, with a word from God, there is light. Within six days, God turns nothing into everything: sky, earth, and oceans; fish, birds, and animals; and, on the final day, Adam and Eve, the two all-too-human beings who, according to this ancient text, become the parents of us all.

Whether or not you adhere to a literal interpretation of Genesis, there's no denying the power of its creation story. This miracle is the basis of Judaism as well as Christianity, addressing not just how we got here but also the fact that we're disobedient and imperfect. By extension, it

The Earthly Paradise and the Fall of Adam and Eve, by Jan Brueghel and Peter Paul Rubens (c. 1615)

WHO KNEW?
According to a 2013 Pew Research Center survey, 60 percent of American adults accept evolution; about a third of those believe a supreme being guided the process.

ONE MIRACLE, TWO VERSIONS

Did Adam have more than one wife?

Religious scholars have long pondered two apparently conflicting, almost back-to-back accounts of creation, in the first and second chapters of Genesis. To reconcile the two stories, some traditions suggest that Adam had two wives. The first, Lilith, is not mentioned in Genesis and may be based on ancient Sumerian myths; her story gained popularity in the medieval era. The second is, of course, Eve.

	LILITH	EVE
Torah verse	"So God created humankind in his image, in the image of God he created them; male and female he created them." Genesis 1:27	"And the rib that the Lord God had taken from the man he made into a woman and brought her to the man." Genesis 2:22
Equals?	Yes; she is created at the same time as Adam.	No; she comes second.
Personality	Seductive, willful	Capricious, curious
Conflict	Since she and Adam are equals, she refuses to be subservient to him; the two don't get along.	Desiring wisdom, she gives in to the serpent's temptation.
Misdeed	She flies out of Eden and refuses to return. She becomes known as a demon who harms babies.	She eats fruit from the Tree of Knowledge and gives some to Adam, leading to their expulsion from Eden.

informs much of Western philosophy, art, and literature.

In the opening passages of Genesis, God creates a man from the dust of the Earth. As he blows into the man's nostrils, the man comes alive. The breath is in itself a remarkable image: the Hebrew word *ruach* can also mean life, spirit, or soul; and some scholars interpret this moment as God infusing man with his own eternal essence. The breath of God distinguishes humans from all other creatures as the only ones to whom God has given this gift.

A Fitting Helper

But breath isn't the only thing God bestows on Adam in Genesis. He also creates a garden for him. In the center are two trees: the Tree of Life and the Tree of Knowledge. Adam is instructed never to touch the Tree of Knowledge, but why would he want to? The Garden has everything he could possibly require: food and water, gold and lapis lazuli, and every kind of animal and plant.

Near the end of his intense burst of creativity, God realizes there is something missing. Although he has created a multitude of creatures to keep Adam company, none of them is a "fitting helper." So he puts Adam to sleep and uses one of his ribs to create a new being. He brings her to Adam, who says:

> This one at last
> Is bone of my bones
> And flesh of my flesh;
> This one shall be called Woman,
> For out of Man this one was taken.

The end of the story is well known: The serpent tempts Eve to eat the forbidden fruit, and Eve, who wishes to know good from evil, can't resist. Angry, God casts his two disobedient human creations from Eden. But God shows a glimmer of compassion. Before he banishes Adam and Eve, he clothes them, offering them some protection from the cold world beyond.

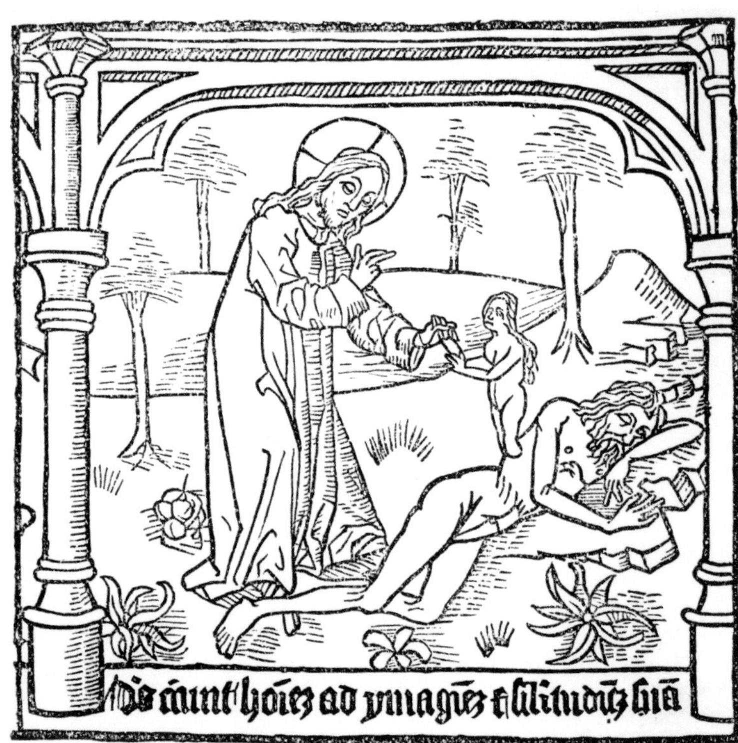

God creating Eve from Adam's rib. Woodcut illustration, origin unknown

Adam and Eve, by Lucas Cranach the Elder (c. 1500s)

CREATION *AND* EVOLUTION?

A group of religious scholars says there's room for both.

You can believe that Adam and Eve were real people and still accept the theory of evolution. That's the conclusion of the BioLogos Foundation, a Christian intellectual group that says scripture can exist in harmony with science.

At first glance, the choice seems to be either/or: Either you accept the genetic evidence that shows humans evolved about 150,000 years ago from several thousand individuals, or you believe the Bible, which says we descended, only about 10,000 years ago, from one couple.

BioLogos suggests three ways these two concepts can be compatible:

→ **Adam and Eve were two specific people** who lived 10,000 years ago. They were chosen out of many others to represent all of humanity to God.

→ **Adam and Eve are symbols** who represent all of the people who lived 150,000 years ago.

→ **Adam and Eve are literary figures** meant to illustrate all humans' relationship to God.

Women at the tomb of Christ are told by an angel of the Lord that Jesus is risen. Book illustration (c. mid-1800s)

WHO KNEW?
In Roman Judea, the crucified bodies of people considered enemies of the state were often left for scavengers or thrown into a ditch. Jesus, however, was entombed after his execution.

"He is not here, but he has risen."

IN THE MYSTERY THAT UNDERPINS CHRISTIANITY, THE FAITHFUL BELIEVE JESUS WAS RESURRECTED AFTER DYING ON THE CROSS.

Christians of all denominations consider it the miracle at the heart of their faith. After Jesus is condemned to death by the Roman governor Pontius Pilate, he is taken to a place called Golgotha. There, Jesus is crucified alongside two others, in the third hour of the day—between 9 AM and 10 AM by our current time conventions. According to Mark, in the ninth hour, Jesus utters "a loud cry, and breathed his last." After that, "the veil of the temple was torn in two from top to bottom"—the result of an earthquake, according to the Gospel of Matthew—and the centurion attending to the crucifixion shouts, "Truly, this was the Son of God!"

A Remarkably Quick Death

Crucifixions were a torturous execution method that sometimes lasted a day or more. The criminal who is put on a cross before Jesus lingers so long that soldiers break his legs to speed his passing. In comparison, Jesus perishes quickly, after a mere six hours. In fact, the soldiers note that he appears dead already, so they pierce his side with a spear. In accordance with Jewish law, which requires burial within 24 hours but forbids burial on the Sabbath, Jesus's body is quickly transferred to a tomb before sundown on Friday and a large stone is rolled across the entrance.

An Empty Shroud

The next day is the Sabbath, when work is forbidden, and early the following Sunday morning, Mary Magdalene, another follower of Jesus, returns to the tomb. The Gospels differ on the exact details. In John she is alone, while in others she is accompanied by other women. To Mary's astonishment, the stone in front of the tomb has been rolled away, and the tomb

MIXED MESSAGES

The Gospels differ considerably in their accounts of what happens on the third day after Jesus is crucified.

EVENT	MATTHEW	MARK	LUKE	JOHN
First visitors to Jesus's tomb	Mary Magdalene and a woman identified only as "the other Mary"	Jesus's follower Mary Magdalene, "Mary the mother of James," and King Herod's niece Salome	Unnamed women who have come with Jesus from Galilee	Mary Magdalene alone
What they find	There is "a great earthquake," and an angel of the Lord rolls back the stone and sits on it. The angel says, "He is not here, for he has been raised."	The stone has been moved. A young man wearing a white robe is there and tells them that Jesus "has been raised, he is not here"; he has gone to Galilee.	The stone is rolled back and two men in dazzling clothes say, "Why do you look for the living among the dead?" "He is not here, but has risen."	Mary finds the stone "taken away."
Whom they tell	The women tell the disciples, but only after Jesus appears to them himself and instructs them to do so.	Mary tells the disciples, but they don't believe her.	Mary Magdalene, Joanna, and Mary mother of James tell the 11 disciples, who don't believe them. Peter alone goes and finds the empty tomb.	Mary finds Simon, Peter, and John and tells them the news. They go and find only his linens and face cloth. After they leave, Mary sees two angels in white sitting where the body of Jesus had been.
Jesus's reappearances	The women leave the sepulcher, and are met by Jesus. He instructs them to tell the disciples to go to Galilee, where they will meet him. There, Jesus orders the men to spread his word.	Jesus appears to two disciples and they tell the rest, who don't believe them. He then appears to all 11 disciples and tells them to go "into all the world and proclaim the good news to the whole creation."	Two disciples encounter Jesus at Emmaus but don't recognize him until he blesses the bread, afterward vanishing from their sight. In the morning, they tell the rest of the disciples, "The Lord has risen indeed." Jesus then appears and shows them his hands and feet.	In the sepulcher, Jesus appears to Mary, saying "Who are you looking for?" She thinks he is the gardener. Later that day, Jesus comes and stands among the disciples, showing them his hands and his side.

Jesus's body is taken to be entombed. Illustration by William Hole in *The Life of Jesus* (c. 1890)

is empty. Depending on the Gospel, one or two men in white robes announce that Jesus is risen.

When Mary tells the disciples what she has seen, they doubt her—but eventually, Jesus appears to them all. "See my hands and my feet, that it is I myself; touch me and see, for a spirit does not have flesh and bones as you see that I have," Jesus says, according to Luke. Then, writes Luke, "while he was blessing them, he parted from them and was carried up into heaven." The disciples finally accept that Jesus has risen from the dead.

The resurrection is the final and ultimate example of Jesus's ability to overcome the bounds of natural law—of death itself—and proof to the faithful of his divinity. It is also an essential fulfillment of the multiple prophesies set forth in the Gospels regarding his fate on Earth.

Jesus and two disciples at Emmaus. Engraving by Pannemaker from a drawing by Gustave Doré (c. 1800s)

RESURRECTION AND REALITY

As with many biblical miracles, scientists and historians have proposed a variety of explanations for the resurrection.

→ **The swoon theory.** Many variations of this hypothesis exist, all suggesting that Jesus only appeared to die on the cross. In 1782, controversial theologian Karl Friedrich Bahrdt proposed that Jesus intentionally feigned his death, using medications to help him endure the trauma of crucifixion. In works published in 1802 and 1828, theologian Heinrich Paulus suggested that Jesus fell into a coma and regained consciousness inside the tomb.

→ **The imposition theory.** Some believe Jesus's body was simply stolen from the tomb. The Book of Matthew predicts that people will suggest the disciples stole the body to fake a resurrection, although Matthew goes on to describe Jesus's appearance to the disciples in Galilee.

→ **The vision theory.** Others suggest that the disciples were familiar with the concept of resurrection and experienced individual or group hallucinations, fantasizing what had been prophesied. Theologian David Friedrich Strauss put forth this idea.

"You are the messenger..."

IN THE DEFINING MIRACLE OF ISLAM, AN ANGEL APPEARS TO MOHAMMED TO REVEAL HIS GOD-GIVEN MISSION.

WHO KNEW?

"Kaaba" comes from the Arabic word for "cube." This holy ancient structure now forms the center of the Grand Mosque in Mecca, Saudi Arabia, and is indeed cube-shaped.

The year is 610 AD. Despite the influence of Christianity from the Byzantine Empire, Judaism from the Levant, and Zoroastrianism from Persia, no monotheistic religion has dominated or unified the peoples of the Arabian peninsula. Instead, distinct tribes worship patron deities. Near the west coast of the peninsula, the city of Mecca is a business hub that draws local merchants and nomads to trade with one another. Within the city, the Kaaba shrine is a sanctuary from tribal conflicts. It attracts a steady stream of pagan Arabs to pray.

This is the world of Mohammed, a caravan driver and merchant from the Banu Hashim tribe. At the age of 40, Mohammed is on a spiritual quest. He is troubled by injustice and the unrest between tribes and has been retreating to the solitude of Hira, a mountain cave about three miles from the city, to pray, reflect, and meditate. It is during one of these solitary trips, in the month of Ramadan, that something unexpected occurs. According to the Sahih al-Bukhari—one of the collections of texts from the Hadith, or the traditional Muslim literature—the angel Jibril (known as

A MAN OF HONOR

In spite of early hardships, Mohammed grew up moral and virtuous.

An Introduction to the Quran, published in 1895, used various versions of *sira*, or biographies from the Islamic tradition, to tell the story of Mohammed.

Before Mohammed was born, his father passed away, and he became an orphan at six when his mother, Amina, died of an illness. Mohammed grew up in Mecca within his Banu Hashim clan, and eventually came into the care of his uncle Abu Talib, the leader of the tribe.

As a youth, Mohammed traveled to and from Syria by caravan with his uncle, learning to become a trader and merchant. His ethical conduct in business earned him the nickname al-Amin, meaning "honest and trustworthy." In fact, when he acted as a business agent for a wealthy widow named Khadijah, Mohammed so impressed her that she proposed marriage. He was 25; she was 40.

Ten years later, the man who would found Islam received a unique honor. Renovations on the Kaaba shrine in Mecca had recently been completed, and the most sacred of icons, an ancient rock called the Black Stone, needed to be ceremoniously returned to its place as the easternmost cornerstone of the building. But who should have the great honor of replacing it? Deciding to leave the selection to fate, the elders agreed to bestow the task on the next man to come through the gates. That man was Mohammed.

Mohammed and the Archangel Gabriel, illustration from the *Siyer-i Nebi* (c. 1700s)

Gabriel in the Bible) appears to Mohammed in human form, embracing him three times and revealing to him the Word of Allah. As Mohammed leaves the mountain greatly awed, he hears, "You are the messenger of God and I am Jibril." Looking back, he sees the angel in a form so grand it appears to fill the sky, which has turned green.

Sharing the Miracle

Returning home, Mohammed tells his wife, Khadijah, of the extraordinary experience. They consult with her cousin, the wise Waraqah ibn Nawfal, a Christian who has learned to read and write Hebrew in order to study scripture. Waraqah affirms that Mohammed has been chosen as a prophet and also predicts that Mohammed will face trouble. The cousin wishes he were younger so that he could advise Mohammed in the future.

Spreading the Word

Three years later, the angel appears to Mohammed again with instructions from God: "Arise and warn, and your Lord glorify." Mohammed knows it is time for him to preach publicly. Over the next 20 years, as he pursues the mission laid out for him, he continues to receive revelations, ultimately accumulating a large volume of divine teachings. Recorded in Arabic and passed on from one scribe to another for 1,400 years, these verses—believed to be the exact words as revealed to Mohammed—comprise the Koran, Islam's holy scripture.

Astronaut Buzz Aldrin steps onto the surface of the moon during the Apollo 11 mission.

LOOKING FORWARD

Does the Koran predict the future? Believers say yes.

→ Splitting of the moon. The Koran verse, "The hour has come near, and the moon has split" has been interpreted as a miracle performed by God through Mohammed in response to skeptics. Different versions vary the details: some say the moon literally split into two distinct bodies, while others describe what we now call a lunar eclipse. Some scholars suggest that the verse is actually a prophesy of the Apollo 11 moon landing. The verse's number, 54:1, predicts the time the lunar module left the moon's surface (17:54:01 UT), taking with it a collection of samples—an act that essentially "split" the moon.

→ Journey with an angel. This miraculous story relates how in 620 or 621 the angel Jibril took Mohammed on a one-night journey from Mecca to heaven, where he met Adam, Moses, Jesus, and other prophets; then to hell; and finally, to the al-Aqsa Mosque in Jerusalem. Mohammed is said to have described the mosque accurately, despite the fact that it wouldn't be built until after his death.

Crossing the Red Sea by The English School.
Gouache on paper (date unknown)

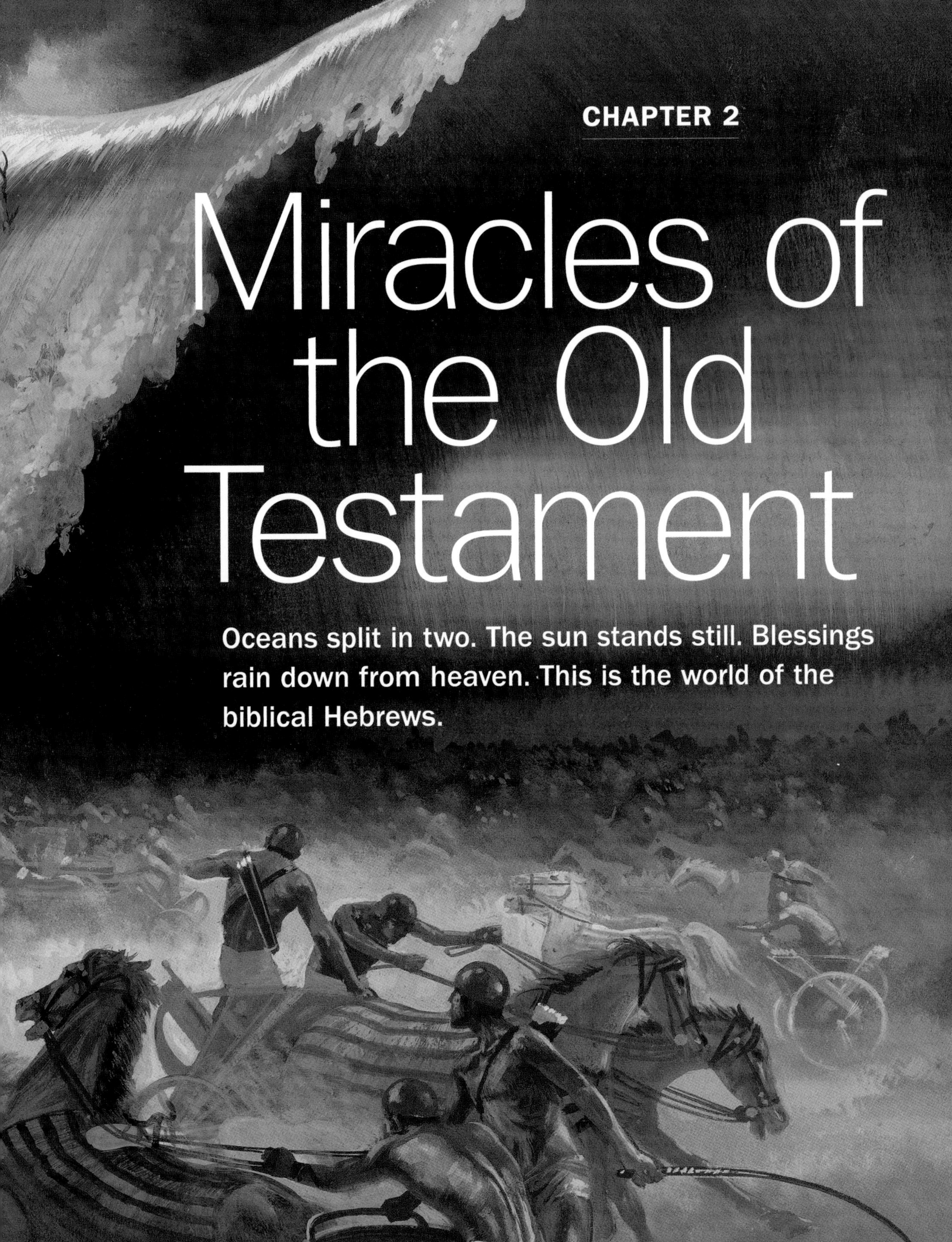

CHAPTER 2

Miracles of the Old Testament

Oceans split in two. The sun stands still. Blessings rain down from heaven. This is the world of the biblical Hebrews.

Flame Thrower

WHEN IT COMES TIME TO LIBERATE THE HEBREWS FROM EGYPTIAN BONDAGE, THE LORD RECRUITS MOSES WITH FIRE.

HOT TOPIC

Scientists have some intriguing explanations for Moses's vision of the burning bush.

For every miracle described in the Bible, there are modern-day scientists looking for explanations in the natural world. The burning bush is no exception.

British physicist Colin Humphreys theorizes that the bush grew just above a volcanic or natural-gas vent in the earth's surface that was the actual source of the fire.

Benny Shanon, a psychology professor at the Hebrew University of Jerusalem, suggests that Moses may have been hallucinating after imbibing a sacred psychoactive tea.

The first time the Lord contacts Moses, the adopted son of Egyptian royalty is living a simple existence. He is married, the father of two sons, and working as a shepherd in a land far from home. He hardly seems the person to be God's chosen prophet. But from his humble position, Moses encounters something miraculous that changes not only his life but the Judeo-Christian story.

Born into Oppression

Moses's entire life has been leading to this moment. At the time of his birth, the Egyptians had been hostile toward the Hebrews for many years. The ruling pharaoh, suspicious of the Hebrews' success and swelling population, had ordered them into bondage and their newborn boys killed.

Moses's Hebrew mother, wanting to save her infant son, placed him in a basket of reeds in the Nile, hoping he would be rescued by an Egyptian. Moses in fact was found and adopted by a young princess, and grew up free and privileged. One day, however, he flew into a rage and killed an Egyptian who was beating a Hebrew slave. Fearing the pharaoh would put him to death, Moses fled to a land called Midian.

A Marvelous Sight

Now years have passed, and the pharaoh has died. One day, Moses is tending his father-in-law's sheep near the mountain of Horeb in Midian when he comes upon a bush engulfed in flames. To his amazement, though the fire rages, the plant is not consumed. Stopping to marvel at the phenomenon, Moses hears a voice coming from the flames: "I am the God of your father, the God of Abraham, the God of Isaac, and the God of Jacob."

God tells the awestruck Moses that he intends to

WHO KNEW?
The ancient biblical land of Canaan is thought to encompass what today is Lebanon, Israel, and parts of Syria and Jordan.

Moses shields his face as God speaks to him from the Burning Bush. Illustration by C.E. Brock (c. 1930s)

THE WORD FROM ON HIGH

In the Old Testament, God communicates directly with Moses, Adam and Eve, and many others.

WHO	WHAT GOD SAID	RESULT
Adam and Eve	"Have you eaten from the tree of which I had commanded you not to eat?" (Genesis 3:11)	Adam blames Eve, Eve blames the serpent, and God casts the couple out of Eden.
Cain	"Where is your brother Abel?" (Genesis 4:9)	God discovers Cain has murdered his brother and curses Cain to endlessly wander Earth.
Noah	"I am going to bring a flood of waters on the earth, to destroy from under heaven all flesh in which is the breath of life; everything that is on earth shall die." (Genesis 6:17)	Noah builds an ark according to God's instructions; when the flood comes, Noah, his family, and his animal passengers are saved.
Abraham	"Take your son, your only son Isaac, whom you love, and go to the land of Moriah, and offer him there as a burnt offering…" (Genesis 22:2)	Abraham starts to do as he is told, but God sends an angel to stop the sacrifice at the last minute and blesses Abraham for his loyalty.
Jacob	"Know that I am with you and will keep you wherever you go, and will bring you back to this land; for I will not leave you until I have done what I have promised you." (Genesis 28:15)	Jacob's 12 sons become heads of the Twelve Tribes of Israel; the family migrates to Egypt, laying the groundwork for the Moses story that follows.

rescue the Hebrews from Egypt and bring them to the land of Canaan, as he promised the Patriarchs of the Torah, Abraham, Isaac, and Jacob. He has chosen Moses to help him. "Come, therefore," God says. "I will send you to Pharaoh, and you shall free my people, the Israelites, from Egypt."

This miracle launches the Book of Exodus, a tale full of wonders, including the 10 plagues visited on the Egyptians and the parting of the Red Sea. Each year during the celebration of Passover, Jews around the world retell the events to remind the faithful that their freedom was hard-won and must remain precious.

WHO KNEW?
Exodus is rife with historical inaccuracies and is less likely a story of one specific migration than a summary of many during the 13th and 12th centuries BC, according to historians.

A Sea Change

IN THE CULMINATING MIRACLE OF THE HEBREWS' ESCAPE FROM EGYPT, GOD PARTS THE WATERS AND MOSES LEADS HIS PEOPLE THROUGH.

As Exodus unfolds, the Hebrews have suffered more than four centuries of bondage under the Egyptians. But with Moses as his messenger, God finally beats down the Hebrews' oppressors with a succession of plagues. He curses them with frogs, flies, locusts, and boils, and ends with the most devestating: the death of the oldest boy in every Egyptian family. Defeated and in despair at the loss of his own beloved firstborn son, Pharaoh summons Moses and his brother, the prophet Aaron. The ruler is finally prepared to give the Hebrews what they have asked for: their freedom.

"Go away from my people, both you and the Israelites!" Pharaoh commands. "Go, worship the Lord as you said!"

Eager to leave, the Hebrews gather up their livestock and collect the silver, gold, and clothing God has earlier urged them to request from their Egyptian neighbors. They pack what food they have ready, including bread dough that hasn't yet risen. Moses takes with him the bones of his ancestor Joseph. Together, the huge group sets out on foot, bound for what God has called the Land of the Canaanites.

The Long Way Home

The group makes its way to an area in northeast Egypt referred to as either the Sea of Reeds or the Red Sea, which will be the final and most serious obstacle to the Israelites' exit from Egypt.

But while the Hebrews have been traveling, the pharaoh has changed his mind about releasing his entire population of slaves. He is now riding with his army in pursuit of the Hebrews. With the water in front of them and the advancing army behind them, the Hebrews are terrified.

Moses tells them to have no fear, and the Lord commands Moses to lift his staff and hold it over the water. When he does so, a strong wind arises from the east and blows all through the night. It splits the water, creating a dry path across which the Israelites travel. Once they are safely on the other side, the waters engulf and drown their Egyptian pursuers.

As recounted in Exodus, "Israel saw the great work that the Lord did against the Egyptians. So the people . . . believed in the Lord and in his servant Moses."

WHO KNEW?

The ancient Philistines were sworn enemies of the Israelites. Philistine territory included the still hotly contested Gaza Strip area of modern Israel.

And Moses Stretched Forth His Hand over the Sea, by Ivan Aivazovsky (c. 1800s)

STAFF DEVELOPMENT

Sticks feature prominently in the Old and New Testaments—and were essential tools in ancient pastoral life.

Moses has a staff; his older brother Aaron, a rod. And God, of course, has both. These tools were necessities among ancient sheepherders. A shepherd would use the rod to defend his sheep as well as to discipline them. It was "an extension of the owner's own right arm," author and herder W. Phillip Keller wrote in his 2007 meditation, *A Shepherd Looks at Psalm 23*. "It stood as a symbol of his strength... in any serious situation."

The longer staff, with its familiar hook-shaped top, was a tool of comfort and compassion. With it, a shepherd could carefully pick up a newborn lamb or reach out to secure a timid animal while remaining at a respectful distance. "Whereas the 'rod' conveys the concept of authority, of power, of discipline, of defense against danger, the word 'staff' speaks of all that is long-suffering and kind," according to Keller. Together, the tools are fitting biblical symbols of God's relationship to humanity.

Moses's staff becomes a snake before Pharaoh. By Robert Leinweber (c. 1845)

Some believe the parting of the Red Sea resulted from receding flood waters.

HOW DID IT SPLIT?

Scientists and historians offer a trio of tantalizing theories about how the water may have pulled back.

→ **It was the wind.** A 2010 computer simulation from the National Center for Atmospheric Research and the University of Colorado at Boulder illustrated how an overnight 63-mile-per-hour gale from the east could have pushed back the relatively shallow water at a specific location: A lagoon off the coast of the Mediterranean Sea. That would have allowed people to walk through mud to the other side.

→ **It was a tsunami.** The volcanic Aegean island of Santorini (then known as Thera) exploded in about 1600 BC. The date of the Exodus story cannot be confirmed, and the date the story originated is not known, but the force of this tremendous eruption north of Egypt and Israel could have triggered extensive flooding in the region.

→ **The water wasn't deep.** Because "Red Sea" is also translated as "Sea of Reeds," some theorists postulate that Moses may have led his people through a swampy area around Suez, Egypt, where it was temporarily drier than usual.

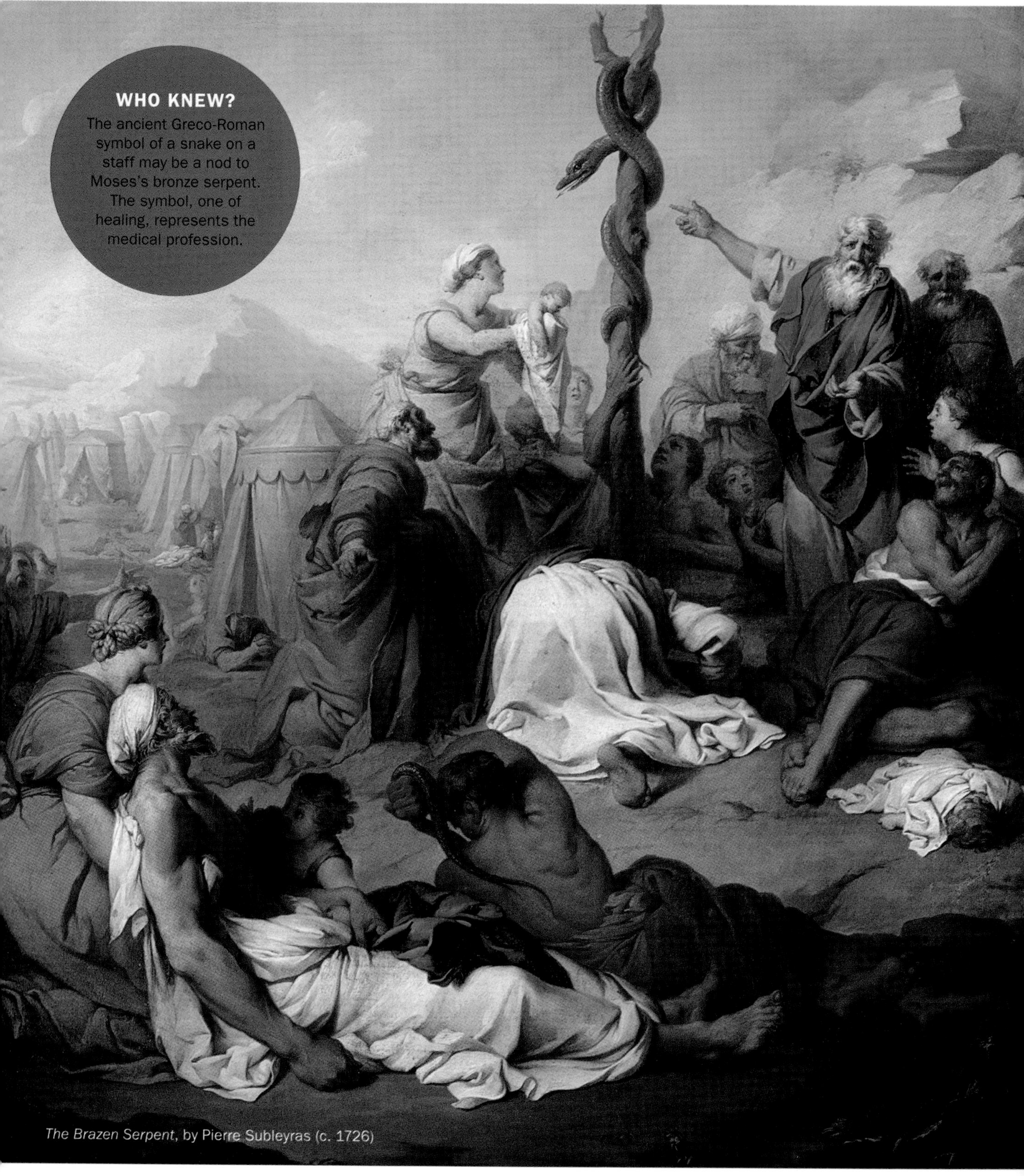

WHO KNEW?

The ancient Greco-Roman symbol of a snake on a staff may be a nod to Moses's bronze serpent. The symbol, one of healing, represents the medical profession.

The Brazen Serpent, by Pierre Subleyras (c. 1726)

Why Did It Have to Be Snakes?

THE HEBREWS' JOURNEY TOWARD THE PROMISED LAND CONTINUES, FRAUGHT WITH TROUBLE. THEN THEY RECEIVE HELP FROM ABOVE.

From the moment Moses is rescued by the Pharaoh's daughter as a newborn floating in the River Nile, his life seems to be a succession of miracles. Perhaps the best-known of these is God's parting of the Red Sea to permit Moses and the Hebrews to flee Egypt unimpeded by the soldiers pursuing them, but the extraordinary interventions by God don't stop there.

The Miracle at Sinai

In the desert wilderness, the miracles continue. God sustains the starving Hebrews with manna, a wondrous honey-wafer substance that floats down daily from the skies above. Still, after three months of wandering, the people are weary, and the Lord intervenes to give them hope.

Amid thunder and lightning, in a thick cloud of smoke and fire, God appears to Moses atop Mount Sinai and imparts to him the Ten Commandments. These simple, powerful rules will become the basis for governing the new monotheistic religious community of Israel.

The magical moment doesn't last once the Hebrews leave Sinai. Numbers, the fourth book of the Old Testament, chronicles this segment of their spiritual and physical journey. Their suffering increases; they fight battles and grow restless with Moses's leadership. They have lapses of faith. As a result of their transgressions, God condemns the Hebrews to wander for 40 more years in the wilderness; the promised "land flowing with milk and honey" will not be delivered until the next generation.

Snakes on a Plain

As the Hebrews move from land to land, they come to Edom, whose rulers refuse to let them pass. Impatient with the journey's hardships, the people criticize God and Moses, demanding to know why they have been brought up out of Egypt only "to die in the wilderness." They complain of eating only manna, fret, lose hope, and rebel.

Angered by their lack of faith, God unleashes a plague of poisonous serpents, and many people are bitten. Realizing they have brought this on themselves by complaining, the people implore Moses to pray to God to remove the serpents. In reply God says, "Make a poisonous serpent, and set it on a pole; and everyone who is bitten shall look at it and live." Moses follows God's command and the bitten Hebrews survive, continuing on their journey toward the Promised Land with renewed faith.

Moses with the Tablets of the Law, by Guido Reni (c. 1624)

Daylight Savings

IN A SHOW OF SUPPORT, GOD STOPS THE SUN FROM SETTING SO THAT THE ISRAELITES CAN DEFEAT THEIR ENEMIES.

Joshua, the sixth book of the Old Testament, chronicles the Israelites' occupation of the Promised Land led by Moses's successor, the charismatic warrior Joshua. Written after the Israelites' exile by the Babylonians, the tales in the book are underpinned by a fervent hope of return.

The Israelites Invade

As the story opens, Joshua has been newly appointed by God to lead the Hebrews into the Promised Land. He dispatches spies to assess enemy morale in the important city-state of Jericho, which the Hebrews must conquer to secure Canaan.

Receiving word that the citizens of Jericho are terrified, Joshua is ready to proceed. He commands his camp's priests to carry the sacred Ark of the Covenant, the chest containing the stone tablets of the Ten Commandments, and to stop in the center of the Jordan River. As the priests step into the waters, the Jordan parts, providing safe passage to the entire Israelite army. The troops circle Jericho's walls once a day for six days. On the seventh day, they continue the pattern. Then, on their seventh round, seven priests blast their ram's-horn trumpets while the Israelites shout thunderously. In a shower of mud and rubble, the walls that surround and protect Jericho crumble, and the Israelite army rushes in to conquer the city.

Next, Joshua vanquishes Ai, another key city-state, and erects an altar to God at Mount Ebal, in the north. The frightened leaders of Gibeon, a prosperous town northwest of Jerusalem, dispatch men disguised as foreign ambassadors to Joshua at his Gilgal camp. The move briefly tricks the Israelites into forming an alliance with the townspeople. When the Israelites discover the ruse, they enslave the Gibeonites.

God's Omnipotence

Soon, the Gibeonites' neighbors, angry at

NOT JUST IN THE BIBLE

Two historical documents from the New World also describe instances in which the sun or moon seemed to stand still.

The *Codex Chimalpopoca*, used by the Nahua Indians of Mexico, documents the pre-European history of the Valley of Mexico and Aztec mythology. The text holds that during a cosmic catastrophe in ancient times, there was an abnormally long night.

The 16th-century Spanish Franciscan friar Bernardino de Sahagun, who traveled to the New World a few decades after Columbus, studied the Aztecs and became known for his massive work *General History of the Things of New Spain*, which included more than 2,000 illustrations by native artists. Sahagun also documented the legend of a great catastrophe in which the sun rose and hovered in one spot just above the horizon.

Joshua urges on his army outside the walls of Jericho as trumpeters proceed around the walls carrying the Ark of the Covenant. Bible illustration (c. 20th century)

Joshua's actions, attack the Israelites. Fighting is fierce, but the Israelites receive miraculous help from God, including "huge stones" from heaven that rain down on the area, which help turn the battle in their favor. As the frenzied fighting continues, Joshua turns his face skyward and pleads, "Sun, stand still at Gibeon, and Moon, in the valley of Aijalon." Miraculously, the heavenly bodies cease their movements until the Israelites vanquish their enemies. As described in the Book of Joshua, "The sun stopped in mid-heaven, and did not hurry to set for about a whole day. There has been no day like it before or since, when the Lord heeded a human voice; for the Lord fought for Israel."

Joshua and the Israelites return to Gilgal in triumph, the five Amorite kings are eventually hanged, and the Israelites continue their conquest of Canaan.

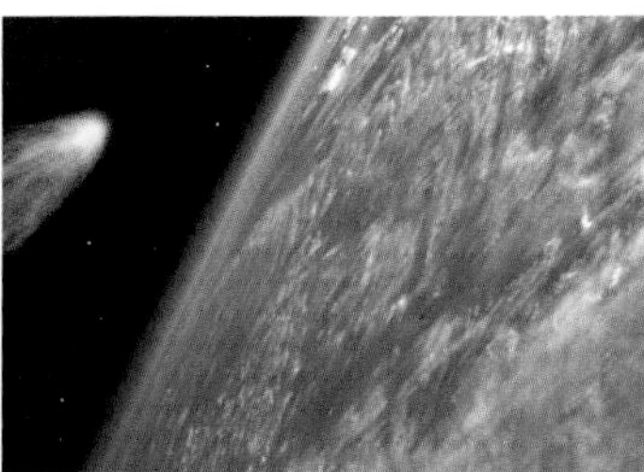

A comet passes near Earth.

DID THE SUN REALLY STAND STILL?

A variety of explanations have been offered for the astronomical miracle described in Joshua.

➔ In his controversial 1950 bestseller *Worlds in Collision*, Russian scholar and psychologist Immanuel Velikovsky hypothesized that the sun appeared to come to a halt because of a comet-like object that passed close to Earth. According to Velikovsky, the body disturbed Earth's rotation and caused widespread cataclysms.

➔ In his 1973 book *The Long Day of Joshua and Six Other Catastrophes*, geographer Donald Wesley Patten suggested that during Joshua's time, Mars passed by Earth in an abnormally close orbit, causing Earth to tilt on its axis and prolonging the daylight over Gibeon.

➔ The Seder Olam Rabba, a chronology of biblical events dating to the 2nd century AD, suggested that the Israelite-Amorite battle took place on the summer solstice, when the sun provides the most daylight.

Wild and Wooly

CALLED TO AN EXTRAORDINARY MISSION, GIDEON ASKS FOR PROOF OF GOD'S POWER, ONLY TO BE TESTED IN RETURN.

The Hebrews have arrived in the Promised Land, but their trials aren't over. Nor are the miracles. The Book of Judges describes a repeating cycle of woe in which the Hebrews first abandon their religion, are punished by God for their transgressions, and then return to Judaism under the leadership of a wise and brave man. In one such cycle, God dispatches an army of Midianites to conquer the Hebrews and destroy their land. God then picks Gideon, a farmer and man of faith, to save his chosen people from their enemy. Gideon is on his way to harvest his wheat when an angel appears before him, speaking for God: "The Lord is with you, you mighty warrior. Go in this might of yours and deliver Israel from the hand of Midian."

When Gideon hesitates, wondering how he, the youngest son of a humble family, can deliver the nation from its powerful conquerors, God responds through his messenger: "I will be with you, and you shall strike down the Midianites, every one of them."

Gideon choosing men from among the Hebrews for his army to fight the Midianites. Engraving by Gabriel Bodenehr (c. 17th century)

Gideon asks for a divine sign, and the angel reaches out his staff. Suddenly, fire bursts up from below the rock where Gideon's meal sits, engulfing the bread and meat. Gideon is convinced. He prepares for his mission, assembling an army of more than 32,000 men.

Heavenly Message

As the day of the battle approaches, Gideon again grows frightened and asks God for another sign that he will vanquish the Midianites: "I am going to lay a fleece of wool on the threshing-floor," Gideon prays. "If there is dew on the fleece alone, and it is dry on all the ground, then I shall know that you will deliver Israel by my hand, as you have said." In the morning, the ground is dry and the fleece soaked, holding enough water to fill a bowl.

Yet Gideon is still doubtful, and again prays, "Let me, please, make trial with the fleece just once more; let it be dry only on the fleece, and on all the ground let there be dew." The following morning, the ground is soaked with dew, the fleece bone-dry. Gideon's faith in his mission is restored.

Now he must comply with a new order that demonstrates God's divine power: He must send most of his warriors home and face the enemy with only a small company of men. "The troops with you are too many for me to give the Midianites into their hand," God tells Gideon. Lest Israel

The Miracle of the Fleece of Gideon, by Nicolas Dipre (c. 1500)

become boastful and say, "My own hand has delivered me," God instructs Gideon to order 22,000 men to return home and take the remaining forces to the river, where God tells him to winnow his troops even further. In the end, just 300 men remain to face the Midianite army.

A Sword for the Lord

Under cover of night, Gideon positions his soldiers, equipped with covered torches and horns, around the Midianite camp. As Gideon sounds his instrument, the 300 troops follow suit, shining their torches and blasting their trumpets. They cry, "A sword for the Lord and for Gideon!"

The Midianite army is thrown into terror and confusion. Thinking they are surrounded by a vast army, the men panic and begin to turn their swords on one another. As they flee, Gideon's little brigade drives them out of the land of Israel. Gideon is chosen to govern the newly delivered land, and there is peace.

A TRIAL AT THE WATER'S EDGE

God helps Gideon determine which of his soldiers are the weakest.

In Judges, Gideon selects his 300 soldiers with help from God. He first asks who among his tens of thousands of men are afraid, and sends home those who say they are—all but 8,000. Gideon then follows a second trial devised by God, and takes the men to a nearby river. "I will sift them out for you there," God says.

When the men reach the water's edge, God directs, "All those who lap the water with their tongues, as a dog laps, you shall put to one side; all those who kneel down to drink, putting their hands to their mouths, you shall put to the other side."

Gideon watches closely and separates the men accordingly. Then God commands him to take into battle only the men who lapped the water like dogs. The idea: If Gideon is surrounded by the least effective soldiers, the victory will be an unmistakable sign of God's favor. Gideon goes forward to face the Midian army with 300 of his worst men and the power of God.

Master of the Beasts

A BABYLONIAN KING IS TRICKED INTO BETRAYING DANIEL, BUT GOD INTERVENES TO SAVE THE DEVOUT ADVISOR.

THE ROYAL ROAR

A lion's den was a common feature of ancient palaces.

It is unclear whether the biblical characters of Darius and Daniel were true historical figures. However, the lion's den in the story is not a metaphor. Kings at the time kept lions for sport, as a means of carrying out death sentences, and sometimes both at once.

The lions were imprisoned in cages, or in a pit in the ground near the palace. This environment, so unlike their natural habitat, kept the creatures restless, unhappy, and vicious. The lions were also usually underfed, ensuring that they would be ferocious when put on display for crowds.

Around 586 BC, the mighty Babylonian King Nebuchadnezzar II conquers Jerusalem and expels most of the city's Jews, sending the best and the brightest, including skilled workers and scholars, back to his base in Babylon. Nebuchadnezzar instructs the palace master to bring him a group of the most outstanding conquered Jews to be his servants: "Young men without physical defect and handsome, versed in every branch of wisdom, endowed with knowledge and insight," according to the Book of Daniel.

The elite attendants are given new names, taught the conquering language and customs, and assigned jobs. One man, Daniel, is a devout nobleman with a talent for prophesy and interpreting dreams. He is assigned to work for Nebuchadnezzar and performs his tasks admirably. Daniel is so respected that he keeps his position after a new people, the Medes, rises to power and their leader, Darius, takes over the throne. He is even allowed to continue practicing Judaism.

As time passes, Darius increasingly relies on Daniel's wise guidance and thinking, and makes plans to elevate him to second-in-command over the entire kingdom. Three of Daniel's peers are consumed with jealousy and try to ruin him by digging for examples of wrongdoing or corruption. Finding none, they instead concoct a plot to use Daniel's piety against him.

The servants know Daniel goes up onto the roof of his house three times a day to pray and give thanks to God. They approach Darius and suggest that the ruler test his subjects' loyalty by forbidding all in the kingdom from bowing before any god or man for 30 days. Anyone caught doing so should be thrown into a den of lions, the servants say. In his vanity, the king is pleased with the idea and signs it into law.

Because Daniel has developed a special relationship with the king, he believes he is exempt from the decree and allowed to continue to pray. He goes as usual to his roof, where the conspirators lie in wait. They observe Daniel bowing before God and rush to Darius to report what they have seen: "Daniel, one of the exiles from Judah, pays no attention to you, O King, or to the interdict you signed."

Divine Intervention

Distraught, King Darius seeks a way to excuse his most trusted advisor, but the conspirators remind him that the injunction can not be changed—not even by the king himself. The king realizes he has been tricked. "May your God, whom you faithfully serve, deliver you!" Darius tells Daniel.

In accordance with the edict, guards bring Daniel into Darius's den of lions.

WHO KNEW?
Daniel's many visions included predictions about the duration of various empires and the fate in store for the Hebrews.

Daniel in the den of lions. Illustration from *Brown's Self-Interpreting Family Bible* (c. 1880)

A stone is placed over the mouth of the den, and the king himself seals it with his signet. After a sleepless night, Darius hurries to the lair to see if his advisor has survived. "O Daniel!" he calls. "Has your God whom you faithfully serve been able to deliver you from the lions?"

Daniel's voice rings out strong and clear: "O King, live forever! My God sent his angel and shut the lions' mouths."

The king is overjoyed. He commands that Daniel be raised up out of the lion's den and replaced by the men who have plotted against him. The lions leap upon the men as they fall, catching them out of the air and devouring them, bones and all. And Darius issues a decree that the whole kingdom respect the God of Daniel, for "He delivers and rescues, he works... wonders in heaven and on earth."

King Nebuchadnezzar II in the Hanging Gardens of Babylon. Illustration by Donald A. Mackenzie (c. 1915)

DREAM JOB

Daniel's first two masters don't get the happy endings they've hoped for.

As a royal diviner to King Nebuchadnezzar II of Babylon, Daniel becomes famous for his vast knowledge and ability to interpret dreams. Called for insight into one of Nebuchadnezzar's dreams, Daniel says: Because you are too arrogant, God will drive you into the wilderness, where you shall live among wild animals. Immediately, the king loses his sanity and for seven years lives as a beast.

The throne then goes to Nebuchadnezzar's grandson, Belshazzar. One night at a banquet Belshazzar commits the sacrilege of serving wine from sacred goblets stolen from the Temple in Jerusalem. A hand appears in the air and writes on the wall: *Mene mene tekel upharsin*. The terrified king summons Daniel, who recognizes the inscription is divine, and translates: "Your kingdom is divided and given to the Medes and the Persians." That very night, the story goes, Belshazzar is slain, the Babylonian Empire is overthrown, and Darius ascends to the throne.

Let This Child Live

AFTER THE PROPHET ELIJAH PERFORMS A LIFE-SUSTAINING MIRACLE, HE MUST TURN TO GOD TO REVERSE A TRAGIC DEATH THAT FOLLOWS.

During time of the prophet Elijah, God becomes incensed by Israel's ruler, Ahab, who has encouraged the worship of another religion, according to the Book of Kings. Elijah warns Ahab that his nation will suffer because of his actions and that soon a terrible drought will descend on Israel. After his message is delivered, Elijah hears the voice of God instructing him to retreat to a secluded spot by the brook Cherith, near the River Jordan, and stay there. The prophet obeys, sustaining himself on water from the brook and the divine provision of bread

SPIRIT A LA CARTE

At the end of his life, Elijah experiences a transformative miracle of his own.

When Elijah senses that his death is nearing, he travels toward Jericho with 50 young prophets. As they reach the Jordan River, Elijah instructs the young men to remain behind while he travels on alone, but one refuses. “As the Lord lives,” declares the prophet Elisha, “I will not leave you.” Giving in, Elijah strikes the river with his cloak and the water parts so that the two of them can cross on dry ground.

When they reach the other side, Elisha asks for a special anointing from Elijah: “Please, let me inherit a double share of your spirit.” Elijah responds that it is difficult to fulfill such a request, “yet, If you see me as I am being taken from you, it will be granted you.” Soon a chariot of fire appears in the sky, drawn by two fiery horses. As Elisha watches, a whirlwind descends, sweeps Elijah up into the flaming chariot, and carries him off to heaven. Elisha dons Elijah's cloak and returns to the group of prophets, who recognize the spirit of Elijah in him, and bow.

Elijah's Ascension to Heaven in the Fiery Chariot, by Peter Paul Rubens (c. 1620)

WHO KNEW?
In addition to his significance to Christians and Jews, Elijah is recognized as a prophet in the Koran and by the Church of Latter-day Saints and the Ba'hai faith.

Elijah Resuscitating the Son of the Widow of Sarepta, by Louis Hersent (1777–1860)

and meat, brought to him by ravens each morning and night.

When the brook dries up, Elijah again follows God's word and travels to the home of a widow in the city of Zarephath. Weary from the journey, he asks the woman for a drink of water and a little bit of bread. "As the Lord God lives," she replies, "I have nothing baked, only a handful of meal in a jar and a little oil in a jug." She has been planning to use these ingredients in a final meal for herself and her little boy before they succumb to starvation.

The Bottomless Jar

Elijah tells the woman to make her cake as she has intended and to bring it to him; then she is to make another for herself and her child, "For thus says the Lord God of Israel: 'The jar of meal will not be emptied and the jug of oil will not fail until the day that the Lord sends rain on the earth.'"

Marveling, the widow prepares one cake—and then another, and another. Elijah remains her guest for many days, and the stores of flour and oil never run low. But the widow's happiness is short-lived: her young son falls gravely ill and dies. She blames Elijah for the death of her boy.

Elijah feels responsible. He carries the child's body to an upper room, lays it upon the bed, and calls out to God in agony, "O Lord my God, have you brought calamity even upon the widow with whom I am staying, by killing her son?" He stretches his own body across the little corpse three times and begs for a miracle. "Oh Lord my God," Elijah cries, "Let this child's life come into him again." God hears the prayers of his faithful prophet and breathes life back into the little boy, whom Elijah returns safely to his mother. The widow rejoices at her son's resurrection. "Now I know that you are a man of God," she tells Elijah, "and that the word of the Lord in your mouth is truth."

Elijah rebuking King Ahab. Lithograph, artist unknown (c. mid-19th century)

BAD KING

The tempestuous ruler Ahab continually challenges Elijah.

→ Ahab is one in a line of several kings of Israel who turn their backs on God; he is described as doing more evil than any king before him.

→ Ahab and Elijah have a contentious relationship. While the king relies on Elijah's prophesies and interpretations, he is often angered when they are not to his liking. After one ill-fated prediction, Elijah appeals to God for the strength to outrun Ahab, who pursues him in a chariot.

→ When Ahab marries Jezebel, a princess from another kingdom, and builds a temple to her god, Baal, a terrible drought descends on Israel.

→ At Jezebel's behest, Ahab plots the death of a neighbor so he can take over his tiny but productive vineyard.

→ When Jezebel dies, she is eaten by dogs just as Elijah had prophesied. Only then does Ahab finally humble himself before God.

Trial by Fire

A PEOPLE'S DEVOTION TO GOD BRINGS A DIVINE GLOW TO THE WORLD.

Ancient Greek coin depicting Roman emperor Antiochus IV Epiphanes

For the Jews, life under Antiochus IV Epiphanes, the tyrannical leader of the Seleucid Empire, is unbearable. Intent on wiping out Jewish culture, the 2nd-century Greek king has outlawed the Sabbath and Jewish sacrificial offerings. He has ordered the burning of all Torahs—Judaism's most important sacred text—and condemned to death anyone found possessing a copy. He also has banned circumcision, a ritual required of all Hebrew males, making it a capital offense. But a double miracle will soon turn the tide.

Reclaiming Jerusalem

To demean and offend the Jewish people, Antiochus hideously defiles their temple, ordering that a statue of the Greek god Zeus be set atop the altar for the performance of pagan rites. Among these is the sacrifice of pigs, animals that the Jews considered unclean. The despot even forces Jewish leaders to offer sacrifices to his idols.

Outraged, the people of Judea begin to rebel, and the scattered uprisings coalesce into in a large-scale revolt. Led by Jewish priest Mattathias the Hasmonean and his five sons—known as the Maccabees—the people launch a guerilla war against the Seleucids. Miraculously, the ragtag collection of dissidents triumphs over the mighty Antiochus IV.

Rededicating the Temple

When the victorious Maccabees return to Jerusalem, they find "the Temple abandoned, the altar profaned, the gates burned down, the courtyards grown up in a forest of weeds, and the priests' rooms torn down," according to the Books of Maccabees. Mattathias and other priests repair and ritually cleanse the building, replace the contaminated altar, and bring in fresh supplies. Their last task is to light the sacred temple lamp, meant to burn eternally, but which has been extinguished.

Combing the wreckage, the priests are able to locate only one undamaged flask of the special kosher oil used to light the lamp. It is enough to burn for a single day, and securing a fresh supply will take at least eight. But when the priests kindle the wick, the oil inexplicably burns for eight days. It is another miracle.

On the 25th day of the Hebrew month called Kislev, the priests offer a sacrifice on the new altar. For eight days, the people celebrate their victory over the Seleucids, their freedom from oppression, and the rededication of their temple. The festival will come to be known as *Chanukah*, the Hebrew word for "dedicate."

WHO KNEW?

The dreidel was originally a ruse used by Jews illegally studying the Torah. When soldiers approached, the students hid their scrolls and started spinning tops, to make it look as if they were gambling.

Fighting between Seleucid Emperor Antiochus IV and the rebel Maccabees. From an illustration in *Histoire de l'Ancien et Nouveau Testament par Royaumont* (c. 1724)

SHINING IN THE DARKNESS

The lamp used to celebrate Chanukah, known as the menorah, is described by God to Moses.

In the Book of Exodus, when God gives Moses the Ten Commandments, he specifies that the Jews must "make me a sanctuary, so that I may dwell among them." The sanctuary must include a source of light, both to illuminate the space and to remind the Jews of Israel's mission to be "a light unto the nations." God provides precise specifications for a very special lampstand, or menorah, to serve these purposes.

It is to be wrought of one talent (about 67 pounds) of pure gold.

It is to include seven oil lamps, six of them on side branches and one in the center.

Pure, consecrated olive oil is to fill the seven lamps, which are to be lit each evening and left to burn until morning.

The Talmud prohibits the use of the seven-lamp design outside of temples, so Chanukah menorahs, lit in homes and elsewhere, have nine lamps: eight side branches commemorating the eight days of the festival and one in the middle, the *shamash*, used to kindle the others. Today's menorahs most often hold candles rather than oil, but they remain a powerful representation of divine light, wisdom, and inspiration.

Children play Chanukah games with spinning tops called dreidels.

THE LIGHTER SIDE OF LIGHT

Chanukah, a joyous holiday, celebrates the rededication of the Temple.

➔ Chanukah is a jubilant opportunity to broadcast the miraculous victory of the Jewish people over their oppressors. Celebrants place menorahs near a door or window in order to share the joy with passersby.

➔ In some Jewish communities, it is traditional to give "gelt," or coins, to children during Chanukah. The youngest members of a household may receive chocolate coins wrapped in foil, while those slightly older will get real coins and are encouraged to donate their gift to charity.

➔ Deep-fried foods are traditional. *Latkes* (potato pancakes), *sufganiyot* (jelly donuts), and *bimuelos* (dough fritters) are some of the treats enjoyed at the holiday.

➔ On Chanukah, Jewish children play games with spinning tops called *dreidels*. A Hebrew letter marks each of the four sides of a dreidel, standing for the Hebrew words "Nes Gadol Haya Sham," which translates as "a great miracle happened there."

Hagar and Ishmael, by Francesco de Mura (1696–1782)

CHAPTER 3

Angels of the Bible

God's messengers visit humans to deliver joyous tidings, thrilling prophesies, and dire warnings.

Chronicle of a Birth Foretold

THREE ANGELS APPEAR TO AN ELDERLY COUPLE TO HERALD ONE OF THE PRIMARY EVENTS OF THE OLD TESTAMENT: THE BIRTH OF A CHILD—AND A NATION.

Abraham, whose story unfolds in the Old Testament book of Genesis, is one of the three great biblical patriarchs and an important figure in Judaism, Christianity, and Islam.

At age 75, this deeply spiritual man is called by God to leave his father's house in Ur, Mesopotamia. He is to migrate with his wife, Sarah, his nephew Lot, some servants, and a few others to Canaan. God promises to make Abraham's offspring as numerous as the stars of heaven. He also establishes a covenant, promising Abraham that he will become the founder of a great nation and that his descendants will inherit the Promised Land. Finally, God promises that Sarah will "give rise to nations" and kings.

Abraham laughs at the prospect. At the time, he and his wife are both very old and childless. How can the two of them possibly give birth to nations?

Three Visitors

The Book of Genesis soon describes Abraham sitting in his tent doorway at midday, near the oak trees of Mamre. This is his encampment near Hebron, southwest of modern Jerusalem. Looking up, Abraham sees three figures approaching and recognizes them as God's angelic messengers.

Abraham runs to meet the visitors, bowing down and humbly imploring them to rest and take refreshment in the shade. After the three guests have eaten, God speaks through one of them; they promise they will return in a year and "your wife Sarah shall have a son."

This time, it is Sarah's turn to laugh. God responds through the angel, "Is anything too wonderful for the Lord?" And indeed, the promised miracle comes to pass: Isaac, the second biblical patriarch, is born.

Saving Isaac

According to the Midrash, a body of Old Testament commentaries compiled by Jewish rabbinical sages between 200 and 1000 AD, on the day Isaac is born, many sick people are healed, prayers are answered, and formerly barren women conceive children.

When Isaac is a child, God tests Abraham's faith by commanding him to sacrifice his beloved son. With a heavy heart, Abraham sets out to obey—but at the last minute, an angel intervenes, again promising that the devout father and son will be the progenitors of a great nation.

The Sacrifice of Isaac, by Rembrandt (c. 1635)

Stained glass showing Abraham and his wife, Sarah, with their newborn son, Isaac. Klosterneuburg, Austria

WHO KNEW?

The 15th of the Hebrew month of Nisan (approximately March or April) has special significance as the day the angels appeared to Abraham and Sarah, Isaac's birthday, and the first day of Passover.

BIBLICAL GEOGRAPHY

Scholars, anthropologists, geologists, and historians have all attempted to pinpoint the locations mentioned in the Old Testament.

Ur: The ancient southern Sumerian city, situated about 140 miles southeast of the site of ancient Babylon, was a center of polytheistic worship. Today it is known as Tall al-Muqayyar. It is located in Iraq, about 200 miles south of Baghdad and 10 miles west of the Euphrates River.

The oaks of Mamre: Genesis mentions this site as the place where Abraham entertained the three angels. According to the Bible, the trees were in Hebron. That ancient city was located about 1.5 miles northwest of modern Hebron, in Israel's West Bank.

Sodom: In Genesis, the sinful city where the angels traveled after leaving Abraham's tent was destroyed, along with Gomorrah, when God rained down "sulfur and fire." Modern geologists believe the devastation was wrought by an earthquake near the Great Rift Valley about 1900 BC. The cities' remains possibly now lie beneath shallow waters near the Dead Sea's southern end in Israel.

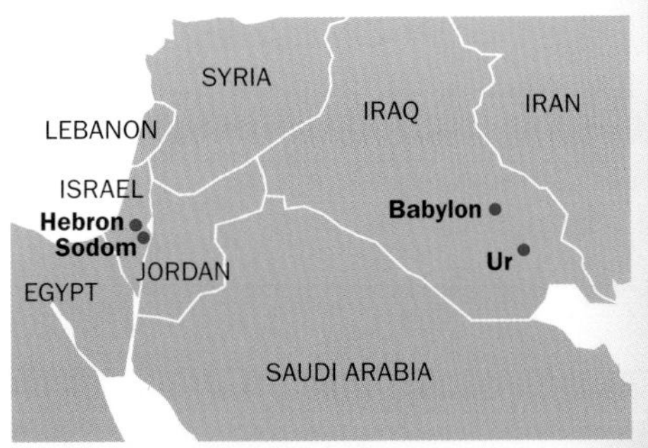

Abraham sends Hagar and Ishmael into the desert. Lithograph (c. 19th century)

"GOD HEARS"

An angel comes to the rescue of another son of Abraham.

Before the childless Sarah gives birth to Isaac, she urges Abraham to father a child with Hagar, her Egyptian maid.

But after Hagar gives birth to a son, Ishmael, Sarah becomes jealous. Abraham banishes Hagar and their child into the desert, where they are soon out of water. In one of the Bible's most heart-wrenching scenes, the desperate Hagar tries to shield the young boy from the brutal desert sun under a shrub. "Do not let me look on the death of the child," she weeps.

An angel appears, commanding, "Lift up the boy, and hold him fast with your hand, for I will make a great nation of him." When Hagar opens her eyes, she sees a well. Ishmael eventually becomes the patriarch of 12 Arab tribes. Tradition holds that he is the forebear of some modern Arab nations.

Truth From a Donkey's Mouth

THE BOOK OF NUMBERS INCLUDES THE STORY OF A WISE MAN TEMPTED BY WEALTH AND THE FAITHFUL ANIMAL WHO SETS HIM STRAIGHT.

STUBBORN AS A MULE

Balaam's animal companion was acting pretty much the way donkeys act.

→ Compared to horses, which are very trainable and compliant, donkeys can come across as difficult, ornery, and stubborn.

→ Donkeys are intelligent and have a very strong self-protective instinct. They evaluate terrain carefully and will not knowingly put themselves in danger. That might explain why Balaam's faithful animal refused to proceed when a furious angel confronted her with a raised sword.

→ Unlike horses, donkeys respect their own limits and will stop following orders when they get exhausted. Horses have been known to continue working until they drop.

The Old Testament diviner Balaam, who lives in the land of Moab, faces a dilemma. The Hebrews, who have been wandering the desert for 40 years, are approaching the area, intent on a battle. Moab's king wants Balaam to put a curse on them. He knows that the Hebrews have successfully defeated their enemies before. But in the Book of Numbers, God tells Balaam, "You shall not curse the people, for they are blessed." Balaam refuses the king's request, but the ruler, whose name is Balak, won't take no for an answer.

Some very distinguished nobles come to Balaam, offering him the king's richest rewards in exchange for the curse. Balaam considers the proposition, and replies, "Stay here tonight, and I will find out what else the Lord will speak to me."

This time, God tells Balaam he can go to Balak, but that God will tell him exactly what to say. In truth, God is angry that Balaam has been tempted by the wealth the king is offering.

An Angel in the Path

Balaam sets off on his donkey, unaware that God has sent an avenging angel to wait for him on the road. When the beast suddenly veers into a field in an attempt to guide Balaam away from the angry—and invisible—angel, the prophet swats the donkey, urging her back to the path.

The angel chooses a new position, where the road narrows to pass between two vineyard walls. Again, Balaam's donkey tries to save him by squeezing against one wall. She squashes her master's foot in the process, and Balaam smacks her again.

Finally the angel finds a passage through which the donkey is unable to maneuver. Out of options, the animal simply lies down in the road. Balaam is furious and strikes her with his staff. At that moment, God blesses the donkey with the power of speech and she says, "What have I done to you, that you have struck me these three times?"

"Am I not your donkey?"

Balaam is astonished, but still angry. "Because you have made a fool of me!" he replies. The beast defends herself. "Am I not your donkey, which you have ridden all your life to this day? Have I been in the habit of treating you this way?" Balaam admits she is right; it is the first time his faithful donkey has been disobedient.

Then God makes the angel visible and Balaam bows down in awe and fear. "I have come out as an adversary because your way is perverse before me," says the angel, speaking for God. "The donkey saw me, and turned away from me these three times. If it had not turned away from me,

Balaam, his donkey, and the angel of God in *The Angel in the Way*, by Julius Schnorr von Carolsfeld (1794–1872)

surely just now I would have killed you and let it live."

Penitent, Balaam turns to make the journey home when the angel redirects him: First, he must go to Balak to deliver God's message. Appearing in the court, Balaam is confronted by the king, who is angry the prophet has not come more quickly. "I have come now to you!" Balaam responds, then blesses the Hebrews instead of cursing them. Balaam has learned his lesson from the donkey. "The word God puts in my mouth, that is what I must speak," he says.

WHO KNEW?
Balaam was a so-called Gentile Prophet, one of six Old Testament prophets who were not members of the Chosen People.

FINDING BALAAM'S BLESSING

An intriguing archeological discovery is thought to be inscribed with the words of Balaam himself.

In Numbers, King Balak tries to force the prophet Balaam into cursing the Hebrews. Instead, Balaam issues a blessing and predicts the Hebrews will enjoy continued success. The passages constitute what is referred to as a pericope—a set of verses, usually from a sacred scripture. The language and style of the "Balaal Pericope" is distinct from the rest of the Book of Numbers.

In 1967, a Dutch archeological expedition working near the Jordan River unearthed plaster fragments inscribed with poetry thought to be from the Balaam Pericope. The fragments date to the late 9th or early 8th century BC—the period corresponding to the story in Numbers—and the language is consistent with the Balaam Pericope's distinctive style. When the fragments were reassembled and translated, they named a seer, "Balaam, son of Beor." The pericope relates the story of a heroic prophet who saved his people by foretelling a catastrophe; it is considered the first archaeological verification of Balaam's existence outside of the story told in the Bible.

Standing in the Heat

WHEN SHADRACH, MESHACH, AND ABEDNEGO ARE SENTENCED TO THE FURNACE, GOD SENDS AN ANGEL TO PRESERVE THEM.

King Nebuchadnezzar II, who ruled Babylonia from 605 BC to 562 BC, is portrayed in the Book of Daniel as having a very high opinion of himself. So high, in fact, that the king erects an enormous golden statue of himself and orders all government officials to attend the dedication. When music sounds in celebration, citizens across the land are ordered to bow down before the statue. "Whoever does not fall down and worship, shall immediately be cast into a furnace of blazing fire," Nebuchadnezzar decrees.

In the days following the ceremony, a group of the king's close advisors comes forward with a disturbing report: Three Hebrew officials are defying the edict. Instead of bowing to the statue, Shadrach, Meshach, and Abednego are praying to their own Hebrew God.

Royal Wrath

Nebuchadnezzar is furious. He summons the three Hebrews and warns that their misdeeds will be punished severely: "If you do not worship, you shall immediately be thrown into a furnace of blazing fire; and who is the god that will deliver you out of my hands?"

But Shadrach, Meshach, and Abednego are unafraid. Their faith in their religion is deep. "If our God whom we serve is able to deliver us from the furnace of blazing fire and out of your hand, O king, let him deliver us," respond the men. "But if not, be it known to you, O king, that we will not serve your gods and we will not wor-

WHO WAS NEBUCHADNEZZAR?

The king who witnessed the miracle of the fiery furnace also created the biblical Hanging Gardens of Babylon.

Nebuchadnezzar II was the son of Nabopolassar, who freed Babylon from Assyrian rule and annexed nearby Syria and Phoenicia. During his father's reign, Nebuchadnezzar led many great battles and built upon his legacy by invading Egypt and subduing a Hebrew uprising. He also oversaw the destruction of the Temple in Jerusalem. During this period, many Hebrews came to live and work in Babylon, some willingly, some as slaves.

As king, Nebuchadnezzar brought peace with the neighboring superpower of Midia by marrying the Midian king's daughter Amytis. He is perhaps most famous for creating the lush Hanging Gardens of Babylon, one of the seven wonders of the ancient world, to remind his wife of her beautiful homeland.

WHO KNEW?

Nebuchadnezzar's golden statue is described as 60 cubits high. That would be about 90 feet tall, or approximately the height of a nine-story building.

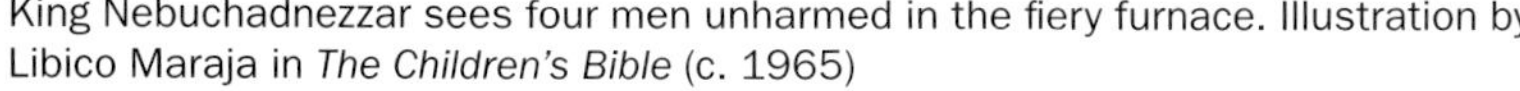

King Nebuchadnezzar sees four men unharmed in the fiery furnace. Illustration by Libico Maraja in *The Children's Bible* (c. 1965)

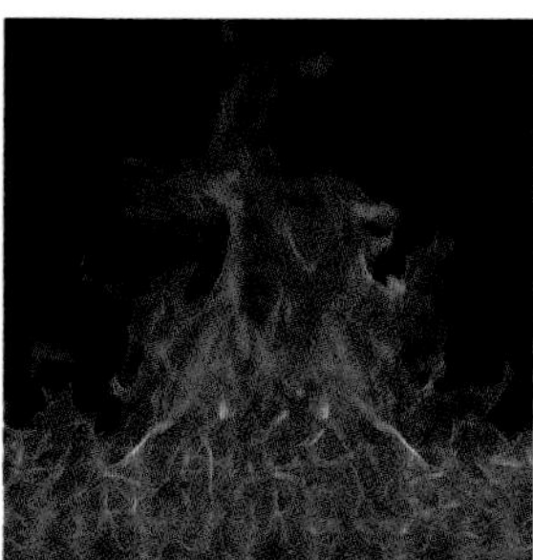

FLASH POINT

If the miracle of the fiery furnace actually came to pass, there would be little scientific explanation for it.

➔ Humans cannot survive temperatures higher than 212 degrees Fahrenheit, according to the National Fire Protection Association.

➔ Like others caught in fires, Shadrach, Meshach, and Abednego would likely have died from smoke inhalation, respiratory burns, or inhalation of toxic gas produced by the fire, rather than the flames themselves.

➔ Even firefighters in full gear would have had problems in Nebuchadnezzar's furnace: Their standard gear is designed to withstand temperatures up to 500 degrees, but only for five minutes. At higher temperatures, the protective clothing will last about eight seconds before melting.

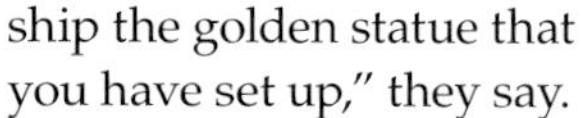

ship the golden statue that you have set up," they say.

Nebuchadnezzar, in a rage, orders the furnace heated to seven times its usual temperature. Shadrach, Meshach, and Abednego are bound with rope and cast into the flames. The blaze is so hot that the men who toss the three rebels in are themselves killed by the radiant heat. The king watches, eager to see his defiant prisoners suffer the same fate. What unfolds astounds him.

He shouts, "I see four men unbound, walking in the middle of the fire and they are not hurt; and the fourth has the appearance of a god." Nebuchadnezzar calls to Shadrach, Meshach, and Abednego to come out. They do so, unharmed.

None of the men bear any sign of the fire. Their clothes do not even smell scorched. The king interprets the fourth man in the furnace as a heavenly messenger, or an angel, sent to watch over the Hebrews.

"Blessed be the God of Shadrach, Meshach, and Abednego, who has sent his angel and delivered his servants who trusted in him," says the king in awe. From then on, Nebuchadnezzar vows to protect the three officials and sees that they lead prosperous lives.

Answered Prayers

AN ANGEL BRINGS GOOD NEWS TO AN INFERTILE COUPLE, LEAVING THE FATHER-TO-BE ABSOLUTELY SPEECHLESS.

Zechariah is visited by the angel Gabriel after lighting incense in the temple. Bible illustration by James Tissot (c. 19th century)

In the New Testament gospel of Luke, a Jewish holy man, Zechariah, is chosen to burn incense in the temple, an honor that is extended only once in each priest's life. Zechariah is obedient to the Lord and performs the rite despite his sorrow: He and his wife Elizabeth are getting on in years but have not been blessed with children. As Zechariah lights the incense, an angel appears next to the altar, startling him.

"Do not be afraid, Zechariah, for your prayer has been heard," says the angel. "Your wife Elizabeth will bear you a son, and you will name him John." The angel goes on to prophesy that Zechariah's son will be special. Not only will his birth bring "joy and gladness" to his parents, he will also be "great in the sight of the Lord" and will grow up to be a prophet who prepares the people for the coming of the Messiah.

Zechariah can't believe what he is hearing. How can this be true, he asks: He's an old man, and his wife, too, is aging. This expression of doubt turns out to be a mistake.

"I am Gabriel," the angel answers. "I stand in the presence of God, and I have been sent to speak to you and to bring you this good news. But now, because you did not believe my words, which will be fulfilled in their time, you will become mute, unable to speak, until the day these things occur."

A Blessed Visitor

Sure enough, Zechariah is unable to tell anyone what has transpired, because he is unable to speak. But just as the angel has promised, Elizabeth becomes pregnant. When she is six months along, her cousin Mary comes for a visit with her own blessed news to share. Mary is also to bear a child—the Messiah himself. Mary's presence makes Elizabeth's unborn baby move joyfully within her; he recognizes the Holy Spirit. Elizabeth cries out to Mary, "Blessed are you among women, and blessed is the fruit of your womb."

"His name is John."

Elizabeth gives birth to a son. His relatives assume she will name him Zechariah, after his father. But she says "No; he is to be called John." At this, everyone is surprised: John is not a family name. They ask Zechariah which name he prefers.

Still unable to speak, Zechariah takes a tablet and writes, "His name is John." And with that, the curse is lifted, and he begins to relate a prophecy in beautiful poetry: John will prepare the world to receive the Messiah as a sign of the mercy of God, Zechariah says. "to give light to those who sit in darkness and in the shadow of death, to guide our feet into the way of peace." The miracle son goes on to become John the Baptist.

The Naming of John the Baptist, by Rogier van der Weyden (c. 1450s)

WHO KNEW?

While all four New Testament gospels include accounts of John the Baptist's preaching, only Luke tells of the angel who foretold his birth.

A SPECIAL OFFER

When Zechariah lights incense in the temple, he is performing a rite so sacred that no man may do it more than once.

In biblical times, an offering of incense was made daily to symbolize the prayers of the godly people of Israel. The task was assigned by the drawing of lots, and a priest could only be selected once. Though Zechariah was in his old age and considered most righteous, he had never before been chosen.

After admitting the people to the temple for the morning worship, the chosen priest entered an inner chamber and stood alone before the altar. When the moment was right, the priest lit the *ketoret*, a kind of incense made of valuable perfume, and prostrated himself before the altar; the smoke arising would signal to the congregation that the offering had been made, and they, too, would bow in prayer until the priest came out.

On the day the angel appeared to Zechariah, everyone must have wondered what was taking him so long. Because the angel rendered him mute, he was unable to tell them of his experience until nine months and eight days later.

Salome Receives the Head of John the Baptist, by Michelangelo Caravaggio (c. 1610)

NO ORDINARY MAN

John the Baptist lives an eccentric life and suffers a bizarre death.

➔ As an adult, John goes off to live in the wilderness, wrapping himself in camel skin, eating wild honey and locusts, and preaching from the Book of Isaiah.

➔ Jesus comes to John asking to be baptized, a practice John has adopted to symbolize the forgiveness of sins. During the baptism, the Holy Spirit appears in the form of a dove. The voice of God says, "This is my beloved Son, with whom I am well pleased."

➔ John publicly condemns King Herod for having an incestuous affair. Herod has John arrested.

➔ At Herod's birthday banquet, the king's niece Salome performs a provocative dance and, prompted by her treacherous mother, requests the head of John the Baptist on a platter as her reward. Herod has John beheaded and grants his guest the prize.

➔ For a while, as Jesus continues teaching and performing miracles, many people believe that he is in fact John, back from the dead.

The Three Marys at the Tomb, by Hubert van Eyck and/or Jan van Eyck (c. 1425–35)

CHAPTER 4

Miracles of the New Testament

In Christianity, the most astonishing events spring from Jesus himself.

AVE

Mary's Visitor

A STUNNING BIRTH ANNOUNCEMENT CHANGES THE LIFE OF A YOUNG WOMAN—AND THE ENTIRE WORLD—FOREVER.

The story of Jesus Christ begins with Mary. Before she is chosen as the Mother of God, Mary is simply a young woman in Nazareth, a small mountain village in what is now northern Israel. She is utterly unaware of the part she will play in a prophecy to which her people have clung for generations—the coming of the Messiah. She is just a typical bride-to-be preparing for her wedding to a local carpenter named Joseph, a descendant of King David of Israel.

Then, according to the Gospel of Luke, an angel appears before her. "Greetings, favored one!" the angel Gabriel thunders. Mary is understandably frightened. "The Lord is with you," he reassures her. "Do not be afraid, for you have found favor with God. And now, you will conceive in your womb and bear a son, and you will name him Jesus."

Gabriel goes on to quote the old prophecies: "He will be great, and will be called the Son of the Most High, and the Lord God will give to him the throne of his ancestor David. He will reign over the house of Jacob forever, and of his kingdom there will be no end."

Mary can hardly believe her ears. The first question she asks is an entirely prosaic one: "How can this be, since I am a virgin?"

The Annunciation, by Teodor Kolbay (c. 1863)

The angel Gabriel visits Mary in *The Annunciation*, by Jan van den Kerckhove (c. 1707)

Nothing Is Impossible

Gabriel explains that Mary's baby will not be conceived in the ordinary way. Instead, he says, the child will be conceived through the Holy Spirit and will be the Son of God.

As further testament to the miracle he describes, Gabriel tells Mary that her older cousin, Elizabeth, who has up until now been infertile, is six months pregnant. Elizabeth will eventually give birth to a son, John, who will become the prophet John the Baptist and who will spread the Word of the coming of the Son of God. With God, Gabriel says, nothing is impossible.

Gabriel's appearance to Mary is called the Annunciation. In Christianity, the occasion is observed on March 25, nine months before Christmas Day.

Mary responds that she is God's servant and will do whatever the Lord wishes. She says she hopes everything Gabriel has told her comes to pass.

And so it does. Nine months later, Jesus Christ is born in a manger in Bethlehem. Numerous divine signs herald his arrival. Kings, shepherds, and heavenly angels rejoice. As the years pass, Jesus's devoted mother will be present for many of her son's miracles. And Jesus's followers will go on to found a religion that crosses the globe and influences the course of human history.

THE HOLY STEPFATHER

In his role as Jesus's earthly guardian, Joseph has his own encounters with an angel.

When Mary becomes pregnant before her marriage to Joseph, the groom-to-be is embarrassed and upset, according to the Gospel of Matthew: The child is obviously not his. He no longer wishes to marry Mary, but he doesn't want her to suffer public humiliation, so he plans to separate from Mary quietly.

Before Joseph can do so, he is visited by an angel in a dream. "Joseph, son of David, do not be afraid to take Mary as your wife, for the child conceived in her is from the Holy Spirit," the angel tells him. "She will bear a son, and you are to name him Jesus, for he will save his people from their sins."

Joseph is a devout man and recognizes the prophecy in the angel's message. He marries Mary as planned, though the two do not live together as husband and wife until after the baby is born.

The Dream of Saint Joseph, by Stefano Maria Legnani (c. 1708)

Jesus as a child in the temple with the elders, in *Mysteries of the Rosary*, by Campi Vincenzo (c. 16th century)

THE EARLY YEARS

As the mother of Jesus, Mary has a front-row seat to her son's life.

➔ On the night of Jesus's birth, a choir of angels appears to a group of shepherds in their fields to announce his arrival. The shepherds become the first to welcome the baby Jesus.

➔ Soon afterward, Herod, the Roman-installed king of Judea, hears the rumors of a new Messiah and, fearful of threat to his power, orders all male children under age two put to death. God sends an angel to warn Joseph, who flees with Mary and Jesus to Egypt. The family lives there for several years, until the angel informs Joseph that it is safe to return.

➔ When Jesus is 12, the family travels to Jerusalem to celebrate Passover. On the journey home, Mary and Joseph realize their son is missing. After three days of frantic searching, they find him back at the temple, sitting with the learned men of the synagogue. When he sees that they are alarmed, he says, "Why were you searching for me? Did you not know that I must be in my Father's house?"

The Sign of the Wine

AT A WEDDING OF ONE OF HIS RELATIVES, JESUS PERFORMS HIS FIRST PUBLIC MIRACLE AND BEGINS HIS WORK IN THE WORLD.

Mary and Jesus at the wedding at Cana. Church fresco, Abondance Abbey, Haute-Savoie, France

THERE'S SOMETHING ABOUT MARY

At the wedding in Cana, mother knows best.

One of the remarkable things about the story of Cana is the prominent role played by Jesus's mother. Arguably, if it weren't for Mary, the miracle would not have taken place. According to the Gospel of John, Mary is the one who sets the events in motion by insisting that her son do something to remedy the couple's shortage of wine.

Among Jews in biblical times, it was common to celebrate marriages over seven days, opening with an extravagant feast. Invited to a relative's wedding banquet in Cana, a village in Galilee, Jesus arrives with his mother, Mary, some other relatives, and his first few disciples.

Mary goes to help out in the kitchen and learns that there is no wine left, a shortage that's sure to disgrace the happy couple. She quickly informs Jesus, but he appears untroubled. "What concern is that to you and to me? My hour has not yet come," he replies, perhaps suggesting that such earthly and temporal concerns are not important to him. Mary persists, and when Jesus agrees to solve the problem, she instructs the servants to do exactly as he asks.

Nearby stand six large stone urns of holy water used for ritual hand-washing. Jesus asks the servants to top off the urns with water, then pour some into cups and take it to "the chief steward," or host. The steward tastes it, declares it delicious, and summons the groom to compliment him on his hospitality: "Everyone serves the good wine first; and then the inferior wine after the guests have become drunk. But you have kept the good wine until now."

It soon becomes apparent that Jesus has created the wine from water. Not only are the wedding guests amazed by this miracle, but by doing "this, the first of his signs," he has "revealed his glory." The disciples, who had been uncertain of his divinity, are now convinced he is the Messiah.

The Good Wine

Biblical scholars still debate whether the story is meant to be taken literally or allegorically, but they generally agree on its meaning. The tale of the wedding at Cana is not just an example of God's supernatural dominion over Earth; it's a sign of Jesus's divinity. He demonstrates his own ability to mold the physical world.

In some allegorical interpretations, Jesus himself is the "good wine" whose appearance signals the dawn of the messianic age. The wine replaces the water in the stone urns, just as the laws and beliefs of pre-messianic Judaism are replaced by God's grace under Christianity. When the good wine is poured into the wedding cups, the joy of eternal life in heaven is granted to those who believe in Christ. The miracle becomes definitive proof to the disciples that God's promise has been fulfilled, and that the Messiah has arrived on Earth.

WHO KNEW?

Each of the stone vessels would have held 20 to 30 gallons, so Jesus made between 120 and 180 gallons of wine.

Jesus instructs a servant to pour water into the jugs at the wedding feast at Cana. Chancel window (detail), Church of St. Patrick, Bampton Grange, Cumbria, U.K.

Wedding at Cana, by Giotto di Bondone (c. 1306)

HOLY MATRIMONY

A biblical-era wedding was quite an event.

Some theologians say the miracle at Cana shows Jesus's approval of tradition, and of marriage. The feast was only the first event in a massive, seven-day celebration. So, what was a wedding feast like?

➔ It fell on a Wednesday afternoon or evening if the bride was a virgin, and on Thursday if she was a widow.

➔ It didn't include a religious ceremony.

➔ The guests wore special wedding clothes.

➔ The feast took place in the groom's home.

➔ The groom led the bride and wedding party from the bride's home to his own in a ceremonial procession.

➔ A man known as a "steward" presided over the affair, making the preparations, circulating among the guests, and ensuring that all was well.

➔ The mood of the feast was jovial; it was customary for guests to tell riddles, and there was music and dancing.

Five Loaves, Two Fish, One Big Meal

IN ONE OF THE BEST-KNOWN BIBLICAL STORIES, JESUS MANAGES TO FEED A FLOCK OF THOUSANDS WITH JUST A FEW PROVISIONS.

As Jesus's ministry begins, he delivers the Sermon on the Mount, offering unforgettable lessons, and performs miracles that attract disciples. He cures people of a variety of afflictions, exorcises demons, and brings a dead girl back to life. In crisscrossing the region around Galilee, Jesus encounters multitudes who gather hoping to witness his next astounding act.

WHO KNEW?
In addition to bread and fish, the everyday diet in biblical Galilee included olives, figs, grapes, grains, legumes, milk, and honey.

Hungry Souls

After lengthy travels, Jesus decides to give his disciples a rest, and they cross the Sea of Galilee by boat to a place in the desert near the city of Bethsaida. Word of their arrival has spread and swarms of people have "hurried there on foot from all the towns and arrived ahead of them," according to the Gospel of Mark. Before the men disembark, a huge crowd, perhaps as many as 10,000, has gathered on a grassy hillside.

Jesus speaks to them about the Kingdom of God and heals those who come to him seeking cures for their ailments. As evening falls, the disciples suggest that he send the throng, hungry after a long day, into the surrounding villages to buy food. But Jesus wants to show the people the miraculous power of God and commands his disciples, "Give them something to eat."

Dumbfounded, the disciples reply they have no food and that feeding the crowd will require "two hundred denarii worth of bread"—about 200 days' wages. Nevertheless, they obey Jesus's order to collect whatever they can find among the spectators.

After this exercise, one disciple reports, "There is a boy here who has five barley loaves and two fish. But what are they among so many people?" Jesus looks up to heaven, blesses the food, and divides it among his disciples. The disciples, in turn, distribute the bread and fish—astounded to find that there is more than enough to go around.

"Gather up the fragments left over, so that nothing may be lost," Jesus commands. When they are through, they have 12 baskets of leftovers.

The miracle amazes the disciples as well as the crowd. The Jews have long believed that when the Messiah came to Earth, he would feed them with bread from heaven. Jesus senses that the excited mob may soon get out of hand and "would come and take him by force to make him king." Sending his disciples to cross back over the Sea of Galilee, he retreats alone up a mountain until the crowd disperses.

The Feeding of the Five Thousand, by Joachim Partinir (1480–1524)

A DIFFERENT PERSPECTIVE

The Book of John is unlike the other three gospels in both tone and content.

All four gospels narrate the miracle of the loaves and fish. In three of them—Matthew, Mark, and Luke—the accounts have a great deal of details and descriptions in common. The fourth gospel, John, gives the story a different spin.

So it is with the gospels as a whole: John tends to stand alone, while the books of Matthew, Mark, and Luke share a similar approach to the life of Jesus. These three are called the synoptic gospels (the Greek word *syn* translates as "together," and *optic* as "seen").

The synoptic gospels present Jesus's life story, from his birth to his resurrection, as a series of events, relating many of the same anecdotes in roughly the same order. Theologians attribute the similarities to the books' intersecting origins: Matthew and Luke used Mark, written about 70 AD, as their main source of information when they wrote their accounts around 80 to 90 AD. By contrast, more than 90 percent of the material in John (written 90–110 AD) doesn't appear in the synoptic gospels, according to Celia Brewer Marshall and Celia B. Sinclair in *A Guide Through the New Testament*.

The Gospel of John has a more mystical tone and leaves out many of the stories told in the synoptic gospels. In John's telling, Jesus performs fewer miracles but they are more spectacular than in the other accounts. Instead of a preacher of parables and a worker of wonders, he is God on Earth.

Going beyond the facts of Jesus's life, the book contemplates the miracle of his existence and his divine identity as the Son of God. John 1:14 encapsulates His approach: "And the Word [God] was made flesh, and dwelt among us, (and we beheld his glory, the glory as of the only begotten of the Father), full of grace and truth."

Wonder on the Water

WITH A BOATFUL OF HIS DISCIPLES WATCHING ONE STORMY NIGHT, JESUS WALKS UPON THE SEA OF GALILEE.

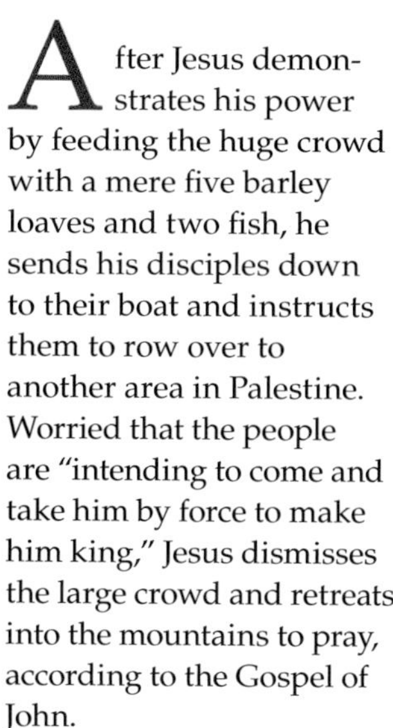

After Jesus demonstrates his power by feeding the huge crowd with a mere five barley loaves and two fish, he sends his disciples down to their boat and instructs them to row over to another area in Palestine. Worried that the people are "intending to come and take him by force to make him king," Jesus dismisses the large crowd and retreats into the mountains to pray, according to the Gospel of John.

A Ghost in the Mist

For the disciples, the winds and waves are rough on the Sea of Galilee, and a treacherous journey lies ahead. When they have rowed about three or four miles, according to John's account, and have been on the water for several hours, Jesus comes to them, "walking on the sea." The disciples fear the apparition, but Jesus reassures them, saying, "It is I; do not be afraid."

Matthew's gospel alone recounts that the disciple Peter replies. "Lord, if it is you, command me to come to you on the water," he says. Jesus responds, "Come." Yet as Peter walks toward Jesus, he is overcome by fear and begins to sink. Jesus reaches out his hand, saying, "You of little faith, why did you doubt?"

When Jesus boards the boat, the seas and winds calm and the men carry on. Once they land, they again find multitudes who have gathered with their ailing loved ones, in hopes that Jesus will heal them. Those who know that the disciples had set off without Jesus the night before marvel at the fact that all have arrived together in one boat, according to John.

Divine Symbolism

From the Christian perspective, the miracle of Jesus on the water is just one of a number of examples of his divine nature, fulfilling the prophecy of Job that God alone "trampled the waves of the sea." The richly symbolic act, demonstrating power over nature, has antecedents in the Old Testament, when God parts the Red Sea for Moses in Exodus and the River Jordan for Elijah and Elisha in Kings.

Similar feats play a role in the legends of other cultures as well. In Roman mythology, the god Neptune rides his chariot upon the sea; and texts detailing the life of the Buddha suggest that he could walk on water, as well as part the seas.

Jesus walks on the water of the Sea of Galilee. Engraving by H. Pisan from a drawing by Gustave Doré, (c. 19th century)

ON THIN ICE

A professor of oceanography weighs in on the Sea of Galilee.

Seeking a meteorological explanation for how Jesus could have walked on water, researchers from Florida State University used temperature records and statistical models to investigate a 10,000-square-foot area of Lake Kinneret, the modern site of the Sea of Galilee.

What they found suggested that the temperature in that region during the time of Jesus likely dropped to around 25 degrees Fahrenheit for a couple of days. So Jesus may have stood or walked on a sheet of ice—which may not have been discernible on a dark night.

"We simply explain that unique freezing processes probably happened in that region only a handful of times during the last 12,000 years," said professor of oceanography Doron Nof, who has written and spoken extensively on physical oceanography. "We leave to others the question of whether or not our research explains the biblical account." Dr. Nof places the chances of this occurring at about one in 1,000, however, "in today's climate, the chance of spring ice forming in northern Israel is effectively zero, or about once in more than 10,000 years."

Fishermen cast their nets on the Sea of Galilee.

SEA OF DOUBT

Those who challenge the idea of Jesus walking on water have alternative explanations.

→ Albert Schweitzer, a Lutheran theologian, philosopher, and missionary, suggested that the disciples actually saw Jesus walking along the misty shore, and that Peter was saved because he was close enough to shore that Jesus could pull him out.

→ Methodist biblical scholar Vincent Taylor, author of the 1957 book *The Gospel According to Saint Mark*, proposes that Jesus was wading through the surf near the shore. The disciples couldn't get a clear picture, though, because the weather was bad.

→ Sherman Johnson, an Episcopalian scholar and dean of the Church Divinity School of the Pacific, hypothesized that Jesus probably walked along a sandbar to a place that merely seemed to be far out into the sea.

Who Touched My Robe?

ON HIS WAY TO SAVE A DYING CHILD, JESUS IS SIDETRACKED BY A WOMAN WHO DESPERATELY NEEDS HIS ATTENTION.

The Twelve Tribes of Israel on the cover of a watch.

THE DIVINE DOZEN

The number 12 is significant in these intertwined miracles: The Rabbi's daughter is 12 years old, and the bleeding woman has been afflicted for 12 years. In fact, this number, said to represent God's divine order, appears almost 200 times in the Bible, including:

→ **12 tribes** of Israel

→ **12 pillars** built in the Promised Land

→ **Jesus is 12** when he questions teachings in the Temple

→ **12 baskets** of leftovers after the loaves and fish miracle

→ Jesus has **12 apostles**

The people of Capernaum, a fishing village on the Sea of Galilee, have witnessed Jesus perform a number of healings during his previous visits. So a large crowd is waiting for him when he returns with his disciples. According to the Gospel of Mark, Rabbi Jairus, a leader of the local synagogue, comes forward and falls to the ground in front of Jesus, imploring him for help: "My little daughter is at the point of death. Come and lay your hands on her, so that she may be made well, and live."

Desperate Measures

But before he can get to the home of this important and powerful man, Jesus is interrupted. As he walks with Jairus, the crowd follows, crushing up against Jesus. At one point, according to Mark, Jesus stops and asks, "Who touched my clothes?"

His disciples are bewildered, replying, "You see the crowd pressing in on you; how can you say 'Who touched me?'" But, according to Luke, Jesus persists: "Someone touched me; for I noticed that power had gone out from me."

At last, a woman emerges from the crowd and admits to touching Jesus's clothing in hope of healing the bleeding illness from which she has suffered for 12 years. Jesus replies, "Daughter, your faith has made you well; go in peace."

She's Only Sleeping

But as Jesus speaks with the woman, bad news comes from the home of Rabbi Jairus. A messenger tells Jairus, "Your daughter is dead; do not trouble the teacher any longer." When Jesus hears this, he assures the grief-stricken rabbi, "Do not fear. Only believe, and she will be saved."

Jesus arrives at Jairus's house to find a group of wailing mourners. According to Mark's account, Jesus addresses them: "Why do you make a commotion and weep? The child is not dead but sleeping." They begin to laugh at this preposterous notion, at which point Jesus insists that everyone leave the house except the girl's parents and his own disciples, Peter, James, and John.

> "Do not fear. Only believe, and she will be saved."

Jesus approaches the motionless child and takes her hand, intoning, "Talitha cum!"—in Aramaic, "Little girl, get up!" The rabbi's daughter arises immediately and begins to walk. Jesus instructs her astonished parents to give her something to eat, and to tell no one what has happened. But inevitably, details of the event spread throughout the area.

WHO KNEW?
The details of New Testament episodes can vary from gospel to gospel—just as with news accounts today. In Matthew, Jairus's daughter is already dead when he first approaches Jesus.

Jesus Raising of the Daughter of Jairus, by Paolo Veronese (c. 1546)

A DESPERATE ACT

There's a reason why the bleeding woman had to touch Jesus's clothing surreptitiously.

The woman who secretly grasps the fringe of Jesus's cloak has been suffering for years from what various Bible translations describe as hemorrhaging or an "issue of blood." Though the exact condition is open to speculation, it is regularly interpreted as a gynecological disorder resulting in continuous bleeding.

According to biblical law (which is still followed today in a few cultures), a menstruating woman is considered "ceremonially unclean" and is not allowed to touch anyone, nor to enter a synagogue. On those days, she is "untouchable."

So, given her condition, the woman in this story has lived as an outcast for 12 years. By breaking a sacred rule and defiling Jesus with her touch, she commits a bold, desperate act to get well. Jesus forgives the transgression, viewing it as evidence of her deep faith.

Conquering Death

JESUS'S RESURRECTION OF LAZARUS PREFIGURES HIS OWN FATE AND IS CONSIDERED BY MANY TO BE DEFINITIVE PROOF OF HIS DIVINITY.

A detail of *The Raising of Lazarus*, by Tintoretto (c. 1581)

The Gospel of John describes one of Jesus's most powerful acts: the raising of his friend Lazarus from the dead. It is the only account of the miracle in the four gospels and is the last such feat discussed in John.

Lazarus is living with his sisters Mary and Martha in the town of Bethany, about two miles southeast of Jerusalem. When he falls sick, the women send word to Jesus, asking him to come quickly. But Jesus does not set out for two days, saying, "This sickness is not unto death, but for the glory of God, that the Son of God might be glorified thereby."

Even when Jesus learns that Lazarus has died, he is not troubled: He will soon show people what the miraculous power of God can do. He knows death isn't the end for those who have faith.

When Jesus arrives in Bethany, Lazarus has been dead for four days and his body entombed in a cave. His sisters and friends have gathered to mourn. Upset that Jesus has not come sooner, Martha complains, "Lord, if you had been here, my brother would not have died." Reassuring her that all will be well, Jesus makes a promise: "I am the resurrection and the life. Those who believe in me, even though they die, will live, and everyone who lives and believes in me will never die," according to John.

"Take away the stone."

Jesus and Martha go to Lazarus's hillside grave, where her sister Mary and the other

Resurrected

Only Lazarus and a few other people in the Bible return to life.

The 66 books of the Old Testament and New Testament recount hundreds of miracles, but, aside from Lazarus and, of course, Jesus, only seven others are said to have been raised from the dead.

SON OF A WIDOW IN ZAREPHATH

MIRACLE WORKER: Elijah

A widow is sheltering Elijah in her home when her son dies. She turns on the prophet, who helps her anyway and raises her son from the dead.

YOUNG MAN IN SHUNEM

MIRACLE WORKER: Elisha

Elisha has prophesied that a barren woman will bear a son. She does, and when her son later dies, the woman feels betrayed by the prophet, who then acts to give the boy life.

ANONYMOUS MAN IN SAMARIA

MIRACLE WORKER: Elisha's bones

Elisha dies and is placed in a sepulcher. At a later date, marauders interrupt a burial ceremony nearby. The mourners throw the body into Elisha's tomb and it touches the prophet's bones. The man is resurrected.

The Raising of Lazarus, by Carl Heinrich Bloch (c. 1871)

mourners join them. The profound grief of the crowd moves him so deeply that "Jesus wept" even though he knows what is to follow. He tells the mourners, "Take away the stone" that covers the mouth of the cave. As they roll it away, Jesus commands Lazarus to come out and, to the amazement of the crowd, the resurrected man emerges in his burial shroud.

Faith and Fear

For many of the witnesses, the miracle of Lazarus proves that Jesus is the son of God. Some, however, are uneasy about the holy man's growing fame and report the incident to the Pharisees, a Jewish sect that sees Jesus as a threat to their power. "If we let him go on like this," the Pharisees agree, "everyone will believe in him: and the Romans will come and destroy both our holy place and our nation." Knowing the Pharisees want to kill him, Jesus withdraws to the city of Ephraim with his disciples and, according to John, performs no further miracles.

The Pharisees also consider the living Lazarus as evidence of Jesus's divinity, and therefore a threat to their leadership. They plot to have him killed as well, though the Bible never mentions his fate.

HOLY LIFE AFTER DEATH

What in the world happened to Lazarus?

Several legends concern the unknown fate of Lazarus after Jesus's crucifixion. One medieval version connects the resurrected Lazarus to a historical bishop of the same name. According to this legend, Jews hostile to Christianity set Lazarus and his sisters adrift on the Mediterranean Sea in a leaky boat. As the story goes, the siblings land in southeastern Gaul (now France), where Lazarus becomes the first Bishop of Marseille. Decades later, the Roman Emperor Domitian has Lazarus beheaded; the Roman Catholic and Eastern Orthodox churches now revere him as a saint.

SON OF A WIDOW IN NAIN

MIRACLE WORKER: Jesus

Jesus encounters a funeral outside the city gates. He touches the dead boy's bier; the boy rises.

JAIRUS'S DAUGHTER

MIRACLE WORKER: Jesus

Jesus brings the dead girl to life.

TABITHA (DORCAS), IN JOPPA

MIRACLE WORKER: Peter

A wake for Tabitha, a widowed follower of Jesus, is underway at her house. Her friends ask the apostle to come, and Peter restores Tabitha to life.

EUTYCHUS, IN TROAS

MIRACLE WORKER: Paul

Listening to a sermon by Paul, Eutychus falls asleep and tumbles out of a second-story window to his death. The apostle embraces the body and says the man is still alive; Eutychus awakens.

Faithful Healers

THE BOOK OF ACTS RECOUNTS THAT AFTER JESUS ASCENDS TO HEAVEN, HIS DISCIPLES PERFORM MIRACLES IN HIS NAME.

Once Jesus has left the earthly realm, the apostles know that it is time to go forth and spread his message. Peter, John, and the others return to Jerusalem, where they set about persuading their fellow Israelites that Jesus is the Messiah. On the first day of their mission, the apostles convert 3,000 people to their new faith—and these are joined by many more as the days pass.

One afternoon, Peter and John head for the Jewish temple just as people are flooding in for afternoon prayer. Their plan is to speak to the crowd in order to gain more converts. Seated outside one of the gates is a man who can't walk. As Peter and John approach him, he asks them for money without even looking up.

St Peter, accompanied by John the Apostle, heals a disabled man at the gate of the temple in Jerusalem. Engraving by H. B. Hall after a 1655 painting by Nicolas Poussin.

"Look at us," Peter says, and the man does, expecting that John and Peter are about to give him some coins. But Peter says, "I have no silver or gold, but what I have I give you; in the name of Jesus Christ of Nazareth, stand up and walk." Peter takes the man's hand.

The transformation is instantaneous. The man leaps to his feet and, for the first time in his life, walks with Peter and John into the Temple courtyard, where he jumps up and down and praises God. The onlookers, who recognize the man as a regular presence at the gate, are "filled with wonder and amazement at what had happened to him."

Peter tells the crowd that he has not performed the miracle—Jesus has. The beggar has been healed because Peter uttered Jesus's name.

This good deed does not go unpunished: Peter and John are thrown in jail for a night for disturbing the Temple worshippers. But the miracle is effective: They soon welcome 2,000 new converts to Christianity.

Wakeup Call

While Peter is performing numerous impressive feats, the apostle Paul travels to Greece and Macedonia to serve as the conduit for God's miracles there. "When the handkerchiefs or aprons that had touched his skin were brought to the sick, their diseases left them, and the evil spirits came out of them." After a couple of years, Paul visits Troas, a Greek coastal city in what is now Turkey. On his last night there, he addresses a roomful of people, going on past midnight. A young man named Eutychus, who is

Paul resuscitating the young Eutychus, in a 19th-century fresco

A WOUNDED GOD

What does it mean that Jesus returns to Earth with his wounds in evidence?

Jesus's body sustains profound damage during the crucifixion. When he later appears to his disciples at the Resurrection, it is with a stab wound to his side from a Roman soldier's lance, and mangled hands and hobbled feet from being nailed to the cross. That he returns impaired, and not as his former able-bodied self, is deeply significant, according to theologian Nancy Eiesland, author of the now-classic *The Disabled God: Toward a Liberatory Theology of Disability.*

The Bible often depicts the disabled as sinners whom God has punished, as noble martyrs or as pitiful charity cases. But Jesus after the Resurrection projects an entirely different image. In Eisland's words, his "disability indicates not a flawed humanity but a full humanity."

sitting in a window, dozes off and plummets three stories to the ground outside. Paul rushes downstairs and puts his arms around Eutychus where he lies. "Do not be alarmed," he tells the crowd, "for his life is in him."

Today, there is some disagreement over exactly what Paul meant—whether Eutychus was dead and Paul revived him, or whether Paul was simply informing the crowd that the young man had survived his fall. Either way, the upsetting incident doesn't slow Paul down. He goes back upstairs, has something to eat, and continues talking until dawn.

ILLNESS AS METAPHOR

In the Bible, disabilities sometimes have unflattering symbolic meanings. Healing of physical problems can stand for healing of the spirit as well.

BIBLICAL AFFLICTION	SYMBOLIC SIGNIFICANCE
BLINDNESS	Ignorance, lack of faith
DEAFNESS	Stubborn refusal to do what God says
MUTENESS	Doubt in God's word
LEPROSY	Sin, uncleanliness
PARALYSIS	Negligence, weakness

WHO KNEW?

While in prison, apostles Paul and Silas have a chance to escape but don't; they know their jailer will be killed if they flee.

Heavenly Rescue

WHEN THE APOSTLE PETER IS ARRESTED, IT TAKES A MESSENGER OF GOD TO FREE HIM.

Since his days as a disciple of Jesus, Peter has been a dedicated leader of the early Christians, preaching Jesus's gospel in Galilee and Judea and overseeing the organization of the first Church. But the Jewish religious leaders dislike the new Christian faith. And Herod, the tyrannical, Roman-appointed ruler of Judea, is on their side for political reasons. A few days after ordering the murder of Peter's fellow apostle James, brother of John, Herod arrests Peter. He plans to make an example of one of Jesus's chief followers by punishing him publically on the last night of Passover, as a deterrent to any others attracted to the new movement. Peter finds himself in prison, while church members gather in secret to pray for his protection and deliverance.

Faith Unchained

As the Book of Acts tells it, on the night Herod plans to punish him, Peter is sound asleep, chained to a soldier on each side, his cell guarded by four squads of armed men. An angel suddenly appears in his cell.

"Get up quickly!" says the angel, as his chains fall away. "Wrap your cloak around you and follow me." Sleepy, confused, and terrified for his life, Peter fears the figure is a product of his imagination. But his faith

The Liberation of St. Peter, by Raphael, 1514.

Roman soldiers attack a Christian service held secretly in the Roman catacombs. Illustration by Selmar Hess, c. 1880.

DANGEROUS FAITH

Back when Christianity was a minority religion, its followers were persecuted relentlessly.

➔ Roman citizens viewed the early Christians as trouble-makers. Christians refused to participate in traditional pagan festivals, and people were suspicious of their new beliefs and unfamiliar religious practices.

➔ Angry mobs often threw stones at Christians, and local authorities beat Christians or imprisoned them.

➔ For 10 years, beginning in 303 AD, a series of four Roman emperors ordered churches destroyed, church leaders arrested, and scriptures burned. Scores of Christians were imprisoned, tortured, beheaded, fed to beasts, or crucified.

➔ During this Great Persecution, Christians were forced to meet and worship in secret; some held services in the catacombs beneath Rome.

➔ Finally, in 313 AD, Constantine the Great issued the Edict of Milan declaring religious tolerance in the Roman Empire, restoring the legal status of Christians and granting them freedom to worship as they pleased.

proves greater than his fear. He follows the angel through the lines of soldiers and all the way to the city gates, which open by themselves to allow the pair to pass through. When they enter, the angel leads Peter to a side street, then vanishes.

"Now I am sure that the Lord has sent his angel and rescued me from the hands of Herod," Peter says to himself as he hurries to the house where church members have gathered to pray. He knocks on the door, and the servant woman who answers, named Rhoda, is so shocked to see him that she runs to tell the flock without letting him in! Naturally, they do not believe her. It must be Peter's angel, they conclude. How could Peter have come to them while they were in the very act of praying for his deliverance?

Peter keeps knocking until he is finally admitted, to everyone's astonishment. Peter explains to them that no, he is not an angel, but he has seen one. In fact, an angel set him free.

St. Peter in Prison (The Apostle Peter Kneeling), by Rembrandt van Rijn, 1631

Crucifixion of St. Peter, Church of San Michele in Bosco, Bologna, Italy (c. 16th century)

"I AM NOT WORTHY"

The man who would become the first pope served the church throughout his life and was humble even in his death.

The apostle Peter traveled throughout the Roman Empire preaching the gospel of Jesus to Jews and Gentiles alike. Under the emperor Nero, who ruled from 37 AD to 68 AD, Peter, along with many other Christians, was arrested and put to death. The motivation for Peter's execution remain a mystery, but some scholars believe he was killed in 64 AD, in response to the great fire that destroyed Rome that year, which Nero blamed on the Christians.

The most well known aspect of Peter's martyrdom is its form. He was crucified—as were other Christians during the period—but Peter insisted that he be crucified upside down. He is believed to have said, "For I am not worthy to die in the same way as my Lord."

Peter was buried near the site of his crucifixion, in Caligula's Circus, at the foot of what is now Vatican Hill. In the 4th century, the Emperor Constantine constructed a basilica on the site that lasted for a thousand years. Pope Nicolas V began a restoration project there in the 15th century, and in 1506 the architect Donato Bramante was commissioned to build a new basilica on the site. After Bramante's death, several architects worked on St. Peter's and eventually Michelangelo took over, designing its famous dome. The St. Peter's that we know today was dedicated in 1626.

The Virgin of Vladimir, from the collection of the State Tretyakov Gallery, Moscow (c. late 15th century)

CHAPTER 5

Miracles of Mary

The most venerated of saints is said to appear periodically to the faithful and blessed.

Manifesting Mary

WHENEVER THE MOTHER OF GOD DECIDES TO PAY THE WORLD A VISIT, BELIEVERS PAY RAPT ATTENTION.

WHO KNEW?
The Greek Orthodox Church refers to Mary as *Theotokos*, or God-bearer. In the Koran, Mary is known as Maryam and Jesus as Isa.

Since the birth of Christianity, Mary, Jesus's mother and the most venerated of saints, has appeared from time to time to those blessed enough to see her.

The Roman Catholic, Orthodox, and Anglican Churches have sanctioned more than a dozen of these metaphysical events, known as Marian apparitions or Marian visions, recognizing them as "worthy of belief," or bona fide miracles. Many other Marian visions have been reported but not officially recognized.

The era, time of day, and even location of Mary's miraculous appearances have been unpredictable. She has reportedly manifested on an arid hill in 16th-century Mexico City, a convent in 19th-century Paris, and the rural woods of 19th-century Wisconsin. Her seers have been peasants and clergy, children and adults. But across the centuries and around the world, there are certain similarities among Church-sanctioned Marian apparitions.

Chosen Visionaries

To begin with, Mary seems to choose pious people to visit. The Catholic Church particularly reveres Mary and views her as a deeply important religious figure. Those who have the visions tend to be already deeply committed to Catholicism and become more so following the experience.

After witnessing multiple visits by the Blessed Virgin in 1917 Portugal, for example, a trio of peasant children adopted spiritual practices normally associated with religious ascetics. They tied their waists tightly with cords, fasted, and beat themselves with stinging nettles—all acts of penance.

Though Mary often appears more than once over a period of time in the same location, she tends to be visible only to one seer or a small group of them—but there have been exceptions. For several years beginning in 1968, thousands claimed to have witnessed the luminous figure of Mary hovering regularly in the night sky above Cairo, Egypt.

All Aglow

There are similarities in Mary's appearance, too. She is almost always bathed in brilliant light. Sometimes rays emanate from her body or clothing. She is often clad in white. She may hold an object, such as a goblet, or stand on something, such as a shining globe. She may be silent or she may speak, bidding witnesses to

Mary is almost always bathed in brilliant light. Sometimes rays emanate from her body or clothing. She is often clad in white. She may hold an object, such as a goblet.

Apparition of Virgin Mary in Lourdes at the Church Basilica del Carmine in Padua, Italy

perform some task. It could be to build a church or find converts. One French nun in the 1830s was asked to create a piece of jewelry.

On occasion, Mary will leave behind a souvenir. In the 1531 Mexico City apparition known as Our Lady of Guadalupe, the Blessed Virgin provided her seer, a peasant named Juan Diego, with proof of her presence: Her image, burned into the fabric of his cloak.

While Mary herself is seen as a manifestation of love, peace, and maternal kindness, her messages can be ominous. Sometimes she warns of coming war or destruction that can only be averted with prayer, conversion, and repentance. The visionaries who in turn share Mary's warnings with the world at large aren't always received positively.

Discredit, Belief

A common thread woven through the Marian miracle stories is that they are often dismissed altogether at first or viewed as disruptive to the community.

That's especially true if the visionary begins to attract a following or if the site becomes a destination for flocks of pilgrims seeking spiritual experiences of their own. Family, friends, and neighbors may ridicule the visionaries, questioning their sanity or motives.

In Lourdes, France, in 1858, a 14-year-old miller's daughter named Bernadette Soubirous claimed to have seen Mary numerous times in a local cave. At first, she was dismissed by many as dull-witted or mentally ill, but over time, Bernadette attracted a following of people who attested to the miracles she was describing.

Today she is recognized as a saint, and the sanctuary that was built at the site of her Marian visions is now one of most visited religious places in the world.

"Build Me a Church"

Mexico City, Mexico, 1531

St. Juan Diego, by Miguel Cabrera, c. 1700s

THAT CLOAK IS DIVINE

A peasant's humble clothing became the canvas for a miraculous sacred image.

Juan Diego's cloak was a *tilma*, an article of men's clothing typical of the time that could be worn in various ways. Peasants like Juan Diego sometimes used theirs as a sort of apron to carry things.

Juan Diego's tilma is considered a sacred relic and is displayed at the Basilica of Our Lady of Guadalupe in Mexico City. In 1977, investigators examined it using infrared and digital-enhancement technology but were unable to determine how the image of Mary was made.

Juan Diego Cuauhtlatoatzin was on his way to church one day in 1531. Walking through an area of Mexico City called Tepeyac Hill, the 57-year-old peasant, a native Aztec who had converted to Catholicism, heard strains of beautiful music. Then he saw a woman, who called out to him, "Juanito... Juan Dieguito."

Juan Diego asked the woman who she was. According to lore, she responded in his native tongue, "Tlecuatlecupe," meaning "the one who crushes the head of the serpent." The woman also identified herself as "the perfect and perpetual Virgin Mary, Mother of Jesus, the true God, through whom everything lives, the Lord of all things near and far, the Master of Heaven and Earth." She asked that a church be built on the site in her honor and sent Juan Diego to convey her request to his local bishop.

A woman prays in front of Our Lady of Guadalupe, patron saint of Mexico, at Guadalupe's Basilica in Mexico City.

Bishop Juan de Zumarraga was a protector of Mexico's indigenous people, whom Catholic Spain had conquered a decade earlier. He doubted Juan Diego's story but agreed to reflect on the matter. When Juan Diego came back a second time, the bishop told him to bring proof that the vision had been real. Juan Diego reported this back to Mary, who told him to return to her the following day.

But Juan Diego had to care for a dying uncle and was unable to make the appointment. The day after that, he avoided Tepeyac Hill, ashamed. But Mary appeared and told him not to worry: His uncle had been cured, and Juan Diego should not be discouraged by the task he had been assigned. She told him to use his cloak to gather roses from the hilltop and bring them to the Bishop. Miraculously, not only did Juan Diego find roses on the normally barren hill, but they were of a variety found not in Mexico but in Spain.

When Juan Diego opened up his cloak to reveal the roses, the Bishop wept. There, emblazoned on the fabric, was the image of Mary.

The Bishop saw to it that Mary got her church: The Basilica of Our Lady of Guadalupe, built near Tepeyac Hill, is now a national shrine in Mexico. And in 2002, Pope John Paul II recognized Juan Diego as a saint.

WHO KNEW?

In Juan Diego's language, Nahuatl, the name "Tlecuatlecupe" sounds similar to the Spanish place-name "Guadalupe," which is how "Our Lady of Guadalupe" got her name.

The Basilica of Our Lady of Guadalupe was built on top of Tepeyac Hill, Mexico City.

"Make a Medal"

Paris, France, 1830

Though she was baptized Catherine Labouré, her family actually called her Zoe, after a minor 3rd-century saint on whose feast day Catherine was born.

Catherine Labouré's visions began the night in 1830 that she ate a relic.

One evening, in the convent of the Daughters of Charity of Saint Vincent de Paul in Paris, where Catherine was a novice, her Mother Superior gave her a scrap of fabric from the surplice worn by the order's founder. Catherine, 24, did something unusual. She split the bit of cloth in half, stashing one piece in her prayer book and swallowing the other. Then she prayed to Saint Vincent for a visit from the Virgin Mary.

Later that night, Catherine awoke to the vision of a young child summoning her to the chapel. There, she heard the sound of rustling silk. She looked up to find Mary seated before her. As Catherine knelt at the Virgin's feet, Mary warned that terrible times were ahead: The streets of Paris would run with the blood of a revolution. A little over a week later, a three-day surge of protest and violence would result in the dethroning of the French king.

Four months after that, Catherine was meditating in the chapel and again heard the rustling of silk. This time, Mary appeared surrounded by an oval frame with golden lettering. A voice instructed Catherine to have the image made into a medal people could wear around their necks. Everyone who wore it, the voice said, would receive grace. Though it took Catherine two years to convince her superiors of the need for such a medal, the Bishop of Paris eventually ordered 20,000 of them to be made and distributed.

In February 1832, a cholera epidemic hit Paris. As citizens began to succumb to the disease, nuns distributed the medals. Though thousands died, the medal seemed to work wonders: Cures were reported, as were conversions. Now referred to as the Miraculous Medal, Catherine's creation is still worn today by believers worldwide, a symbol of the power of faith and trust.

Detail of Catherine Laboure and the Virgin Mary in the Chapel of Our Lady of the Miraculous Medal, Paris, France

SHE'S A VISION

Each symbol on the Miraculous Medal, officially known as the Medal of the Immaculate Conception, appeared in Catherine's vision of Mary.

The Medal text reads, "O, Mary, conceived without sin, pray for us who have recourse to thee," assuring the wearer that Mary will intercede with God when asked for help.

She showers rays of divine grace on the world.

Mary crushes a serpent, representing Satan, under her feet.

The globe represents Earth.

The date may refer to the year of Catherine's vision or the start of a new battle between good and evil.

WHO KNEW?

The water at Lourdes is said to have cured more than 7,000 people of illness or infirmity. As of 2011, the Church had accepted 69 of these healings as official miracles.

Crowds gather to watch 14-year-old Marie-Bernarde "Bernadette" Soubirous (1844–1879), a poor French girl, experience one of her visions of the Virgin Mary in the grotto of Massabielle in Lourdes.

"Heal the Sick"

Lourdes, France, 1858

It was a chilly afternoon in Lourdes, France, in 1858 and Marie-Bernarde "Bernadette" Soubirous was out with friends collecting firewood. When Bernadette, 14, looked up from the alcove where she had stopped, she saw the young Mary standing near a wild rosebush, dressed in brilliant white with a blue waistband, yellow roses on each foot. Bright light and golden clouds surrounded her. She reached out to Bernadette, who took out her rosary beads and prayed. Mary smiled, then disappeared, but only temporarily. Over the next few months, the Virgin Mother would reappear to Bernadette 17 more times.

Bernadette's Vision at Lourdes. Mural painting, Lourdes, France (c. 1890)

The alcove was an odd place for a holy vision. It was located on public land at the foot of the Pyrenees Mountains and primarily was used to graze farm animals and dump garbage. When Bernadette got home and described what had happened, her mother told her not to go back. Still, Bernadette found herself returning to the grotto again and again, each time greeted by Mary, who told her, "I do not promise to make you happy in this world but in the other."

Word of Bernadette's visions spread through town, and she found herself followed by a growing band of locals who watched her go into trances and receive her visions. Authorities tried to contain the excitement, accusing Bernadette and her family of perpetuating a hoax from which they could profit.

When, on one occasion, Bernadette dug into the mud of the grotto and drank the dirty water, her followers began to doubt her sanity. But as she drank, the water began to run clear. When a visitor came a few days later and plunged her injured arm into the water, she regained movement. The water in the grotto—now a shrine—is still said to have healing properties, and the site attracts more than six million visitors a year.

"Teach the Children"

Green Bay, Wisconsin, 1859

WHO KNEW?
As of 2014 Adele Brise was not on the path toward sainthood, though there were people lobbying the Church on her behalf.

"I do hereby approve these apparitions as worthy of belief," Bishop David Ricken of Green Bay, Wisconsin, announced in December 2010. His audience at the Shrine of Our Lady of Good Help applauded and cried. The historic moment marked the first-ever Church-sanctioned vision of Mary in the United States, on that very spot, a century and a half earlier.

Adele Brise had been carrying a sack of wheat to the mill, on a four-mile walk through farmland in what is now the community of Champion. Suddenly, she saw a woman standing among the maple and hemlock trees, radiating light. The woman was clothed in white with a yellow sash and had a crown of stars on her flowing hair. The vision scared Brise, 28, who had emigrated from Belgium with her farmer parents. She prayed until it disappeared.

A woman was standing among the maple and hemlock trees, radiating light. The woman was clothed in white with a yellow sash and had a crown of stars on her flowing hair.

A week later, Brise was walking the 11 miles to mass and saw the woman again. She was no less frightened. After church, she sought out the priest, who told her to ask the apparition what it wanted.

When the woman appeared a third time, Brise followed the priest's instructions. "Gather the children in this wild country," said Mary, "and teach them what they should know for salvation."

Brise was not a nun, but she began to spend her days tirelessly walking miles to her neighbors' homes and teaching them the Catholic doctrine and traditions. By 1868, Brise's father had built a chapel on the site where Mary had appeared; it became known as *Notre Dame de Bons Secours* ("Our Lady of Good Help" in French, the family's native language). A convent of the Sisters of St. Francis of Assisi was constructed, as was a boarding school where Brise could continue her teaching.

In 1871, the most devastating forest fire in American history ripped through northeast Wisconsin, burning over a million acres and killing 1,500 people. As the flames raged, Brise took as many people as she could into the church. When the fire died, the landscape surrounding the five-acre compound was charred black—but the property and people Brise had sheltered had been spared.

Adele Brise's Catholic teaching ministry was prompted by Marian visions.

"Prepare for Trouble"

Fátima, Portugal, 1917

If you were a peasant child in Portugal a century ago and reported having multiple visions of Mary, you might have been tossed in jail and told you would be boiled in a big vat of oil. At least, that is what happened to Lúcia de Jesus Dos Santos, age 10, and her cousins Francisco Marto, eight, and Jacinta Marto, six.

Lúcia, Francisco, and Jacinta began witnessing holy visits in 1916, as World War I raged through Europe. On several occasions, the three were out tending sheep near their village about 80 miles northeast of Lisbon when an angel materialized. They decided to keep those experiences to themselves. But a year later, when Mary appeared before them, Jacinta felt she must tell her mother, who repeated her daughter's "tall tale" to some neighbors. Within hours, all of the villagers of Fátima had heard the story.

Sanctuary of our Lady of Fátima, Fátima, Estremadura, Portugal

Mary appeared again to the three seers and divulged a trio of prophesies the children said she'd told them not to repeat. As word spread and thousands of believers flocked to Fátima, a local politician had the children arrested and interrogated. Still, they would not reveal the content of Mary's messages. They were released, and though Jacinta and Francisco both perished in the Great Influenza Epidemic of 1918, Lúcia went on to become a nun. She finally revealed Mary's communications to Church officials in 1941, because, she said, it was time to do so.

Called the Three Secrets of Fátima, the messages Lúcia detailed were alarming. The first was a description of hell: a vast fiery sea, Lúcia later wrote in a memoir, seething with human souls screaming in agony. The second included a warning: If people did not stop sinning, there would be another, even worse war. Lúcia revealed those in 1941, at the request of her local bishop, but she asked Church officials not to make the third secret public until after 1960. In fact, they did not do so until 2000.

The third secret included the prediction that a Pope would be assassinated, something that nearly happened in 1981. But many continue to believe that the Church has held back part of the prophecy. Does it reveal a coming apocalypse? Only the Vatican knows for sure.

Lúcia de Jesus Dos Santos and her cousins Francisco and Jacinta Marto, ages 6 to 10, witnessed apparitions of the Virgin Mary a number of times, at the Cova da Iria in Portugal.

A GRATEFUL POPE

John Paul II credited the Blessed Virgin with saving his life.

On May 13, 1981, in Vatican City, on the annual feast of Our Lady of Fátima, a would-be assassin shot Pope John Paul II, hitting him twice in the lower abdomen. Though the Pope lost a lot of blood, he survived. Proclaiming that Our Lady of Fátima had been watching over him, the Pope gave one of bullets to the Sanctuary of Our Lady of Fátima, a shrine on the site of Mary's appearances in Portugal.

"Keep the Faith"

Cairo, Egypt, 1968

The Coptic Orthodox Church is an Egyptian form of Christianity distinct from Roman and Eastern Orthodox Catholicism. It has about 18 million believers.

Egypt is primarily Muslim but it holds a special significance to Christians as the place to which Mary and Joseph fled with the newborn Jesus, seeking refuge from the murderous King Herod. Egypt's first Marian apparition was reported in 1968, at a time when the nation was in turmoil following a war with Israel. One night, a glowing figure appeared above the domes of the Virgin Mary Coptic Orthodox Church in Cairo's Zeitoun district. It returned regularly, witnesses said, until 1971.

The apparition took many forms. Sometimes the figure appeared as a full body, other times as a bust surrounded by a halo of light. On occasion, other bright lights appeared in the shape of doves. Local news stations broadcast footage of the seemingly supernatural event, and police who searched the surrounding area for any sign of equipment that could have been used to manufacture such an apparition came up empty. Crowds of all faiths and professions witnessed the vision.

"Two important aspects accompanied these apparitions," Pope Kyrillos IV, head of the Coptic Orthodox Church of Alexandria, wrote in an official statement. "The first is an incredible revival of the faith in God, the other world, and the saints, leading to repentance and conversion of many who strayed away from the faith. The second are numerous miracles of healing which were verified by many physicians to be miraculous in nature." The apparition is considered valid by the Coptic Orthodox Church.

"Pray and Repent"

Kibeho, Rwanda, 1981

With hands folded, the beautiful woman appeared before Alphonsine Mumureke in Kibeho, Rwanda, in 1981 with a message: There was going to be a terrible war. A student at a Catholic boarding school, Alphonsine, 16, understood right away that she was having a vision of the *Umubyeyi w'Imana* ("Mother of God"). Over the next eight years, Mary would appear dozens of times to Alphonsine and several times to two classmates, Anathalie Mukamazimpaka and Marie Claire Mukangango. In the visions, Mary was serene but called for prayer and repentance.

During the same period, ethnic hatred was intensifying among the Hutu, a group that made up the majority of Rwanda's population, toward the elite Tutsi, the powerful minority. In 1990, Pope John Paul II visited Rwanda and encouraged Catholics there to pray to Mary for unity and peace. But in 1994, a plane carrying Rwanda's Hutu president was shot down, triggering a civil war and genocide that would lead to the death of 800,000 Tutsi, as well as to thousands of Hutu who objected to the violence. Alphonsine, Marie Claire, and Anathalie, as well as those who believed in their visions, saw the genocide as the heartbreaking realization of Mary's warnings.

Marie Claire was killed in a massacre in 1995. Alphonsine and Anathalie went on to do religious work. In 2001, the Church approved the visions of the three girls, making them the first sanctioned Marian visions in Africa.

The icon of the Our Lady of Kazan, in Russia

SHE'S ICONIC

Christians in Eastern Europe regard some paintings of Mary as miraculous in their own right.

In the Orthodox Church, certain paintings of the Blessed Virgin are deeply important. Called icons, these representations, often painted on wood, are accepted as what believers call "windows into the kingdom of God."

OUR LADY OF KAZAN

THE STORY
In Kazan, Russia, in 1579, Mary appeared to a young girl and told her to unearth a painting that had been lost for 300 years. The girl discovered the icon, wrapped in red cloth, beneath a burned home near her own.

SAMPLE MIRACLE
As the icon was carried with great ceremony through the city, it healed two blind men.

WHERE IS IT NOW?
It was stolen in 1904 and is believed to have been destroyed. Copies, also considered holy, can be found in Russia.

THE BLACK MADONNA

THE STORY
Said to have been created by the apostle Luke, this painting resurfaced in 1382 in the home of a Polish prince. Under attack by Tatar invaders, the prince fled with the icon, stopping to rest in the town of Czestochowa, Poland. When it was time to continue on, his horse refused to budge—a sign, the prince decided, that the icon should remain there.

SAMPLE MIRACLE
The icon is said to have helped protect Poland from Swedish invaders in 1655, thus changing history.

WHERE IS IT NOW?
Battle-scarred and soot-blackened (hence its name), the painting is in a monastery in Czestochowa.

THE VLADIMIR ICON

THE STORY
As with the Black Madonna, Church legend maintains that the apostle Luke painted this portrait of the Virgin, which was kept for a time in the city of Vladimir, Russia. However, it's really the work of an anonymous 12th-century Byzantine artist. It was brought to Moscow in about 1395 and is considered the most sacred icon in Russia.

SAMPLE MIRACLE
The icon allegedly saved Moscow from Mongol attack on three separate occasions.

WHERE IS IT NOW?
The painting is on display at the Tretyakov Gallery in Moscow.

When Art Cries

WHAT IS THE SIGNIFICANCE OF RELIGIOUS STATUES AND PAINTINGS THAT SEEM TO WEEP REAL TEARS?

Hoaxers around the world have created holy "tears" using calcium chloride, animal fat, or vegetable oil, but many weeping icons have never been debunked or explained as anything but miraculous.

In October 2013, the elderly village women who clean the Sacred Church of the Archangel Michael in Rhodes, Greece, noticed something strange. Tears seemed to be streaming from the eyes of Michael in a painting that hung on one of the church's walls. The women informed the church vicar, and soon news of the crying icon spread throughout the island.

The local Orthodox Church leader, His Eminence Metropolitan Kyrillos of Rhodes, visited the icon to see the miracle for himself. Finding no signs of tampering or a hoax, he instructed that the icon be moved to Ialyssos' Sacred Church of the Dormition of Theotokos so that the church leaders could observe how the phenomenon evolved.

The painting is said to have wept on and off since then, drawing crowds of believers to the new location. Many have reported witnessing the tears of the archangel Michael, whose name means "Who is like unto God" in Hebrew and who is widely seen as a defender of Christianity against the dark forces of Satan. Some believe that the icon cries as a warning of dark days to come.

Leaps of Faith

Though reports of "crying" icons aren't unusual in Eastern Orthodox churches, there is growing skepticism about the phenomenon. Most recent cases have been debunked as practical jokes, naturally occurring phenomena, or outright frauds. At best, scientific tests have been deemed inconclusive.

Weeping or not, icons have played a crucial role among the Orthodox faithful for more than 2,000 years. They are viewed as sacred windows to heaven that help worshippers' prayers reach whichever holy figure they depict—from Jesus and the Virgin Mary to angels and saints. They are also seen as God's way of bestowing his grace and mercy upon the world.

In the Eastern Orthodox Church, the emphasis is not so much on the tears as on the impact they have on believers. "The miracle is...how praying in front of that icon changes people's lives," said Father John Matusiak, editor of *The Orthodox Church*, the official publication of the Orthodox Church of America.

The Roman Catholic church also investigates cases of miraculous activity centered on holy objects, and Catholic officials have declared a number of cases of weeping and bleeding icons to be hoaxes over the years. Still, many believers continue to be drawn to the sculptures and paintings in question. "I think we need to respect people's experiences through the eyes of faith, and God does use these things to bring us closer to him," one Catholic priest, Father James Murphy of the Sacramento, California, diocese, stated in 2005.

An icon of Jesus and the Virgin Mary at Kykkos monastery, Cyprus

ISLAND CURE

Thousands of devout Greek Orthodox Christians make a pilgrimage to the Greek island of Tinos in hopes of a miracle cure.

The Greek island of Tinos is famous throughout Greek Orthodoxy as the home of the Church of the Panagia Evangelista and its miraculous healing icon. Tinos's renown dates to 1822, when a local nun, Pelagia, said Mary had appeared to her in a series of visions. Mary had ordered her to search for an icon in the long-buried church of St. John the Baptist. Pelagia convinced the locals to start excavation that September, and the ruins of the Byzantine chapel were soon uncovered, along with an icon of the Annunciation. A new church was built to house the icon in 1823, and since then it has attracted a steady stream of the faithful, many of whom crawl up the hill from the ferry wharf on their hands and knees in hopes of a healing cure. Among the miracles attributed to the icon is the cessation of a cholera epidemic that decimated the island population in 1822–23.

A pilgrim is dragged on his back to the shrine at Tinos.

The Madonna of Medjugorje in Civitavecchia, Italy, reportedly cries tears of blood.

CRY ME A RIVER

The Roman Catholic view of weeping icons.

Catholic officials have declared some weeping and bleeding icons hoaxes, but such incidents continue to surface.

→ **In June 1973,** Sister Agnes Sasagawa of the Handmaid of the Eucharist convent in Akita, Japan, had visions of the Virgin Mary and received the stigmata (wounds mimicking Christ's on the cross). A wooden image of the Virgin Mary in the church bled from its hands, then produced tears. The local bishop has authorized veneration of the icon, but the Roman Catholic Church has not approved it.

→ **In early 1992,** Roman Catholic priest James Bruse of Lake Ridge, Virginia, received the stigmata. Soon, religious statues started to weep in Father Bruse's presence, according to congregation members. "Maybe it's plaster sweating, maybe it's hysterical reaction on the part of the observers. It's not me. . . . It's Christ working through me," Father Bruse told a reporter.

→ **In February 2014,** Amira Khoury, a Lebanese Christian in Tarshiha, Israel, saw a statue of the Virgin Mary covered in oil. Thousands of believers then descended on the village, convinced that the statue was weeping on its own.

Saint Anthony Preaching to the Fish by Paolo Veronese (c. 1580)

CHAPTER 6

Amazing Saints

Recognized for their holy ways and amazing acts, these extraordinary men and women have inspired the faithful for centuries.

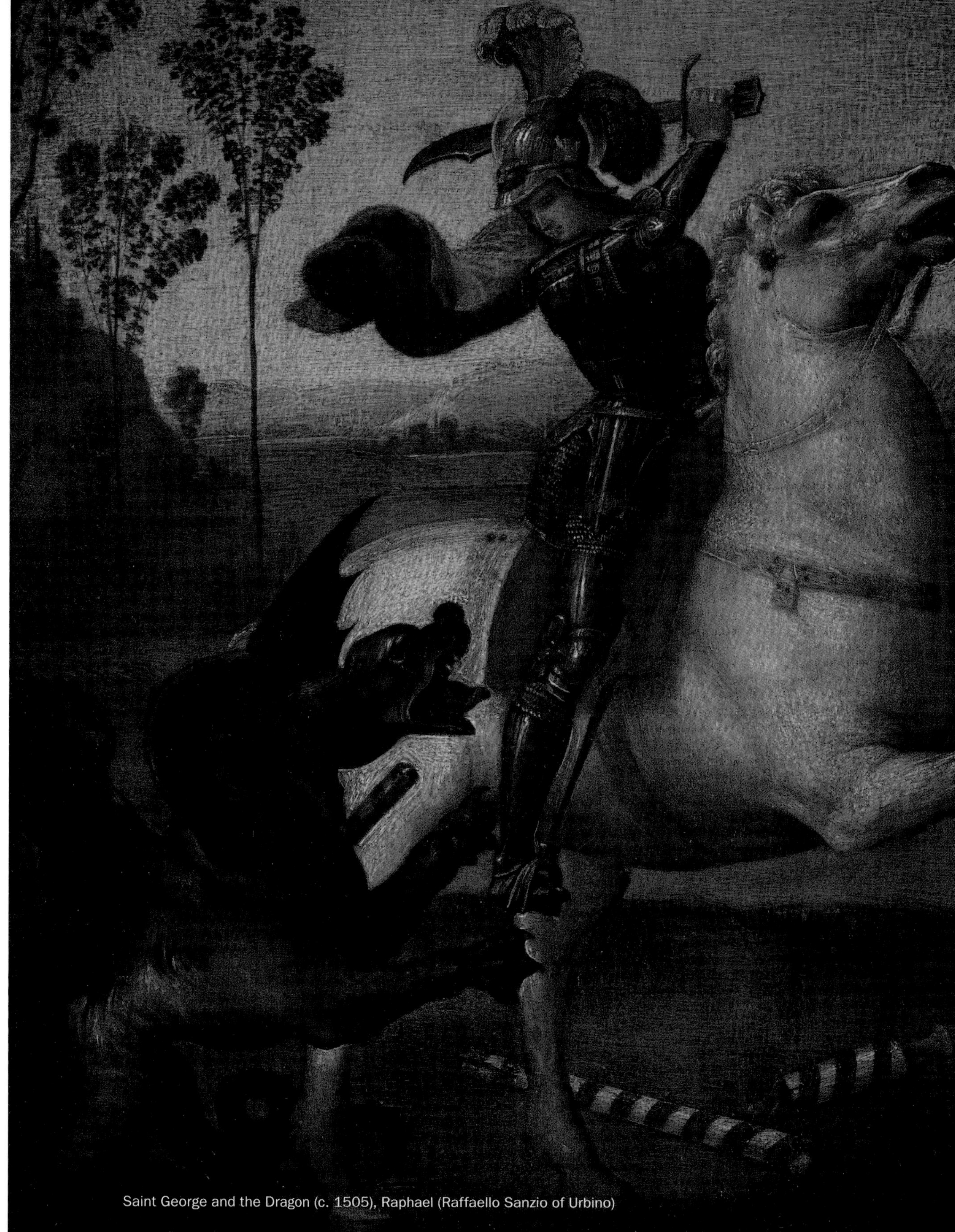

Saint George and the Dragon (c. 1505), Raphael (Raffaello Sanzio of Urbino)

Onward, Christian Soldier

A MYTHIC MILITARY HERO OF THE ROMAN ERA ENDURED HARDSHIP, TORTURE, AND A DRAGON.

The dragon was the least of it. By the time George was executed in 303 A.D., he had battled not only a fire-breathing beast, but all manner of misery at the command of a Roman emperor. Or so the legend goes.

George, a soldier and Christian martyr, is one of the most beloved saints in the world. Historians agree that only a few facts are known about him, and some of his supposed feats, including the battle with a dragon, are obviously fiction. The roots of St. George and his legend do lie in fact, however: It is generally agreed that he was born around 280 A.D. in what is now the city of Lod, Israel—a part of the Roman Empire at the time.

George came from a Christian military family; his father, who died when George was just 14, was an official in the Roman army and a favorite of the emperor, Diocletian. George wished to follow in his footsteps. In his late teens, George traveled to the eastern capital city of Nicomedia, in what is now Turkey, to become a Roman soldier.

George soon distinguished himself, rising to become an officer in the imperial guard. Around this time, tales of his deeds shade into legend. According to some stories, he is said to have killed a dragon in a Libyan city after making the sign of the cross. In awe and gratitude, the entire city converted to Christianity.

Historians do agree that in 303 A.D., Diocletian, the Emperor of the Eastern part of the Roman Empire, made a decree. Wishing to restore the Empire to its former glory, Diocletian set about re-establishing the dominance of the Roman gods. To do that, he had to eliminate all minority religions, including Christianity. He ordered churches torn down; burned Christian texts; and fired Christian officials and soldiers, including George. When George protested, Diocletian ordered his execution.

WHO KNEW?

The symbol of Saint George, a red cross on a white background, is incorporated into the Union Jack, the flag of the United Kingdom.

Courage and Pain

The emperor went to truly gruesome lengths to destroy George, according to lore. He had George stabbed with swords, plunged into boiling water, and ripped with hooks. The warrior's wounds were rubbed with salt. He was bashed in the head with a hammer, forced to drink poison, and cut into little pieces that were tossed into a well. But George would not die. According to legend, God was on his side and told George that he would die three deaths before finally getting to heaven.

So the torture continued. George had hot metal poured into his mouth, nails pounded into his head, and was cut in two, and still he refused to denounce his religion. Every time death was upon him, God would preserve him until, finally, George was decapitated. At last, God allowed him to float up to heaven. But before he went, George prayed for his fellow Christians.

Beheading St George, from *Episodes from the Life of St George*, by Altichiero, 1379-1384

A TALE OF TWO CHURCHES

The two biggest branches of Catholicism diverge along the division of what was once the eastern and western Roman Empire.

For the first two centuries A.D., the Roman Empire encompassed vast swaths of what is now Europe, the Mediterranean, Asia Minor, and the Middle East. But by the end of the 3rd century, the formerly unified empire had essentially split into two separate parts: The Greek-speaking Eastern Empire and the Latin-speaking Western Empire. As centuries passed, the halves grew estranged, and their religious beliefs diverged, leading to the Great Schism, in 1054, in which the Church divided into eastern and western branches.

The main differences between eastern (Orthodox) and western (Roman) belief has to do with two issues: the authority of the Pope and the nature of the Holy Spirit. Both traditions believe in the Christian Trinity and the Holy Spirit as an element of that Trinity. The divide is over exactly where that "Holy Spirit" emanates from.

Pope John Paul II and Romanian Orthodox Patriarch Teoctist embrace at Patriarchal Cathedral, Bucharest, May 7, 1999.

ORTHODOX CATHOLIC		ROMAN CATHOLIC
300 million	**Number of followers**	1.2 billion
Eastern Europe, including Greece, Russia and Ukraine	**Primary regions**	Latin America, Western Europe, Africa
22, including Greek Orthodox	**Denominations**	One
His is no holier or more important than any other bishop.	**How important is the Pope?**	He's the boss of the Church.
Just God ("the Father")	**Where does the Holy Spirit come from?**	God and Jesus ("the Father and the Son")

The tomb of Saint George inside The Church of Saint George, Lod, Israel.

A SAINT FOR ALL SEASONS

Catholics, Protestants, and Muslims all revere Saint George.

It's rare that multiple faiths venerate the same figure, but George is one of those cases, possibly because so little is known about him that he can fit into a number of legends. His shrine, the Church of Saint George in Lod, Israel, is Greek Orthodox but also incorporates a mosque. In Islam, George is often conflated with a mythic figure named al-Khidr, who is believed to appear in the Quran as a servant of God who talks with Moses. He is the patron saint of Protestant England and shares similarities with Sigurd, a mythic Anglo-Saxon dragon-slayer. And he is also a Roman Catholic saint, canonized in 494.

Saint Underdog

BORN INTO A WORLD OF PREJUDICE, A PERUVIAN MAN ROSE ABOVE HIS OBSTACLES, LITERALLY.

Saint Martin de Porres relic preserved in Santo Domingo church, Lima, Peru

THE GOOD LIFE

Although never officially ordained, Martin de Porres led the ascetic, self-sacrificing existence of a devoted monk.

➔ He didn't eat meat.

➔ He fasted regularly.

➔ Once, when his monastery needed money, he suggested that they sell him as a slave.

➔ When a sick, near-naked homeless man covered in sores showed up needing a bed, de Porres gave the man his own.

➔ He begged for food and money every day to distribute to the poor.

He could levitate. He could communicate with animals and be in two places simultaneously. Yet, in Lima, Peru, Martin de Porres was reviled by many simply because of the color of his skin. Local law even forbade him from becoming a full member of the religious order to which he devoted his life. He was able to join a Dominican monastery, wear the robes, and live among the other residents—but only as a worker who cleaned and did laundry.

Spurned by His Father

In the late 16th century, few Peruvians would accept a mixed-race illegitimate child, so the deck was stacked against Martin from the moment he was born, in 1579. His father, a Spanish nobleman, refused to marry his mother, a freed slave from Panama. Martin and his younger sister, Juana, grew up poor, socially demeaned, and unacknowledged by their father.

But Martin was a remarkable person. Trained as a barber and a healer at a time when the two professions were customarily practiced together, Martin developed a reputation for saving people's lives. He was frugal, humble, and devout—so much so that after he had served his order faithfully for eight years, he was made an unofficial priest. Martin had to be forced to accept the position, believing himself too lowly for such an honor.

Incredible Gifts

Martin was said to be able to pass through locked doors. He was spotted in faraway countries, including Mexico and Japan, despite never having left his monastery in Peru. And it was said that he could teleport: Once, when he and a group of novices found themselves miles from the monastery and late to prayer, he asked them to take his hands. In an instant, the group was back home.

Martin's boundless compassion extended even to the lowliest of creatures. In a famous episode known as the Miracle of the Rats, he was told to set out poison to rid the monastery of pests, but it pained him to do so. He went into the garden and called to the rats quietly. When they appeared, he warned them not to eat the poison and said he would be happy to feed them in the garden every day, as long as they stopped bothering the monks. From then on, the rats behaved themselves.

OPPOSITE: *St. Martin De Porres*, by Dunstan St. Omer (c. 1985)

WHO KNEW?

Martin de Porres is the patron saint of Peru, hairstylists, the poor, interracial harmony, social justice, television, and the State of Mississippi.

Martin de Porres is also called "The Saint of the Broom" for his belief in the holiness of menial labor.

SAINT MARTIN

Pope John XXIII canonized Martin de Porres in 1962. These officially confirmed miracles proved him worthy, though he is credited with many others:

→ **In 1948,** an elderly woman in Paraguay survived a heart attack and intestinal blockage after her daughter prayed to de Porres.

→ **In 1956,** Antonio Cabrera Pérez-Camacho, a six-year-old Canary Islands boy, fell while climbing around on a house under construction. His leg was pinned under a 60-pound block of cement. Told by doctors the leg would have to be amputated, Antonio's mother prayed all night to Martin. In the morning, Antonio's circulation had returned. He healed and grew up to be a dentist.

Holy Locals

LATIN AMERICAN CATHOLICS HAVE A UNIQUE RELATIONSHIP WITH THEIR SAINTS, NOT ALL OF WHOM ARE SANCTIONED BY THE CHURCH.

For much of the four centuries that Latin Americans have practiced Catholicism, they have venerated not only the Church's official saints but also more than a few of their own whom the Vatican doesn't recognize. These folk saints may have lived their lives as traditional healers, political figures, local heroes, indigenous deities from older religious traditions, or simply extraordinarily compassionate individuals. Some are fictitious characters.

Believers flock to elaborate chapels and roadside shrines erected in the folk saints' honor to pray for small miracles: a new apartment, relief from a toothache, or other everyday requests. Offerings often relate to the saints' own stories or to the mystical powers they are said to possess: Difunta Correa of Argentina, who died of thirst in the 1830s, regularly receives bottles of water from supplicants hoping for safe travels. Guatemalan schoolchildren offer books, notebooks, and pencils to Pedro Sangueso, murdered in 1963 at age 6 and believed to help them with their studies.

Some folk saints are even said to safeguard those on the wrong side of the law. Sarita Colonia, who in the early 20th century miraculously escaped a rape attempt, supposedly watches out for prostitutes in Peru; while in Mexico, Jesús Malverde, a possibly fictional late-1800s bandit who stole from the rich to give to the poor, is believed to grant favors to drug traffickers. Drug traffickers also venerate San Pascualito Muerte.

Faith Healers

Many folk saints are generalists, thought to deal in all human hopes and worries from romance to finance. Others have particular areas of expertise, such as warfare or agriculture. A common specialty is curing the sick.

In the 1890s, the people of Juazeiro, Brazil, spread

CURE-ALLS

In Mexico and parts of Latin America, folk healers are said to work miracles.

Traditional Mexican and Latin American shamans, known as *curanderos*, use herbal medicine and prayer in their practice. Their centuries-old techniques are designed to correct imbalances of the body, mind, and spirit, so the curanderos are consulted for spiritual as well as physical maladies. Their patients credit them with such feats as lifting curses and restoring sight and speech.

Timiteo Lauriso, a curandero, performs a Quechua ceremony for a successful roundup of vicuña in the Andes mountains.

A typical treatment might combine magic, divination, and prayer; the use of local herbs, spices, and fruit; and treatments such as massage and aromatherapy. A curandero might also employ Catholic symbols such as holy water, candles, and crucifixes, and prescribe prayer to recognized saints as well as local ones.

Some renowned curanderos are themselves considered folk saints, even while still alive. One example was El Niño Fidencio, a 20th-century curandero famous for performing painless operations without anesthesia and for curing the president of Mexico of a form of leprosy.

This shrine in Culican, Sinaloa, Mexico, is dedicated to Jesús Malverde, who stole from the rich to give to the poor.

the word that a local priest named Cícero Romão Batista offered a remarkable communion service: The bread he used for the Catholic holy ritual turned to blood in parishioners' mouths. Padre Cícero was said to have miraculous healing powers, and today, millions of ailing Brazilians visit his chapels and shrines each year.

Born in Northern Mexico in 1873, Teresita Urrea, La Santa de Cabora, fell seriously ill as a teenager and had a series of religious visions. When she recovered, Teresita began healing hundreds of patients a day by laying her hands on them. She also spoke out against the oppression and mistreatment of her fellow Yaqui and Mayo Indians. Eventually exiled, she moved her healing practice to the southwestern United States. Surviving at least three assassination attempts, Teresita died of consumption in 1906. Today, the Yaqui and Mayo peoples, and women in particular, venerate her.

Venezuelans in need of medical miracles appeal to José Gregorio Hernández, a top doctor at a Caracas hospital from the 1890s through the 1910s. A deeply religious man, Hernández was unwell himself but ministered to the poor without charge, even buying medicine for them. After his death in 1919, Venezuelans who prayed to him reported being healed. Today, his adherents place a fresh glass of water near a lit candle in the evening and ask him to infuse the water with any medication they might need. The next morning, they take three sips of the water and pour out the rest on their doorsteps.

"Our Lady of the Holy Death," Santa Muerte idol

DAY OF THE DEAD

Two mythic skeleton-saints symbolize a Latin American fascination with death.

Venerated in Guatemala, San Pascualito Muerte, a mythic skeleton-saint, is symbolized by a skeleton wearing a crown.

Saint Death, as he is sometimes called, has various abilities, including the power to wipe out illness. He appeared, the story goes, to a Guatemalan man dying of a 17th-century plague. Described by the man as a tall skeleton in glowing robes, the specter identified himself as Saint Paschal Baylon, a Catholic saint of 16th-century Spain.

In return for veneration by the local people, San Pascualito promised to end the epidemic. He said that although the man to whom he appeared would die, the plague would end in nine days. Sure enough—nine days later, the man was gone, but so was the plague.

These days, San Pascualito Muerte and his female counterpart, Santa Muerte — Our Lady of the Holy Death— are Latin American cult figures. Believers ask their help in all manner of extreme situations.

I Need a Miracle

FOR BELIEVERS, SAINTS MAKE ORDINARY LIFE EXTRAORDINARY.

If you wandered into a Catholic home in the mid-20th century, or lived in one yourself, chances are you spotted some saints scattered around—say, perched on a mantel, in a niche, or hanging on a wall. Many Catholics still appeal to popular saints to watch over loved ones and influence daily events.

ANNE Mary's mother watches over housewives and pregnant women. She also protects against poverty and infertility.

JOAN OF ARC The Patron Saint of France

CATHERINE OF PADUA
The Patron Saint of Italy

JOSEPH The Patron Saint of Happy Homes, he's also said to help sell a house in a tough real estate market.

CHRISTOPHER Put him in the car; he looks after drivers and travelers.

NICHOLAS OF MYRA The Patron Saint of Happy Marriages and Newlyweds

Every Day

FRANCIS OF ASSISI The Patron Saint of Animals will guard your pets. He's also a protector of families.

PATRICK The Patron Saint of Ireland

ISIDORE OF SEVILLE The Patron Saint of the Internet is there to ensure smooth surfing.

ANTHONY OF PADUA The Patron Saint of Lost Items does double duty as the patron of expectant mothers.

RITA The Patron Saint of the Impossible

JUDE The Patron Saint of Lost Causes and Desperate Situations

MICHAEL THE ARCHANGEL Saint Michael watches over the sick. He also helps people avoid temptation.

Saving Face

ACROSS MILES AND HUNDREDS OF YEARS, A 17TH-CENTURY MOHAWK WOMAN IS CREDITED WITH RESCUING A BOY FROM DEATH.

WHO KNEW? Kateri Tekakwitha, Elizabeth Seton, and Katharine Drexel are the only three American-born Catholic saints.

It is fitting that Kateri Tekakwitha (pronounced gah-dah-LEE degh-agh-WEE-dtha) was made a saint after healing a Native American boy afflicted with a fatal flesh-eating bacteria. She herself was a Native American who as a child had suffered from a deadly disease that affects the skin: smallpox.

The daughter of a Mohawk chief, she was born in 1656 in what is now upstate New York. When she was four, tragedy struck in the form of the fearsome virus, which killed her parents and little brother. The little girl survived, but the disease attacked her face and eyes, leaving her with scars and poor vision. Her tribe gave her the name "Tekakwitha," which means "she who bumps into things," and she went to live with an uncle.

At the time, missionaries were already at work in the New World trying to convert Native Americans to Christianity. Tekakwitha's late mother had been a Catholic, and the orphan was intrigued by the

FATAL EPIDEMIC

A virus brought to the New World by European settlers devastated the Native American population.

One of the most powerful weapons the New World settlers brought with them was not guns but smallpox. The highly contagious disease, known by its characteristic skin rash, entered the body through the mouth or nose and destroyed the immune system within days. Those it didn't kill were sometimes left blind or covered with disfiguring scars.

In 17th-century Europe, where smallpox had existed for eons, many people had developed a natural immunity to it. But the indigenous populations of the Americas, including the Incas, Aztecs, and Native Americans, had never been exposed to the disease. According to some estimates, 20 million of these native peoples, or up to 95 percent of them, succumbed to smallpox in the generations following the arrival of the Europeans.

By the time the disease was eradicated in 1977, it had taken the lives of hundreds of millions of people worldwide, over many centuries.

Pontiac, an Ottawa Indian, confronts Colonel Henry Bouquet, who had authorized his officers to spread smallpox among Native Americans by deliberately infecting blankets. Painting by Benjamin West (c. 1764)

A carving of St. Kateri Tekakwitha stands in St. Peter's Chapel at the National Shrine of Saint Kateri Tekakwitha in Fonda, New York.

religion. Privately, Tekakwitha took a vow of chastity and, though her uncle forbade it, at age 18 began to study Catholicism in secret. Eventually she was baptized, taking the name Kateri in honor of Saint Catherine of Siena. Harassed and threatened by her family and peers, Tekakwitha left her tribe to join a settlement of Catholic Native Americans in Canada, where she helped care for the ill and the elderly.

Tekakwitha's pious life ended far too soon; she died of an illness just before her 24th birthday. But witness at her death reported a miracle: Her face, scarred for 20 years from smallpox, became smooth, glowing, and beautiful.

Parallel Universe

On a February Saturday in 2006, in Ferndale, Washington, a five-year-old boy named Jake Finkbonner cut his lip while playing basketball. The cut seemed minor at first, but within a day, Jake was in the hospital, infected by lethal bacteria that had entered through the cut and spread rapidly. After four days, a priest administered last rites and a doctor told Jake's family there was little they could do besides pray.

So they did. Jake's father, Donny, was a member of the Lummi Nation, a tribe native to Washington State. A local priest suggested that the family pray to Kateri, who shared a similar story and heritage. As days passed and Jake continued to battle the infection, he was visited by a local nun named after Kateri, who prayed with the family and laid a relic on Jake's body. Almost immediately afterward, the infection retreated. Jake's parents believe that his life was saved that day.

In October 2012, Jake, by then a healthy and athletic 12-year-old, traveled with his family to Rome to witness something his miracle had made possible: the canonization of Kateri Tekakwitha, his very own patron saint.

Statue of Kateri Tekakwitha at the Cathedral Basilica of St. Francis of Assisi in Santa Fe, New Mexico

THE KATERI CURE

Hundreds of spontaneous healings have been attributed to Kateri Tekakwitha.

→ **Pneumonia.** In 1681, a 40-year-old Canadian man, Claude Caron, was in dire condition from "a great oppression of the chest." A visiting priest urged him to pray to Kateri. After the priest left, Caron collapsed. His caretakers got him into bed, where he slept for half an hour, awoke feeling much better, and made a full recovery.

→ **Intestinal blockage.** In 1695, Louis Fortier, 13, was treated with various medications at a Montreal hospital for an acute stomach condition. As his health worsened, his mother begged a priest to appeal to Kateri for her son's cure. The priest did, the medicines began to work, and the boy was healed.

→ **Smallpox.** Around 1703, Joseph Kellogg, a young Puritan from Deerfield, Massachusetts, fell ill with the dreaded disease. A Catholic priest told the teen that if he converted, the priest would cure him with a religious relic: A sliver of wood from Kateri's coffin. The boy agreed, the relic was produced, and Joseph recovered.

Hear Our Prayers

TWO FAMILIES APPEALED TO AN AMERICAN NUN IN HEAVEN TO HELP THEIR CHILDREN OVERCOME DEAFNESS. BOTH TIMES, SHE ANSWERED.

Robert Gutherman prayed to the Mother Katharine Drexel and his hearing was restored.

Robert Gutherman was 14 in 1974 when he developed an ear infection that was more than just agonizingly painful. "The doctor told my mother that the infection had eaten away two of the three bones in my right ear, and that I'd be deaf in that ear for the rest of my life," Gutherman said years later. With no way to cure the damage, the Bensalem, Pennsylvania, boy and his family prayed nightly to the late Mother Katharine Drexel, a local nun whose order had run a nearby chapel where Gutherman and his brothers had served as altar boys.

One night about a month after beginning the prayers, Gutherman heard a voice calling his name, "Bobby." He was certain he'd heard the sound in his right ear. The damaged bones seemed to be somehow repairing themselves, and by September his hearing was restored. The family credited Mother Katherine, the miracle worker in their own backyard.

WHO KNEW?
The late Mother Teresa, missionary to the poorest of the poor and winner of the Nobel Peace Prize, is not a saint (yet).

The Banker's Daughter

Born in 1858 in Philadelphia, Katharine Drexel was the second daughter of a prominent investment banker who was worth millions. She and her siblings were taught that their extraordinary wealth was a gift to be shared. The family opened their home to people in need, and the girls taught Sunday school to neighborhood children.

The reading and traveling Drexel did as a young woman left her distressed by the plight of African Americans and Native Americans. In 1889, the heiress took her vows—including the pledge of poverty—and entered a convent.

In 1891, Drexel founded the order of the Sisters of the Blessed Sacrament, dedicated to serving black and Native American populations. By the time she died in 1955, Drexel's order had grown to 500 sisters in 51 convents. Thanks to the Gutherman miracle, she was beatified by Pope John Paul II in 1988.

After learning about Gutherman's story in 1993, Constance Wall, a Pennsylvania mother, was also inspired to pray to Drexel for her intercession. Wall's one-year-old daughter, Amy, had been born with nerve deafness in both ears. In 1994, after months of prayer, Amy started to hear normally. It was this second miracle that paved the way for Mother Katharine's sainthood. She was canonized in 2000.

It's a lovely parallel that both of Saint Katharine's miracles were related to hearing. "I think," explained Monsignor Alexander Palmieri, of the Archdiocese of Philadelphia, "it's almost as though God's saying to us through Katharine Drexel, 'Open your ears, the ears of your heart.'"

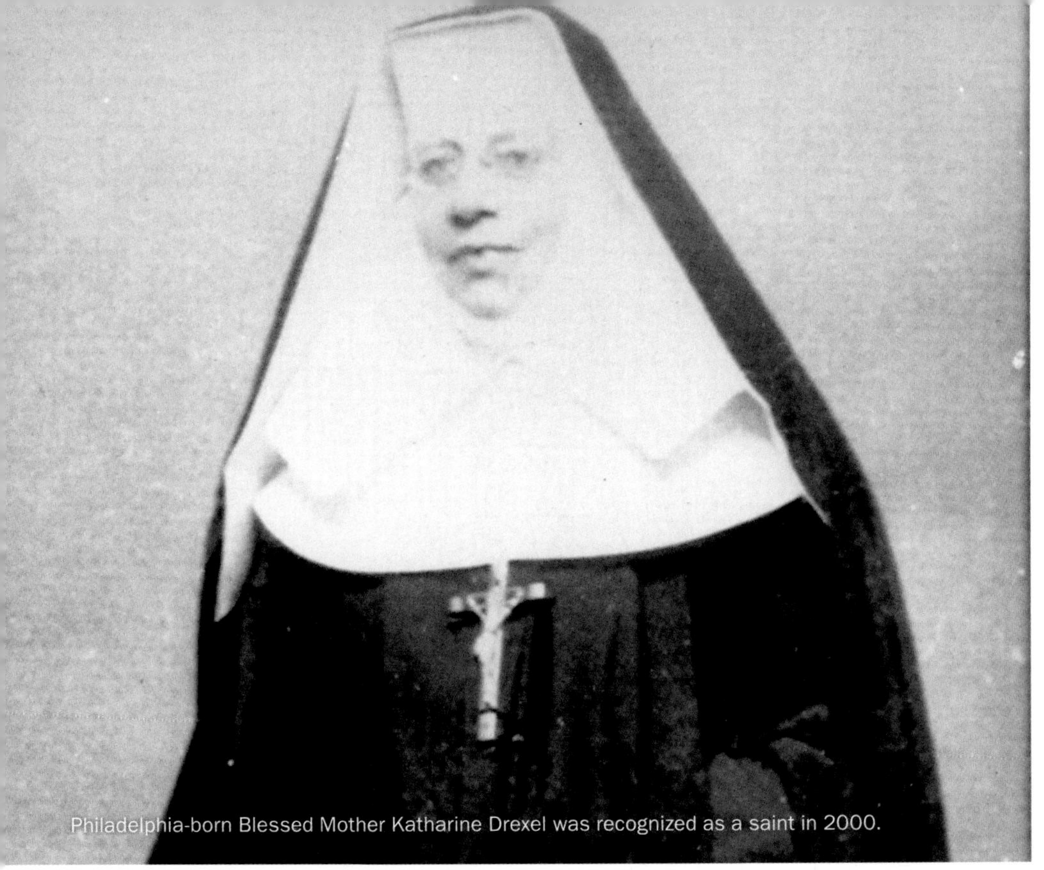
Philadelphia-born Blessed Mother Katharine Drexel was recognized as a saint in 2000.

PHYSICIAN-APPROVED

When the Vatican wants to be sure a true medical miracle has taken place, they call in the doctors.

It isn't a miracle until the Vatican says it is—at least in the case of Catholic miracles. So before the Pope gives his stamp of approval, the event in question is vetted to be sure it meets the Church's three criteria: A miracle must be instantaneous, absolute, and defy scientific explanation. In the contemporary age of skepticism and spectacular medical advances, proving that something is scientifically inexplicable requires expert opinions from professionals.

Thus, all potential medical miracles are scrutinized by a five-person panel from the Consulta Medica, a board of 100 physicians. Typically, the panel reviews each healing, assessing medical reports, x-rays, and other files related to the case. Three of the five doctors must deem the cure medically unexplainable.

Most of the Consulta Medica doctors are Catholic. Still, they maintain a healthy skepticism. "I myself, if I did not do these consultations, would never believe what I read," Dr. Raffaello Cortesini, a renowned heart and liver-transplant surgeon and a former president of the Consulta Medica, once said. "You don't understand how fantastic, how incredible—and how well documented—these cases are.... Science fiction is nothing by comparison."

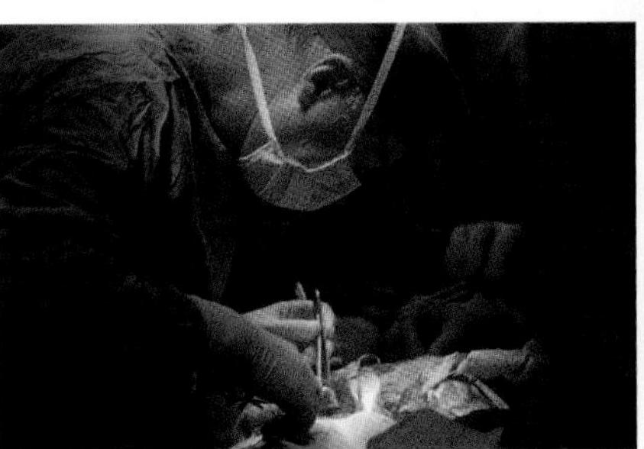
Raffaello Cortesini, a former president of the Consulta Medica, performing a kidney transplant

LET THE SAINTS COME MARCHING IN

A number of women have been canonized for their good works.

➔ **Elizabeth Ann Seton** was born in 1774 to a high-society New York City family. Raised Episcopalian, Seton converted to Catholicism as an adult and was shunned by friends and family. She moved to Maryland, opened the first free Catholic school in the U.S., and founded the Sisters of St. Joseph, the nation's first Catholic sisterhood. Pope Paul VI canonized her in 1975, making her the first American-born saint.

➔ **Marianne Cope** was born in Germany in 1838. Two years later, her family emigrated to Utica, New York. As a child, she worked in a factory to help support her family, joining the Sisters of Saint Francis in 1862. Eventually she traveled to Hawaii, where she spent the rest of her life caring for people with leprosy and managing hospitals, schools, and shelters. Pope Benedict XVI canonized her in 2012.

➔ **Mother Frances Xavier Cabrini** Born in Italy in 1850, Cabrini was influenced by her parents' strong faith. She founded the Missionary Sisters of the Sacred Heart in 1889, then sailed for the U.S., where she opened orphanages, schools, and hospitals for Italian immigrants. Pope Pius XII canonized her in 1946.

The Patron Saints of Minor Aggravations

SUFFERING FROM THE SNIFFLES, A HANGOVER, OR DANDRUFF? AN APPEAL TO THE RIGHT ADVOCATE MIGHT CURE WHAT AILS YOU.

In Catholicism, a patron saint is a heavenly advocate who can pray to God on behalf of a human on earth. People might appeal to a patron saint for prosperity or luck, but often the request has to do with a health problem. For instance, Peregrine Laziosi, the 13th-century Italian priest said to have cured himself of a deadly leg infection through prayer, is the patron saint of people with cancer, heart disease, and AIDS. And Dymphna, murdered as a teenager by her Irish-nobleman father in the 7th century, is the patron saint of the mentally ill.

While it's not surprising that a person with a debilitating or life-threatening health condition might appeal to an appropriate go-between for help, there are patron saints for a whole host of minor aggravations as well. Sometimes there's an obvious connection between the saint and these lesser ailments, sometimes not.

COMMON COLD

MAURUS This gifted 6th-century healer from Italy cured numerous people's illnesses through prayer.

HEADACHE

TERESA OF AVILA

This 16th-century Spanish saint suffered from years of debilitating illness after contracting malaria.

DANDRUFF

GENESIUS OF ARLES

In 3rd-century Rome, this court secretary refused to write an edict demanding the persecution of Christians. He was beheaded.

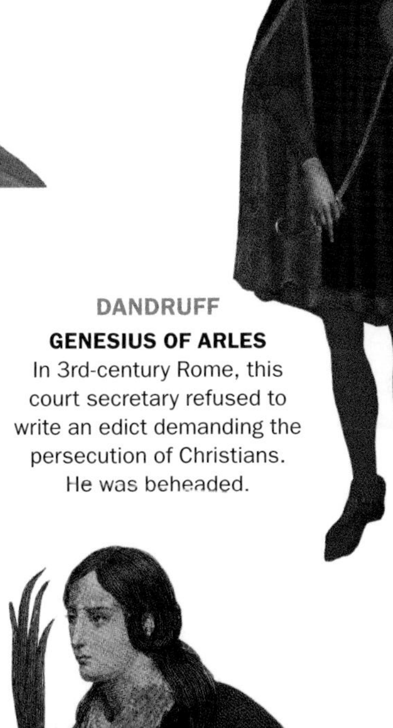

SORE THROAT

BLAISE

An Armenian who lived in the early 4th century, Blaise once saved a boy who was choking on a fish bone.

HANGOVER

BIBIANA

A 4th-century Italian virgin who chose death over forced prostitution. A plant that grew on her grave in Rome was said to cure a number of ills.

HEMORRHOIDS

FIACRE OF BREUIL

A 7th-century Irish monk and herbalist, Fiacre of Breuil had many followers. France's Cardinal Richelieu believed the monk's relics were a cure for this condition.

BACK PAIN

GEMMA GALGANI This 19th century Italian saint is said to have received holy stigmata and to have levitated. She contracted spinal meningitis but miraculously survived.

IT'S THEIR JOB

There is a patron saint for pretty much every occupation, and even one for those seeking work.

Flight Attendants:
BONA OF PISA
Born in Italy around 1156, Bona of Pisa started traveling as a 14-year-old, when she went to the Holy Land to visit her father, who was fighting in the Crusades. She led numerous pilgrimages throughout her life.

Mechanics:
ELIGIOUS OF NOYON
The 6th-century French Saint Eligious of Noyon was a skilled metalworker said to have painlessly removed—and replaced—a horse's leg in order to shoe the animal more easily.

Politicians: **THOMAS MORE**
In the 1500s, English statesman Thomas More held the country's second most powerful office after King Henry VIII. When Henry declared himself—not the Pope—the leader of the Church of England, More's ethical objection cost him his head.

Scientists:
ALBERT THE GREAT
Albert the Great, born in 1206 in what is now Germany, was a highly educated theologian who wrote extensively on biology.

Teachers:
JOHN BAPTIST DE LA SALLE
The 17th-century founder of the Christian Brothers schools, John Baptist de la Salle of France, established numerous educational traditions, including dividing students into grades.

The Unemployed: **CAYTANEO**
A nobleman in Venice in the 16th century, Caytaneo founded the Bank of Naples to serve destitute clients who would otherwise have had to borrow money from loan sharks.

Angel of Mercy

IN A NAZI CONCENTRATION CAMP, ONE CATHOLIC PRIEST SERENELY MADE THE ULTIMATE SACRIFICE FOR A STRANGER.

The entrance to the Auschwitz-Birkenau death camp, where Father Kolbe was imprisoned

It was July 1941 at Auschwitz, the notorious World War II concentration camp built in Poland by the Nazis. When the guards called roll, three prisoners from Block 14A did not respond and it was presumed the men had escaped. Karl Fritzsch, the captain in charge of the death camp, announced that the blockmates of the missing captives would pay for the offense. He sentenced the 10 men who remained behind to die by starvation and dehydration in an underground cell.

One of the condemned, a Catholic army sergeant named Franciszek Gajowniczek, cried out, "My poor wife! My poor children! What will they do?" At this, another prisoner calmly stepped forward and requested to be sent for punishment in Gajowniczek's place. As surprised as anyone by this gesture, Fritzsch accepted the exchange, sending Maximilian Kolbe, a Franciscan friar from Poland, with the other nine men to the starvation cell.

Father Maximillian Kolbe in 1939

Leading a Holy Life

Kolbe joined the Conventual Franciscan order at the age of 13, attended seminary, and was ordained as a priest in 1918, when he was 24. He spent his life tirelessly spreading the word of Christ throughout Poland and in Asia, all the while suffering with chronic tuberculosis. In 1927, he founded a monastery near Warsaw. After the Nazis invaded Poland in 1939, the monastery published anti-Nazi literature and provided shelter for thousands of Polish refugees, including Jews.

The Nazis shut down the monastery on February 17, 1941, sending Kolbe to Auschwitz on May 28. There, he was branded prisoner 16670, sentenced to hard labor, and viciously beaten. Through it all, Kolbe maintained an aura of selfless generosity, lifting the prisoners' spirits by leading prayers and hearing confessions.

The Ultimate Sacrifice

In the starvation cell, Kolbe offered spiritual comfort to the condemned men. As they died one by one of hunger, thirst, and attacks by guards, Kolbe, a janitor later noted, prayed ceaselessly and always greeted his captors peacefully.

By August 14, the cells were needed for other prisoners, and an executioner was ordered to inject each remaining prisoner with a lethal dose of carbolic acid. Kolbe, the only one still alive, extended his arm as he prayed.

A decade after the war ended, the Catholic Church officially recognized Kolbe's holy deeds, designating him a Servant of God. The Polish-born Pope John Paul II, who described Kolbe as having won "a spiritual victory like that of Christ himself," canonized him as a martyr-saint in 1982.

WHO KNEW?
Father Kolbe's officially sanctioned posthumous miracles include the curing of a woman's tuberculosis in 1948 and the clearing of a man's arteriosclerosis in 1950.

STILL STANDING

When the United States dropped an atomic bomb on Nagasaki, Kolbe's monastery there was spared.

In 1930, Maximilian Kolbe and four other Franciscan brothers left Poland for East Asia, landing in the southern Japanese seaport of Nagasaki. There, although they spoke no Japanese, they met with Buddhist and Shinto monks and lived modestly in a hut while getting to know the country. Eventually, they founded a small monastery outside of the city amid the foothills of Mount Hikosan. In a few short years, it became the largest Catholic monastery in Japan, and Kolbe returned to Poland in 1936. Nine years later, at 11:01 AM on August 9, 1945, the United States dropped an atomic bomb on Nagasaki, killing as many as 75,000 people and destroying a four-square-mile swath of the city. But Kolbe's monastery sustained little damage beyond a few broken windows. It still stands today.

Ruins of Nagasaki, Japan, following the detonation of the atomic bomb

Father Kolbe became the first Catholic "Martyr of Charity."

THE MAKING OF A MARTYR

Sainthood is automatically conferred on Catholic martyrs—those who are killed for refusing to denounce their religion. But the specifics of Kolbe's death left room for debate.

→ **When he was young,** Kolbe had a vision of Mary, who offered him two crowns, a white one symbolizing purity and a red one symbolizing martyrdom. "I said that I would accept them both," he reported.

→ **Fiercely patriotic,** Kolbe originally hoped to pursue a career in the military after finishing his Catholic education. But after his parents decided to devote themselves to religion, Kolbe did, too, not wanting to let them down.

→ **After Kolbe's death,** some argued that he was not killed specifically because he was Catholic, so therefore wasn't a martyr. To settle the matter, Pope John Paul II created a new category, "Martyr of Charity."

WHO KNEW?
Father Kolbe is the patron saint of political prisoners, journalists, and drug addicts.

St. John the Wonderworker

Saint John the Wonderworker

A ZEALOUSLY ASCETIC MONK RENOWNED FOR MIRACULOUS HEALINGS WAS ALSO A LEADER OF THE SOVIET ÉMIGRÉ COMMUNITY THROUGHOUT THE WORLD.

Michael Maximovitch was born to an aristocratic family in 1896, in Adamovka, a Russian village in what is now northeastern Ukraine. He parents named him for an archangel, an act that seemed to influence his life: He was fascinated from an early age with life at a nearby monastery and took to dressing his toy soldiers as monks. Growing up, he devoured biographies of the saints and sought to emulate their lives of humility, compassion, and abstinence even as he attended a Russian military academy and studied law at a local university.

In 1921, following the Russian Revolution, Michael and his family immigrated to Belgrade, Yugoslavia, where he returned to university and graduated with a theology degree. He discovered a mentor in Archbishop Anthony Khrapovitsky, later the founding chief hierarch of the Russian Orthodox Church Outside Russia.

Saint John suffered from a speech impediment. In 1934, when he said he thought it rendered him unfit to be bishop, his superiors reminded him that he shared that challenge with Moses.

A Bishop in Shanghai

In 1926, Michael took the first steps to becoming a monk and a priest in the Russian Orthodox tradition; he received the name John, was ordained a hieromonk (priest-monk), and became a schoolteacher. Though children warmed to John, he was quite strict and practiced a daily regimen of self-mortification, including fasting, walking barefoot, all-night prayer, and sleeping on the floor. He was known for frequenting hospitals and visiting suffering people.

Upon being ordained as a bishop in 1934, John was assigned to Shanghai, China, home to a large Russian Orthodox community made up of a variety of warring factions, including those who had roots in China dating to the late 17th century and refugees from the Bolshevik Revolution of 1916. Bishop John began to heal the deep divisions and win the devotion of his parishioners. He developed a reputation for an ability to heal

Icon of St. John Maximovitch the Wonderworker, Archbishop of Shanghai and San Francisco

through prayer and his followers believed he was a clairvoyant. Bishop John was so admired that when two leaders of the Russian Orthodox were killed for resisting the Japanese occupiers during the Sino-Japanese War in 1937, Bishop John assumed leadership of the terrified community and eventually was named Archbishop of the Russian Orthodox Church in China.

A Displaced Flock

The community's trials continued, however, and when the Communists assumed power in China in 1949, Christians across the country, including the Russian Orthodox, were persecuted. The Russians fled to the Philippines, and Bishop John successfully lobbied the American government to allow the émigrés to make the United States their home.

In 1962, he became Archbishop of San Francisco, Russian Orthodoxy's largest parish outside of the Soviet Union, and again united a divided community. Archbishop John died four years later, while visiting Seattle, Washington, and was buried in a sepulcher in the Holy Virgin Cathedral in San Francisco.

In 1994, he was canonized. A shrine in the cathedral contains some of his relics.

IN THE FOOTSTEPS OF THE SAINTS

Of all the holy men Saint John sought to emulate, two influenced him the most.

Saint John's forbear and namesake, Saint John of Tobolsk, was born **John Maximovitch** in 1651 in Nezhin, central Russia, to a noble family. He studied theology and was ordained a monk in 1680. He was appointed head of a monastery in Chernihiv, a flourishing city near Kiev, in 1695, and in 1697 he was made an archbishop. A devout ascetic, Saint John established a college, wrote poetry and prose, and founded a religious printing press. In 1711, he was appointed Archbishop of Tobolsk, in Siberia, and he ran a Latin school, established icon-painting classes, did missionary work, visited prisons and widows, and cared for the ill and impoverished.

Michael Leontovich was born in 1784 in Stara Stanzhara, a village in Russia's Poltava district. After graduating from a St. Petersburg theological academy in 1814, he became a monk, was ordained as a priest, and became renowned for his strict asceticism, countless good deeds, and missionary work. Eventually, Leontovich rose to become Archbishop and was appointed to the cathedral of the cities of Kharkov and Akhtyr (now part of northeastern Ukraine) in 1835. He abstained from sleep and spent his nights standing motionless, arms uplifted in prayer, and is said to have foretold the precise day and hour of his own death.

Icon of St. John of Tobolsk

The Russian Orthodox Church in Shanghai, China

HEALING GIFTS

Thousands of cases of Saint John's healings and clairvoyance have been documented by the Russian Orthodox Church.

→ During the two years that Saint John and the Russian émigrés spent at a camp in the Philippines, no typhoons threatened the area. "Your holy man blesses your camp from four directions every night," was the local Filipinos' explanation. Soon after John and the Russians left, a devastating typhoon destroyed the camp.

→ In the 1950s in Paris, Saint John prayed over and gave communion to a young man with a skull fracture. When the man's head was subsequently x-rayed, the fracture had disappeared and he quickly recuperated, dumbfounding his doctor.

→ In May 1966, Saint John told a San Francisco congregant, "I will die soon, at the end of June—not in San Francisco, but in Seattle." Four days before his death, he told another astonished follower, "You will not kiss my hand again."

Pillars encircled with hieroglyphics form a column through the interior of the Cenotaph Temple of Seti I at Abydos, Al-Balyana, Egypt, where Dorothy Eady believed she had been a priestess in an earlier life.

CHAPTER 7

Feats of Reincarnation

When people claim to have lived past lives, they can be hard to believe, but also hard to ignore.

Mummies in the Egyptian Galleries at the British Museum, London

Return of an Egyptian Priestess

A BRITISH TODDLER TAKES A TUMBLE AND WAKES UP WITH A FASCINATING STORY TO TELL.

When the young Englishwoman Dorothy Eady began writing down details of her dreams in the 1930s, she filled about 70 pages with ancient Egyptian hieroglyphics. Eady claimed that a spirit named Hor-Ra had appeared to her, dictating the story of her life, but that she'd known since toddlerhood that she was a reincarnated Egyptian.

Knocked Unconscious

Dorothy Eady was born in England in 1904. When she was three, she fell down the stairs and was knocked unconscious. Her parents frantically summoned the family doctor, who declared her dead. But when he returned to the house with the child's death certificate, he found her sitting up in bed, playing. After that, the little girl began to have strange recurrent dreams and repeatedly pleaded to be taken back to her "real home." On a visit to the Egyptian Galleries in the British Museum, four-year-old

WHO KNEW?
Omm Sety, a.k.a. Dorothy Eady, once discovered a cobra inside the Temple of Sety. To the alarm of the temple guards, she began feeding it.

Eady rushed around to the statues of the gods and goddesses, kissing their feet and shouting to be left "with my people."

As she grew, Eady learned to read hieroglyphics and was fascinated with Egyptian archaeology. In her 20s, she went to work for an Egyptian magazine in London, where she met her husband, an Egyptian. The couple moved to Egypt in 1933; when they arrived, Eady kissed the ground, declaring that she had come home to stay.

"Sixth Sense"

The couple had a son, whom they named Sety, but within two years the marriage was over. Eady continued having visions, including visitations from Hor-Ra. Landing a job as an archaeological research assistant with the Egyptian Department of Antiquities, she contributed to scholarly articles about ancient painting and earned recognition for her unerring insight. In 1956, she relocated to work in Abydos, the site of the Temple of Sety I and her alleged past life as a priestess. By that point a serious devotee of ancient Egyptian religion, she prayed at the temple each morning and evening.

Eady was popular with the Abydos villagers, who called her Omm Sety ("mother of Sety"), a name she ultimately adopted. She wrote articles tracing modern Egyptian culture back to the customs of ancient times, claiming her expertise was based more on memory than research. Despite such unscientific claims, Omm Sety had the respect of academics such as Klaus Baer of the Oriental Institute, who noted that she "understood the methods and standards of scholarship, which is usually not the case with nuts."

Indeed, Egyptologist Kent Weeks wrote that Omm Sety's colleagues "never doubted the accuracy of her field observations." She once demonstrated her past-life recall for an officer of the Antiquities Department, deciphering, in near-total darkness, a mysterious wall painting in the Temple of Sety. Her "uncanny sixth sense about the terrain on which she walks," as one colleague put it, also seemed apparent when she pointed out the site of the temple's lost garden, which awestruck archaeologists then unearthed.

Omm Sety died in 1981, leaving behind a body of work that many Egyptologists still use as source material. The mystery of her supposed reincarnation also lingers. As James P. Allen, curator of Egyptian Art at the Metropolitan Museum of Art, commented, Omm Sety "knew that some people looked on her as a crackpot, so she kind of fed into that notion.... She believed [in her reincarnation] enough to make it spooky, and it made you doubt your own sense of reality sometimes."

BUMPED INTO ANOTHER LIFE

Did Eady really live twice—or did brain trauma make her believe she had?

Dorothy Eady took her reincarnation seriously, but she was aware of the skepticism buzzing around her story. Happy to joke about it, she once told a journalist from *The New York Times* that some people said of her "when I fell downstairs, it knocked a screw loose."

One psychiatrist speculated that Eady's childhood fall may in fact have damaged her locus ceruleus, a part of the brain that controls learning and memory, perhaps facilitating the quick absorption of Egyptological information. Other brain changes may have made Eady more emotionally flexible and less inhibited, allowing her to separate from her current life and switch her attention to another.

Howard Carter and Lord Carnarvon at the opening of King Tutankhamun's tomb in the Valley of the Kings, Egypt, 1922

Egyptian Sculpture Gallery in the British Museum, London

EGYPTOMANIA!

Did England's fascination with all things Egyptian worm its way into Dorothy's subconscious?

When Dorothy Eady was born, England had been obsessed with Egypt for decades. British archaeologists announced one discovery after another throughout the 19th century, culminating in the discovery of the tomb of Tutankhamen in 1922, when Eady was 18.

Though Eady's reincarnation story remains one of the most convincing ever recorded, some are skeptical. She was an intelligent, creative young person, they reason. Perhaps she simply absorbed information from the hullabaloo around her. In Eady's day:

→ **Many English tourists** published intriguing accounts of their travels to Egypt.

→ **Egyptian themes** pervaded literature and film.

→ **Ancient Egyptian imagery** and aesthetics permeated fine arts, architecture, and design.

→ **Egyptian motifs** appeared on everything from tableware and furniture to fashion and advertising.

→ **Garbed in Egyptian-style** costumes, revelers attended Egypt-themed parties.

→ **Amateur Egyptologists** held pseudo-scientific "mummy parties," where guests unwrapped actual mummies purchased for the occasion.

A Double Life

WHEN AN AMATEUR HYPNOTIST HELPED A COLORADO WOMAN REVISIT A PAST LIFE, HE UNLEASHED A FRENZY OF INTEREST IN REINCARNATION.

Poster from the movie adaptation of *The Search for Bridey Murphy*

THE BRIDEY BUNCH

"Bridey Murphy Puts Nation into a Hypnotizzy," trumpeted the headline of a 1956 article in *Life*.

In the late 1950s, American pop culture burst with everything Bridey:

- A movie adaptation starring Academy Award–winning actress Teresa Wright was released in 1956.
- Bridey-themed pop tunes hit the airwaves, including Perry Como's "Did Anyone Ever Tell You, Mrs. Murphy?"
- A jig-like Bridey Murphy dance became popular.
- Hosts threw "come as you were" costume parties, where guests enjoyed parlor hypnosis and Bridey gags.

It was October 1952, and a cocktail party was underway at a home in Pueblo, Colorado. In attendance were 28-year-old homemaker Virginia Tighe, a middle-class mother of three who enjoyed playing bridge, and 36-year-old Morey Bernstein, a successful businessman who dabbled in hypnotism. One of the guests suggested that Bernstein put someone under his spell, and Tighe decided to be a good sport. Soon she was in a deep trance, recalling the events of her childhood. The delighted onlookers laughed and toasted the parlor trick.

Tighe had no particular interest in hypnotism, but a few weeks later she agreed to let Bernstein hypnotize her again and tape-record the results. Bernstein hoped to explore the idea of reincarnation: Do we live many lives, and if so, is it possible to recall a past one? To protect Tighe's privacy, Bernstein gave her the pseudonym Ruth Mills Simmons.

Looking Back

Between November 1952 and October 1953, Tighe met with Bernstein six times. During each session, he later wrote, he asked her to go "back, back, back... until oddly enough you find yourself in some other scene, in some other place, in some other time." The trance would take hold, and in an Irish brogue sprinkled with colorful expressions, Tighe unspooled the story of Bridey Murphy, born in 1798 in Cork, Ireland. Her narrative was packed with details.

Tighe revealed that Bridey was a redheaded Protestant who went to Mrs. Strayne's school in Cork and took a childhood trip to the Glens of Antrim. She married a young Catholic lawyer named Sean Brian McCarthy and lived with him in a cottage in Belfast; they never had children. Through Virginia, Bridey spoke of the region's currency and crops, told local folk tales, and sang her favorite Irish songs. In response to a post-hypnotic suggestion from Bernstein, Tighe danced the "Morning Jig" that Bridey had described in a trance. Bridey said she died in 1864, after breaking her hip in a fall, but lived on "in the spirit world," where there was no need to sleep or eat and no pain or fear. She stayed there until she was reborn as Virginia Tighe.

Bernstein chronicled the "Ruth Simmons" sessions in his book *The Search for Bridey Murphy*, published in 1956. On the *New York Times* bestseller list for six months and translated into more than 30 languages, the book sold millions of copies. Priests prayed for Tighe's soul and crowds gathered outside her home, hoping to catch a glimpse of her. According to *The New York Times*, the exhausted Tighe once said, "If I had known what was going to happen I would never have lain down on the couch." Although Tighe never underwent hypnosis again and never came to believe in reincarnation, she told the *Denver Post* years later, "Well, the older I get the more I want to believe in it." Tighe passed away in 1995. Bernstein, who by then had given up hypnotism and become a recluse, died four years later.

WHO KNEW?

A popular joke of the day: Did you hear about the man who read *The Search for Bridey Murphy* and changed his will? He left everything to himself!

Morey Bernstein poses with his hypnotism subject Virginia Tighe.

ALTERNATE THEORIES

Is the Bridey Murphy story evidence that we live many lives, or might there be another explanation?

In the nearly 60 years since Morey Bernstein published his bestseller, researchers and journalists have looked into the remarkable story, visiting the scenes of Tighe's childhood and traveling to Ireland. Believers insist they've found confirmation of reincarnation, while skeptics have poked numerous holes in her story. Some scientists explain Tighe's "memories" as *cryptomnesia*, the reemergence and reconfiguring of subconscious memories from childhood. Plenty of critics, including the popular math and science writer Martin Gardner, referred to the episode a hoax. "Almost any hypnotic subject capable of going into a deep trance will babble about a previous incarnation if the hypnotist asks him to," Gardner wrote in *Scientific American*.

BRIDEY WAS REAL	TIGHE HAD CRYPTOMNESIA	IT WAS A HOAX
Bridey said her father-in-law, John MacCarthy, had been a lawyer in Cork. Public records of the period included a barrister from Cork named John MacCarthy.	As a child, Tighe lived across the street from a Bridie Murphy Corkell.	Tighe liked to act and was involved in high school theater productions.
Bridey recalled shopping at the Belfast stores of John Carrigan and William Farr. A Belfast librarian confirmed merchants by those names existed in the 19th century.	Bridey said one of her brothers died when she was four years old. Tighe's brother died when she was five.	It was no surprise that Bridey could do a jig: Tighe was a proficient dancer who liked to perform Irish jigs.
Bridey stated that Catholics were allowed to teach at Queen's University in Belfast, a Protestant institution. American investigators doubted it, but it was common knowledge in Belfast at the time Bridey supposedly lived.	Bridey gave her Belfast address as Dooley Road. As a young student, Tighe recited a monologue called "Mrs. Dooley on Archer Road." There was no Dooley Road in Belfast.	It was well known that Tighe could do a skillful imitation of an Irish brogue.

The Doctor and the Ghost

ONE OF THE WORLD'S MOST INFLUENTIAL EXPERTS IN DYING CLAIMED TO HAVE HAD A LIFE-CHANGING SUPERNATURAL ENCOUNTER.

The 1969 bestseller *On Death and Dying,* by Elisabeth Kübler-Ross, changed the way the Western medical establishment dealt with an uncomfortable topic. Death, wrote the Swiss-born psychiatrist, was a natural part of life and should be treated as such, rather than feared, lied about, or ignored. As conventional as the idea might seem today, it was controversial at the time and Kübler-Ross long maintained that she was able to weather opposition with encouragement from an unlikely advisor: the ghost of a former acquaintance.

In the 1960s, as an assistant professor at the University of Chicago Medical School, Kübler-Ross interviewed hundreds of terminally ill patients. One of them, a woman named Mary Schwartz, had been discovered to be alive a few hours after a doctor had pronounced her dead. Schwartz told Kübler-Ross that she had been aware of her surroundings while clinically deceased, even accurately recounting a joke the doctor had told in the room. Schwartz's story piqued Kübler-Ross's interest in the idea that there might be a unique state of consciousness between life and death.

Ghostly Advice

About a year and a half after her miraculous recovery, Schwartz died. Ten months after that, in 1969, Kübler-Ross was visiting a colleague at the University of Chicago hospital. Discouraged by the scientific community's criticism of her work, she was seeking advice on whether it might be time to give up on the subject of mortality and find something new to study.

Entering the hospital, Kübler-Ross noticed an oddly familiar woman standing near the elevator. "She was very transparent, but not transparent enough

DYING WORDS

Grieving follows a common human pattern.

Elisabeth Kübler-Ross's most enduring contribution to the study of death was her description of a series of emotional states often experienced by dying people.

Called the Kübler-Ross model, these "five stages" can be applied to all manner of emotional trauma.

1. **Denial** of a terminal diagnosis
2. **Anger** at one's self, caretakers, friends, and the universe or a higher power
3. **Bargaining** in an attempt to avoid the certainty ahead
4. **Depression** and a lack of interest in the remainder of life
5. **Acceptance** and a positive attitude toward the near and ultimate future

Dr. Kübler-Ross interviewing a leukemia patient known as Eva

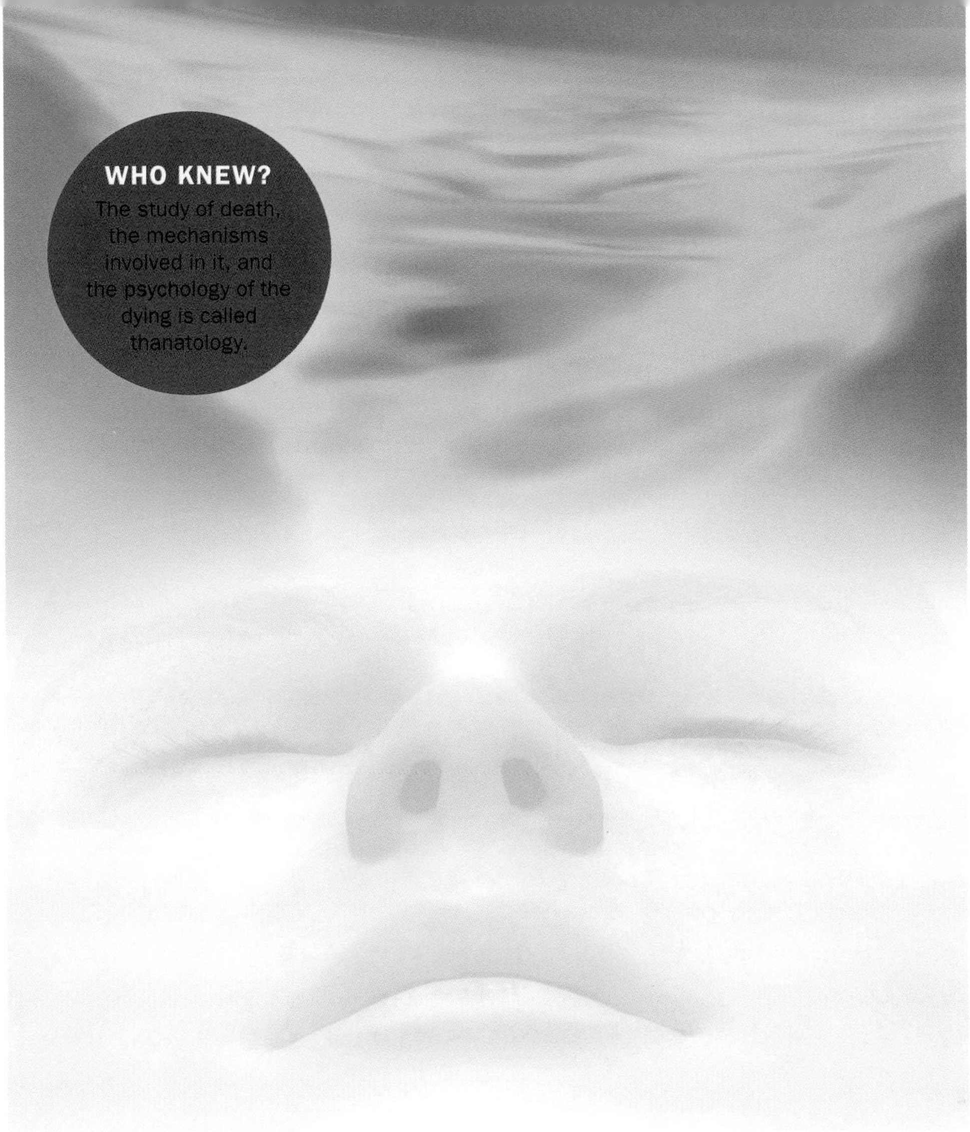

WHO KNEW?

The study of death, the mechanisms involved in it, and the psychology of the dying is called thanatology.

Elisabeth Kübler-Ross investigated the possibility of a unique state of consciousness between life and death.

that you could see very much behind her," the psychiatrist wrote later. To her shock, she realized that the apparition was Schwartz. "I even touched her skin to see if it was cold or warm, or if the skin would disappear when I touched it," she recounted later to lecture audiences.

The apparition spoke, asking for a few minutes of Kübler-Ross's time. Kübler-Ross led the otherworldly visitor to her office. "It was the most incredible walk I have ever taken, not knowing why I was doing what I was doing," she said.

Schwartz had come to thank Kübler-Ross for helping her through the dying process. She also wanted to encourage the psychiatrist to continue her research. "Your work is not finished," Schwartz reportedly said. "We will help you, and you will know when the time is right, but do not stop now. Promise?" She left the office, shutting the door behind her, but when Kübler-Ross opened it and peered out into the corridor, it was empty.

Kübler-Ross credited the visitation with inspiring her to persevere in the face skepticism and opposition throughout her career. As she wrote in *On Death and Dying*, she had transitioned from a feeling that belief in an afterlife was "a form of denial," to accepting wholeheartedly that people can live on after they've gone.

Dr. Elisabeth Kübler-Ross holds copies of her books.

PSYCHIATRIST WITH A PSYCHIC FLAIR

Kübler-Ross's interest in death was coupled with an attraction to paranormal phenomena.

Before her death in 2004 at age 78, Elisabeth Kübler-Ross published more than 20 books, received 18 honorary degrees, and helped launch the U.S. hospice movement. Still, her mid-career interest in psychic events damaged her credibility considerably.

➔ She reported having out-of-body experiences. Once, while severely ill, she participated in a study of relaxation and consciousness at the Menninger Foundation, a psychiatric treatment center in Topeka, Kansas, and said later that she'd experienced the sensation of floating up to the ceiling.

➔ She claimed to have four spirit guides, whom she identified as Willie, Aenka, Salem, and Mario.

➔ She said that she'd had a past life as "Isabel," a teacher during the time of Christ.

Wounded Warriors

WERE THESE YOUNG CHILDREN SOLDIERS IN PAST LIVES? THEIR REMARKABLE MEMORIES SEEM TO INDICATE COMBAT EXPERIENCE.

"We were walking along through the mud. It was damp; it was raining; it was cold. My rifle was heavy. I heard a shot come from behind, and I felt my throat fill with blood." Patricia Austrian of Connecticut vividly remembers the day in 1995 when she heard this story, from a soldier during World War I. The memory was grim, but the fact that the "veteran" relating it was her four-year-old son, Edward, made it positively chilling. Edward was too young to understand war, yet he laid out a detailed memory of dying by enemy fire in France as an 18-year-old.

Post Traumatic Stress?

As a toddler, Edward had always feared cloudy, damp weather. He had persistent throat problems, too, and would refer to the area in which he felt discomfort as the place where he'd been shot. Eventually, doctors discovered a large cyst in the boy's throat.

It was shortly before surgery to remove the cyst that Edward related his war story. At first, Edward's parents thought their boy had a particularly vivid imagination, though they did find it interesting that his cyst was exactly where he described being shot. Then, the cyst—not a type his doctors said would go away spontaneously—suddenly disappeared. The mystified doctors couldn't explain it, but Edward's parents became convinced that their son had been cured by talking about the traumatic events of a past life. Edward's cyst never came back.

"Airplane crash!"

American James Leininger, two, was obsessed with airplanes. The only toys he liked were models of World War II fighter planes, which he would deliberately crash into his family's coffee table to knock off the toys' propellers. In his car seat, he'd don an imaginary headset and facemask, and at home he

NO KIDDING

Do we really walk through this world more than once? Seeking answers, a professor asked children.

For 50 years, until his death in 2007, University of Virginia Medical School psychiatry professor Ian Stevenson studied children who believed they were reincarnated. Stevenson investigated more than 3,000 cases worldwide of children claiming to remember past lives, and discovered some strong similarities among them:

→ Most had their first past-life memories at two to four years of age.

→ Most had vivid memories of specific events in their former lives.

→ Most were born less than two years after their supposed previous persona died.

→ Many described their previous deaths as upsetting.

→ Many feared people and objects connected with their previous deaths.

→ Some had birthmarks or deformities corresponding to past-life injuries.

→ Some possessed inexplicable skills.

WHO KNEW?
U.S. war hero General George Patton believed he had a past life as a Carthaginian soldier several centuries BC.

In 2000, two-year-old James Leininger discussed World War II battles; after turning three, he claimed he had served on the *USS Natoma Bay* in the war.

set up a make-believe cockpit in a closet. When his parents, Bruce and Andrea, took the toddler to a flight museum in 2000, he circled a Corsair fighter, pretending to conduct a pilot's preflight check.

After the museum visit, James would scream out in his sleep, "Airplane crash! Plane on fire! Little man can't get out!" Awake, James told his parents that he was the "little man" in his nightmare, and "the Japanese," whose planes were marked with a "big red sun," had shot him down. The boy's parents were puzzled: How did their two-year-old know about World War II battles?

When he was three, James told Bruce and Andrea that he had been a 21-year-old Navy pilot named James Huston, who had served in the Pacific on the aircraft carrier *Natoma Bay* and had flown a Corsair against the Japanese with his copilot, Jack Larson. During the Battle of Iwo Jima in 1945, antiaircraft artillery hit their plane's engine, and Huston had died in the fiery crash. Larson had survived.

Upon investigating, Bruce found that there had indeed been a *Natoma Bay* in service during World War II, and pilots named James Huston and Jack Larson. Witnesses to the crash confirmed other details of the child's story, and also noted that the propeller had been knocked off Huston's plane.

Huston's 84-year-old sister, Anne, on hearing James's story, said, "This child couldn't know the things he does... I believe he is somehow a part of my brother." In 2009, Andrea and Bruce published a book about James called *Soul Survivor: The Reincarnation of a World War II Fighter Pilot.*

James Leininger, left, visits with Jack Larson, a World War II veteran fighter pilot who flew with the late James M. Huston Jr.

Jim Tucker is a child psychiatrist at the University of Virginia who studies claims of reincarnation.

MARKED FOR LIVES

University of Virginia associate psychiatry professor Jim B. Tucker, author of *Return to Life: Extraordinary Cases of Children Who Remember Past Lives*, has found that 70 percent of such subjects say they died violently in their previous incarnation.

→ **At age two, Charles Porter,** a full-blooded Tlingit from Alaska, insisted that he had been killed by a spear in a clan fight. He named the man who killed him and pointed to the place on his side where the spear had penetrated. Clan records confirmed his story.

→ **As soon as he could speak, D.G.,** an American boy born with an abnormally narrow pulmonary artery, said he had died in a shootout. He didn't know that a group of thugs had killed his grandfather, a security guard, during a robbery, and that one of their bullets had severed his grandfather's pulmonary artery.

→ **Ravi Shankar,** a boy in India, was born six months after a young boy in a nearby village was decapitated. As a toddler, Ravi described the other boy's death, saying the child had been killed by a relative who hoped to claim his inheritance. Ravi had a linear birthmark encircling his neck.

Ghost Gadget

AN ENGINEER INVENTS AN ELECTRONIC DEVICE HE SAYS DETECTS THE PRESENCE OF HIS DEAD DAUGHTER.

WHO KNEW?
Though Melissa Galka's posthumous visits have become less frequent over the years, her father reported in 2012 that "she still shows up on Christmas and her birthday."

Melissa Galka was a pretty high school senior who was on the gymnastics team and hoped to study business and interior design in college. Then, in September 2004, the Granby, Connecticut, 17-year-old crashed her car into a tree. Melissa's parents and sisters, Heather and Jennifer, were devastated by the teen's tragic death. But they soon began to believe that she wasn't far away. "She started doing things like ringing the doorbell, changing TV channels, turning lights on and off," Melissa's father, Gary Galka, told the *Hartford Courant* some years later. "One time she came into my room and I felt her sit on the edge of the bed."

Galka, an electrical engineer with a company that developed testing equipment for electrical devices, had the knowledge and resources to investigate the seemingly supernatural phenomena. He created a handheld device he called the Mel-Meter 8704 (the number referred to the year Melissa was born and the year she died), designed to record what believers in the paranormal say is evidence of ghostly activity in a room.

Special Equipment

Paranormal enthusiasts often use electronic equipment to identify what they say are signs of a spectral presence: minute

CHECK THE WIRES

The Mel-Meter is measuring something, but is that "something" supernatural?

Does the Mel-Meter really prove that ghosts exist? There are perfectly rational explanations for all of the phenomena such devices measure, according to Joe Nickell, Ph.D., a senior research fellow at the Center for Inquiry, an organization that debunks pseudoscientific claims. "All sorts of non-ghost sources" could account for the readings, he said in a 2011 interview, "such as faulty wiring, nearby microwave towers, sunspot activity, and so on." But Galka countered in another interview that the devices gave people hope. "I feel compelled to help other bereaved parents," he said, "to show these parents that they can live beyond the grief and be comforted knowing their child is in a good place."

Joe Nickell

Melissa Galka's parents, Gary and Cindy Galka, bring a Mel-Meter to their daughter's grave in Connecticut.

changes in electric and magnetic energy. They may also use thermometers to pick up on temperature fluctuations and infrared or ultraviolet video cameras to record light-wave activity not visible to the naked eye. The Mel-Meter, an all-in-one handheld device, tracks many of these phenomena simultaneously. It even beeps when it detects the slightest touch—say, of a spirit tapping one's shoulder.

"Hi, Daddy"

For the Galkas, the device provided them with the proof they needed that Melissa lived on in another form. "I've never seen her," Galka said in 2012, "but my younger daughter Heather has seen her three times."

The family has been featured on various ghost-hunting television series. In one, Melissa's mother, Cindy, described hearing an unusual sound as she lay in bed one night. Sure that it was Melissa, Cindy invited her deceased daughter to crawl into bed with her and felt a tingling presence against her body, a kind of hug from beyond. She found out later that Gary was experiencing the same thing at the same time. The episode also included "unaltered footage" of a voice recorded on the Spirit Box, another gadget Galka invented. The voice, identified as Melissa's, said, "Hi, Daddy; I love you."

DREAMS, PSYCHICS, VISITATIONS

Ordinary people claim to have communicated with deceased loved ones in many different ways.

→ **Ten years** after her daughter Lindy's 1974 suicide, Maxine Weaver consulted with a psychic and received a message: "Do you remember the tea bags?" Though she hadn't told the psychic, the Nebraska mother recalled that six months after Lindy's death, she had discovered a note in her tea canister that read, "I love you, Mommy."

→ **In 1997,** when Josh Harris was 12, his grandfather Raymond was dying from lung cancer. One night the Alabama boy awoke to find his "pa-pa" standing next to him, assuring him that everything would be OK. Josh awoke to the telephone ringing with the news that his grandfather had just died.

→ **In 2007,** as her mother was about to be remarried, Anna Sayce, a New Zealand psychic, had a dream in which her great-grandmother said to her, "your mother looks lovely in brown." The next day while Sayce and her mother were dress shopping, her mother said, "Great-granny always used to tell me how nice I looked in brown."

WHO KNEW?
One in three Americans believes in ghosts, according to a 2005 Gallup poll.

The Tian Tan Buddha, at Po Lin Monastery on Hong Kong's Lantau Island, weighs 250 metric tons and is 111.5 feet tall.

CHAPTER 8

The Extraordinary East

Legend has it that as soon as Buddha was born, he walked seven steps, then pronounced: "I am the highest in the world..."

Enlightened and Exalted

THE BUDDHA WAS NOT A FAN OF MIRACLES. BUT IF PRESSED, HE COULD TURN HIMSELF INTO FIRE AND COMMUNE WITH WILD BEASTS.

Departure of Prince Siddhartha. From *Myths of the Hindus and Buddhists*, by Sister Nivedita and Ananda Coomaraswamy (c. 1913)

WHO KNEW?

A yearly Tibetan holy day, the Day of Miracles, commemorates the end of a 15-day span during which the Buddha did something remarkable every day.

Siddhartha Gautama—the man who was to become the Buddha—was born to a wealthy clan in what is present-day Nepal, sometime between the 4th and 6th centuries BC. Legend has it that Siddhartha walked seven steps as soon as he was born, then pronounced: "I am the highest in the world, I am the best in the world, I am the foremost in the world; this is the last birth; now there is no more renewal of being in future lives."

Growing up in the ancient city of Kapilavastu, Siddhartha lead a sheltered existence surrounded by luxury, but he was troubled by the hardships, poverty, and illness he witnessed in his brief travels. Over time, he became increasingly focused on human suffering and longed to find answers.

At 29, Siddhartha renounced his privileged lifestyle. He left his wife and child and retreated to the city of Rajagaha, where he began to beg in the street. For six years he practiced ever more extreme forms of self-deprivation, subsisting on a grain of rice a day and routinely holding his breath until he collapsed.

Eventually, Siddhartha realized that the ascetic life he was leading would not bring him the wisdom he sought. While sitting under a banyan tree, he vowed to meditate until he was enlightened. That night, Siddhartha reached a state of heightened understanding. He was peaceful and free from suffering, and soon sought to help others reach enlightenment.

Unnatural Phenomenon

Some two years later, Siddhartha returned to his father's kingdom of Kapilavastu as the revered Buddha. Upon his arrival, some members of his own clan questioned his divinity and refused to pay homage to him. According to legend, the Buddha responded by performing the *yamaka pa¯tiha¯riya*, or "twin miracle." Rising into the air, he transformed his body so the upper half was made of fire, while the lower half became streaming water. He then reversed the effect, so that the water emerged from his top half and flames from his bottom half; finally, he alternately projected fire and water from his left and right sides. The skeptics were resoundingly convinced.

The Buddha repeated the same astonishing act several times, including five years later in the ancient Indian city of Savatthi, when he conjured a jeweled walkway in the air to stage the miracle.

Trunk Show

Decades later, when the Buddha was 72, his cousin and student, Devadatta, who was bitterly jealous of him, plotted to kill the holy man. Bribing the keepers of an ill-

Great Buddha, Daibutsu, Kamakara, Central Honshu, Japan

tempered elephant with a promise of better work and wages, Devadatta convinced them to release the angry animal when they saw the Buddha coming.

The next day, the elephant keepers saw the Buddha walking with several monks, and they opened the stable door. The elephant raised its trunk and charged. The monks implored the Buddha to hide from the raging animal, but he said, "It cannot happen, that anyone can take a Perfect One's life by violence," according to a biography based on the ancient Buddhist scripture *Pa¯li Canon*. The Buddha then embraced the elephant "with thoughts of loving-kindness." The beast settled down in front of the Buddha, who stroked the animal's forehead. Using its trunk to sprinkle the dust from the Buddha's shoes on its own head, the elephant retreated to the stables, forever tamed.

PARLOR TRICKS

Although he was responsible for more than a few, Buddha said of miracles, "I dislike, reject, and despise them."

The Buddha generally disliked the performance of miracles, calling such displays empty dazzle executed without wisdom. The book *Buddhism: Its Essence and Development* relates a parable of how the Buddha encountered an ascetic who had practiced self-deprivation for 25 years. When asked what he had gained from this discipline, the man stated that he could cross the river by walking on the water. The Buddha replied that this was an insignificant achievement, since anyone could cross the river on the ferry for the equivalent of a penny.

While the Buddha was living in the Indian city of Nalanda, a man named Kevatta pressed him to explain why he didn't perform more miracles in order to awe his followers. The Buddha answered that when done to impress others, such acts were no better than magic tricks. They had no real value because they did nothing to end suffering or help guide people toward enlightenment.

The Buddha tames an elephant with loving-kindness. Detail from *The Life of Buddha* at Jogyesha Temple, Seoul, Korea

GUEST APPEARANCE

During a stay in one village, the Buddha demonstrates his many abilities.

→ The Buddha stays with three monks, each a leader of many disciples. One monk worries that the Buddha's presence will diminish his own standing at an upcoming ceremony. Reading his mind, the Buddha leaves the village for the duration of the ceremony.

→ The monks need more wood to keep their fires burning but are unable to split the logs. They suspect "supernormal" scheming by the Buddha. When the Buddha sees their problem, however, the 500 logs are immediately and inexplicably split.

→ A storm causes water levels in the area to rise and flood the Buddha's quarters, but he makes the waters stand back around him. When one of the monks comes by in a boat to check on him, the Buddha is standing on dry ground.

The Hugging Saint

AN INDIAN WOMAN IS RENOWNED FOR SPREADING THE LOVE—BY EMBRACING THE WORLD ONE PERSON AT A TIME.

SUPER YOGIS

Hindus and Buddhists in a higher state of consciousness experience *siddhis*.

Siddhis, wondrous powers over body, mind, and physical world, are believed to be a natural, inevitable result of perfected yogic practice. Ancient texts mention many siddhis, but eight are canonical:

→ **Anima** the power to grow very small

→ **Mahima** the power to grow very big

→ **Laghima** the power to become very light

→ **Garima** the power to become very heavy

→ **Prapti** the power to go anyplace or attract anything

→ **Prakamya** the power to realize any desire

→ **Istva** the power to create matter

→ **Vasitva** the power to control nature and all objects

Can a single hug transform the world? Millions of devotees—from the desperately poor to celebrities such as Sharon Stone and Russell Brand—believe the answer is yes. They wait in miles-long lines to fall into the arms of Amma ("mother" in Malayalam, Amma's native tongue), who they believe is a living incarnation of the Mother of the Universe.

Born in 1954 to a low-caste family in Kerala, southern India, Mata Amritanandamayi Devi is considered by her followers to be the divine embodiment of pure, selfless, motherly love, able to solve the world's problems through a warm embrace. "She is simply the essence, the embodiment, of compassion," said Roy Strassman, one of the thousands of followers who came to receive *darshan*—Amma's signature hug—in Los Angeles in 2010.

Magic Touch

Devoted to God from early childhood, Amma was so moved to help others that she gave away family valuables to people in need—and was often beaten for it by her father, according to her biography. In her teens, Amma had several visions that prompted her to begin hugging strangers, a defiant act in a culture where women weren't supposed to touch men.

Soon, extraordinary things—miracles—began happening to people and villages who came in contact with Amma. Malignant cancers and leprosy were healed, and a single pot of water was said to be transformed into a bottomless bowl of rice pudding that fed an entire village.

The hopeful began to line up by the thousands to receive *darshan* at the ashram, or spiritual monastery, that Amma founded in Kerala in southwest India. In some cases their waiting time was as long as 15 hours, since Amma was said to rise from her seat only after she had hugged every single person hoping for her blessing—not even stopping to eat or use the bathroom. And she took few days off.

Along with a hug, Amma gives devotees tokens such as flower petals, apples, or Hershey's kisses.

WHO KNEW?
Amma received the Gandhi King Award for Non-Violence from the United Nations in 2002.

Amma, the "hugging saint," smiles during public discourse in Delhi, India, in 2006.

"I'm trying to awaken true motherhood in people, in men and women, because that is lacking in today's world," Amma told *Salon* in an interview. "Today there are two types of poverty. The first is a lack of basic necessities. The second is a lack of love and compassion. As far as I'm concerned, the second is more important because if there is love and compassion then the first kind can be taken care of."

Force for Good

Amma's ashram has grown into a bustling 100-acre community known as Amritapuri. The ashram includes a university, restaurants, temples, and shops, all exquisitely maintained by Amma's legions of local and foreign follower-volunteers. She tours Europe and North America every year, and her Embracing the World global network, which generates $20 million a year, funds orphanages, schools, shelters, and disaster relief.

After the 2004 tsunami in Asia, Amma's organization provided shelter and food to thousands of refugees and victims. Since 2005, her charities have also contributed funds for relief after Hurricane Katrina in the United States, super-typhoon Haiyan in the Philippines, and the earthquakes in Haiti and Japan.

Lines to embrace Amma can stretch out for 15 hours.

THE EMBRACE OF 1,000 GRANDMOTHERS

Huggees describe their experiences with Amma.

➔ "[My hug was like] a jolt of electricity. Her embrace just felt so unconditionally loving and comforting, with no holding back."
—Walt Freese, former CEO of Ben & Jerry's

➔ "The embrace lasted no more than 30 seconds but I was surprised at how good it felt, and while she was hugging me, she whispered, 'My son, my son! God loves you, God loves you.' It was like getting a loving embrace from 1,000 grandmothers."
—John Quinones, *20/20*

➔ "Suddenly, Amma's hands clasped my neck. She planted my head into her upper chest and... stroked my hair, laughed, and began silently chanting words that were indecipherable. It was warm, comfortable, even sweet. She scattered flower petals atop my head and it was over.... It felt like a hug from my grandmother."
—Kurt Streeter, *Los Angeles Times*

Take Me to the River

IN THE MOST SACRED PILGRIMAGE IN HINDUISM, MASSES OF HUMANITY SHARE A SINGULAR SPIRITUAL EXPERIENCE.

Devotees immerse an idol of the Hindu god Ganesha in the Yamuna River during Ganpati festival in New Delhi, India, September 2014.

On January 14, 2013, millions of pilgrims from around the globe gathered in the city of Allahabad, India. It was the holiest pilgrimage in Hinduism, the Kumbh Mela, celebrated four times every 12 years. The 2013 version, at the end of a 12-year cycle, was the Maha Kumbh Mela—the biggest of them all—and was said to be one of the largest religious gatherings in history. It offered the faithful a chance to bathe in sacred waters and to cleanse their souls of sin from this life and those prior. The Kumbh Mela drew crowds of wealthy and poor, devout believers and casual tourists, and some 30,000 holy ascetics known as *sadhus*.

The Legend

When the Kumbh Mela was first written about in the 7th century, it was described as taking place at the confluence of three rivers, the Ganges, Yamuna, and the mythical Sarasvati. According to Hindu legend, demigods known as the Devas worked alongside their enemies, spirits known as Asuras, to churn the ocean and obtain *amrita*, the nectar of immortality. When the pitcher—or *kumbh*—of nectar appeared, the Devas and Asuras fought over it for 12 days. The god Vishnu then flew away with the pitcher, spilling drops of amrita in four places. Today, the Kumbh Mela, or "pitcher festival," takes place at each of those four sites, on dates determined by the positions of the Sun and Jupiter.

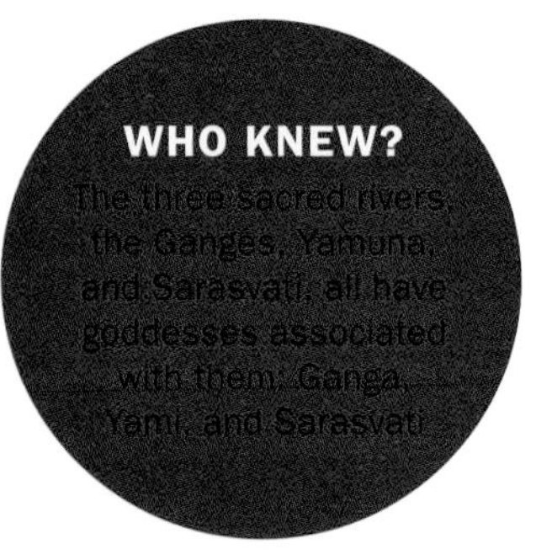

WHO KNEW?
The three sacred rivers, the Ganges, Yamuna, and Sarasvati, all have goddesses associated with them: Ganga, Yami, and Sarasvati.

Cleansing and Liberation

At the appointed time, a makeshift city of tents and camps rises up, full of pilgrims engaged in devotional singing, religious discussion, and feeding of the poor and needy. For most, the focus is a ritual bathing in the sangam, the place where the rivers meet, to achieve a spiritual rebirth. The high point occurs on the occasion of the new moon, when sadhus, naked or covered in ash, lead a procession into the rivers. Having renounced all worldly desires, these holy men depend on the charity of pilgrims, who provide them with food, necessities, and money in exchange for blessings and healings, or just for the opportunity to sit in the presence of an embodiment of the divine—an encounter known as *darshan*.

Pilgrims celebrate Maha Kumbh Mela, Allahabad, India, 2013.

Whatever hopes they bring, the pilgrims can be sure of an extraordinary—and, for most, a once-in-a-lifetime—experience. Having attended the Kumbh Mela in 1895, Mark Twain noted, "It is wonderful, the power of faith like that, that can make multitudes upon multitudes of the old and weak and the young and the frail enter without hesitation or complaint upon such incredible journeys and endure the resultant miseries without repining. It is done in love, or it is done in fear, I do not know which it is. No matter what the impulse is, the act borne of it is beyond imagination."

MILK FOR THE GODS

Miraculous drinking statues attract hordes of believers—and some skeptics as well.

Early in the morning of September 21, 1995, a worshipper went into a Hindu temple in New Delhi. He brought a spoonful of milk up to the mouth of a statue of the god Ganesha; to his astonishment, the figure appeared to drink. By midday, news of this incident had spread across the city, causing gridlock as countless worshippers flocked to the site.

By the end of the day, statues of Ganesha and several other Hindu deities across India and abroad were reportedly drinking milk from spoons and bowls. "Guru buster" Prabhir Ghosh of the Indian Science and Rationalist's Association insisted that the "miracle" could be explained according to a basic concept of fluid mechanics known as "capillary action." The ceramic statues were porous enough to draw liquid in, making it appear as if the statues were "drinking." Believers were not swayed by the explanation.

SADHUS, SWAMIS, AND SAINTS

It is said that Hindu ascetics have been performing miracles for centuries.

Swami Shankarashram I. The second guru of the Chitrapur Sarasvats community of India, this 18th-century holy man performed many miraculous acts. Legend has it that he appeared to a devoted Brahmin in a distant village while never leaving his *matha*, or monastery; he also appeared in dreams and in person to a poor artist, who became very successful after receiving the guru's blessing.

Trailanga Swami. This 19th-century yogi from Varanasi, India, was believed to be an incarnation of the god Shiva. Legends relate that he hovered in the air over the river Ganges for days on end, consuming a bucket of poison with no ill effect; he also repeatedly appeared on the roof of the prison where he had been locked up for walking around in the nude, or *naga*—"sky clad." Trailanga Swami died in 1887, reportedly at the age of 280.

Sai Baba. Claiming to be the reincarnation of Sai Baba of Shirdi, this 20th-century guru reportedly could materialize objects out of thin air, and after suffering a stroke and becoming paralyzed in 1963, healed himself in front of thousands. By the time of his death in 2011, Sai Baba had developed a massive following, and his organization continues to support educational, medical, and social projects.

Camp meeting, Philadelphia. Lithograph by Kennedy & Lucas, after Alexander Rider (c. 1829)

CHAPTER 9

Made in America

Prophets, evangelists and healers have been astounding believers in the United States since Colonial times.

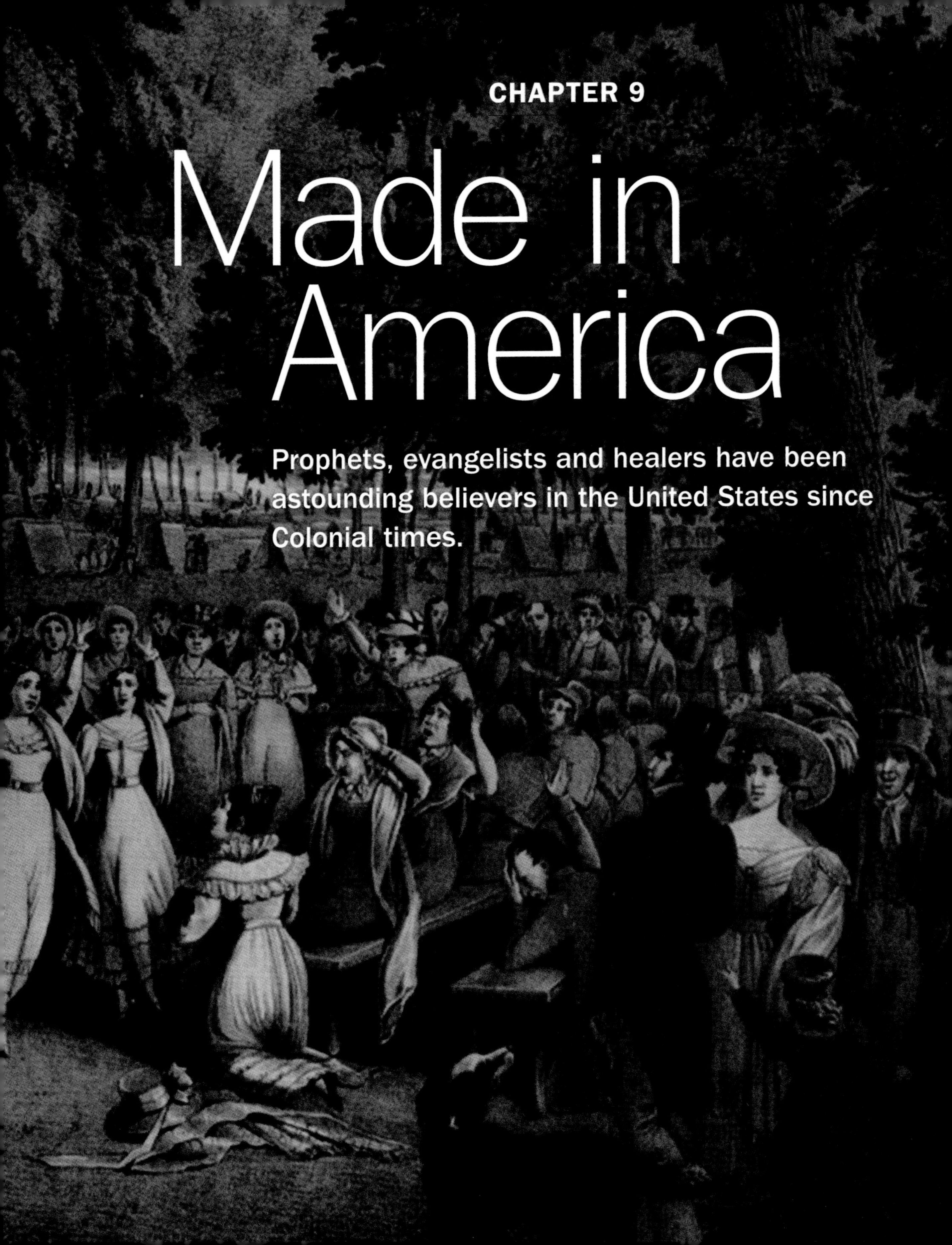

The Birth of a New Faith

ONE OF THE WORLD'S FASTEST-GROWING RELIGIONS AROSE FROM THE REVELATIONS OF A TEENAGE PROPHET IN RURAL NEW YORK.

Joseph Smith's vision started a new religion.

WHO KNEW?
The Book of Mormon, the sacred text of the Church of Jesus Christ of Latter-day Saints, is named after the ancient prophet Mormon, who is said to have written much of it.

They were thin, like sheets of paper, inscribed on both sides, and bound together with rings, like a loose-leaf notebook. But these pages, called "plates," were special. Not only were they made of gold, they were said to contain the sacred writings of prophets who lived centuries ago in what is now America.

It is said that the existence of these plates was revealed to Joseph Smith, the son of a farmer in Palmyra, New York, in 1823. Smith, 17 at the time, was praying when an angel appeared and revealed that a sacred text was buried nearby in a hill. Four years would pass before the young man would finally discover and retrieve the documents, which would become the foundation of a new religion.

Praying in a Wooded Grove

Born to parents who claimed to regularly receive messages from God, Smith became interested in religion at 12 but had questions about the differing claims made by various branches of Christianity. At 15, trying to decide which denomination to join, he went to a wooded grove to pray. As Smith struggled with his thoughts, he said Jesus and God the Father appeared to him with a message. Do not join any of these denominations; none is the true faith, they said.

The golden plates, comprised of the writings of various Native American prophets before and after the birth of Jesus, would provide Smith with the answer. Their language was mysterious, one that Smith called Reformed Egyptian, and he was able to translate them into English, before returning them to the hill in which he found them. Believers say they described the history of Christianity in the ancient Americas.

Exodus to America

Smith's translated text tells of groups of Israelites who made their way from the Holy Land across the ocean to the Americas, centuries before the birth of Christ. The surviving group, the Lamanites, were the ancestors of the Native Americans. This scripture also gives an account of Christ appearing in America shortly after his resurrection. The text, which Smith published in 1830 as the Book of Mormon, became the foundation of a new religion, the Church of Jesus Christ of Latter-day Saints.

The angel Moroni delivering the plates of the Book of Mormon to Joseph Smith. Artist unknown (c. 1886)

Smith soon gained converts and eventually moved with them from Palmyra to Ohio, then to Illinois. After Smith's death, one of his apostles, Brigham Young, led the Mormons to Utah, now headquarters of the thriving Mormon Church. Today, there are 14 million Mormons around the world and 150 million copies of the Book of Mormon in print; it has been fully or partially translated into more than 100 languages.

Brigham Young, who was cured by Joseph Smith in Nauvoo, Illinois, led the Mormons to Utah.

MORMON MIRACLES

The Latter-day Saints doctrine records many wonders.

→ **According to the Book of Mormon,** an early group of Israelites came across the ocean to the Americas in 600 BC with the help of a miraculous compass that pointed them in the right direction and also contained written instructions from God.

→ **Joseph Smith** was said to have healing powers. In 1835, according to eyewitnesses, he instantly healed a dying woman when she was "so much deranged" that she could not recognize her friends and family. In 1839, he is said to have cured numerous ailing members of his settlement in Nauvoo, Illinois, including Brigham Young, by walking among them.

→ **In the 1848 Miracle of the Gulls,** a plague of crickets began devouring the Mormon pioneers' first harvest in Utah's Salt Lake Valley. Suddenly, a huge flock of seagulls—who would have had to travel all the way from the Pacific coast—descended, ate the pests, and saved the crops.

God Heals All

ONE WOMAN WHO FELT THE LORD'S PRESENCE WAS CURED OF TUBERCULOSIS. SHE AROSE WITH A MISSION TO HELP OTHERS.

Sarah Mix, the first known African American healing evangelist, carved out a pioneering role in the American faith community in the 19th century, despite her race and gender.

A Life-Changing Illness

Born in 1832, Mix was diagnosed with tuberculosis in her early 20s, not long after the disease claimed the lives of both her parents. In spite of her ill health, she spent many years as a domestic worker in her native Connecticut, which required long hours of backbreaking chores for little pay. When Mix was about 45, her tuberculosis worsened and she became so weak that even a short walk exhausted her. In December 1877, she encountered Ethan Otis Allen, a well-known faith healer. Allen prayed for Mix, and she recovered. What's more, Allen told her that she, too, was blessed with the gift of healing.

Mix began to travel with Allen throughout New England, praying for the sick as he trained her in the healing arts. Word of her astonishing abilities soon spread through the Northeast, and physicians began referring patients to the "healing home" Mix established.

In 1882, Mix published a small book, *Faith Cures and Answers to Prayer*, which included testimonials from those whom she'd cured. Mix's tuberculosis remained in remission for seven years but returned in 1884. This time, prayer didn't help and she died at age 52.

Tent revivals were a popular forum for faith healing in the U.S. in the 19th and early 20th centuries. Photo c. 1910

A Move Toward the Miraculous

In the 1700s, most Protestants in the U.S. believed in predestination, not miracles; they thought humans too sinful and God too far removed from worldly affairs to allow for such things as spontaneous healing. But in the early decades of the 1800s, attitudes changed radically and many began to embrace the possibility of miracles as evidence of God's presence in the world. The popularity of the divine healing movement was part of this massive shift. By the 1870s, faith healing as practiced by Sarah Mix was part of American culture. Believers attended faith-healing conventions, and magazines were filled with testimonials about the practice.

"Some time since I solicited your prayers for my daughter; now I write to tell that we feel without a doubt that she is cured. Oh, what a wonderful thing this faith cure is," one woman wrote in a letter to Mix, echoing the testimonials of the era.

The mainstream religious establishment remained skeptical of anyone claiming to cure people through prayer—and many con artists did take advantage of the sick and desperate. But some American religious groups—including Shakers, Mormons, and Seventh-Day Adventists—incorporated faith healing into their worship. Many African Americans, drawing on western African traditions, believed in supernatural healing as well. Though far from pervasive today, faith healers can still be found working in different corners of the country.

People raise their hands in prayer while Reverend John Wood touches their heads during a faith-healing session.

MEETINGS IN THE WILD

Rural tent revivals were lively events, with participants dancing, singing, and experiencing visions, supernatural impressions, and spiritual ecstasy.

The U.S. faith-healing movement developed out of camp meetings held in frontier areas at the end of the 1700s and beginning of the 1800s. People who lived far from conventional churches camped out for several days, praying, listening to sermons, singing hymns, and enjoying a rare sense of religious community, often under huge tents.

The first truly influential camp meeting was held at Cane Ridge, Kentucky, in 1801. It drew between 10,000 and 20,000 people in a state with a population of only about 230,000. People fainted and fell to the ground (were "slain in the spirit") or suffered uncontrollable shaking ("the jerks"). One eyewitness reported "sinners dropping down on every hand, shrieking, groaning, crying for mercy, convoluted, professors praying, agonizing, fainting, falling down in distress for sinners, or in raptures of joy! Some singing, some shouting, clapping their hands, hugging and even kissing, laughing...and all this at once." Many behaviors typically experienced at camp meetings, such as "speaking in tongues," swoons, and trances, became associated with the Holiness movement in the late 1800s and the Pentecostal movement in the 1900s.

The Cane Ridge Meeting House, Kentucky

GOD CALLS WOMEN

Sarah Mix was an early, but not the only, female faith healer of her era.

Several women became well-known evangelists in the late 19th and early 20th centuries.

→ **Maria Woodworth-Etter (1844–1924)** began to pray for the sick in 1885, and her meetings became famous for the number of people who fell to the floor in a trance. She was arrested in 1913 in Massachusetts for taking money under false pretenses but was cleared after a spectacular hearing featuring numerous testimonials.

→ **Carrie Judd Montgomery (1858–1946)** was healed by Sarah Mix in 1879 and was inspired to take up the practice herself. In the 1880s, Montgomery opened a "healing home" in Buffalo, New York, that became a model for many others. Montgomery's journal, *Triumphs of Faith*, was popular in faith-healing circles for many years.

→ **Minnie Abrams (1859–1912)** heard God's call and traveled to Bombay, India, in 1887, where she learned the Marathi language and opened a boarding school. Mukti Mission, which she established with a leading Indian Christian social reformer in 1898, became known for eliciting ecstatic experiences.

Curing the Multitudes

ONE OF AMERICA'S FIRST SUPERSTAR EVANGELISTS ATTRACTED DEVOUT FOLLOWERS WHO BELIEVED SHE HAD THE POWER TO HEAL.

Believing in Aimee Semple McPherson required a leap of faith. The evangelical minister, popular in the 1920s and 30s, claimed she had been given divine power that allowed her to cure those people who revered God. Tens of thousands were convinced by the claim, and they flocked to McPherson as she traveled the U.S., performing faith-healing demonstrations in which she allegedly helped hordes of sick and injured people.

Aimee Semple McPherson helped pave the way for nationally famous evangelists like Billy Graham and Joel Osteen.

Her services were dramatic and emotional. She would anoint her hands with spiced oil and touch and pray over the infirm. Then, "The deaf heard, the blind saw, the paralytic walked, the palsied became calm, before the eyes of as many people that could be packed into the largest church auditorium..." reported the *Denver Post.*

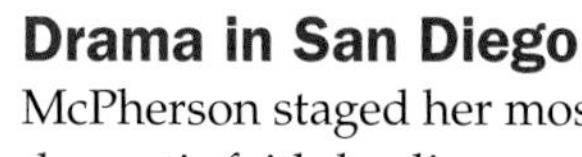

Drama in San Diego

McPherson staged her most dramatic faith-healing demonstration in 1921, in San Diego, California. A few days before the event, the still relatively unknown evangelist strapped herself into the passenger seat of a biplane and dropped 15,000 leaflets onto the city below. "I'm taking my fight against the devil to the skies!" she declared. The publicity stunt worked, and an estimated 30,000 people showed up for the outdoor service at Balboa Park in the hope that McPherson would be able to heal them or a loved one.

McPherson ministered to the ailing and injured multitude for hours. A man tossed his crutches into the crowd and danced. When a woman said to be paralyzed stood from her wheelchair and walked, the crowd went wild. Hundreds of sick and disabled men, women, and children swarmed the stage. McPherson was unable to help everyone in the crowd and emphasized that she was not a miracle worker. "Jesus is the healer," she reminded people, but her career as a national celebrity was launched.

The Fame Game

McPherson quickly became a favorite with media and the public. She entered floats in a parade, created her own radio station, and tried to faith-heal a zoo lion. In 1923, McPherson settled in Los Angeles, where she founded her own Pentecostal religious denomination, the International Church of the Foursquare Gospel. Its headquarters, Angelus Temple, held 5,300 people, and McPherson packed it seven days a week.

Then, in 1926, McPherson disappeared while on a visit near Venice Beach, California. Her distraught followers believed she had drowned while swimming in the ocean. But five weeks later, she reappeared in the Arizona desert and claimed to have been kidnapped and tortured before escaping. Rumors swirled that it was a hoax—that the story was a cover-up for an affair, plastic surgery, or an abortion—and the supposed kidnapping remained unsolved. The skeptical press began to portray her as a huckster, but she remained beloved by her ever-growing flock until her death in 1944.

WHO KNEW?
The Foursquare Gospel Church, founded by Aimee Semple McPherson, now has a worldwide membership of more than 8 million people.

Evangelist Aimee Semple McPherson, far right, standing with raised arms, preaching (c. 1930)

DEATH BY FAITH

A controversial Pentecostal practice has led to a number of fatal accidents.

In February 2014, a venomous snake bit Jamie Coots as the 42-year-old pastor performed a religious service at the Full Gospel Tabernacle in Jesus Name in Middlesboro, Kentucky. It was the eighth and last time Coots was bitten while snake handling. The bite, from a four-foot-long timber rattlesnake, proved fatal.

What do poisonous snakes have to do with Christianity? The answer can be found in the Book of Mark: Believers, it states, "will pick up snakes in their hands, and . . . it will not hurt them."

During this rite, whenever believers say they feel the Holy Spirit enter them, they reach into boxes and pull out venomous serpents. The snakes are held up as the faithful pray, sing, and dance.

Snake-handling services date to 1910, when a Pentecostal church in Tennessee began to offer them, and others in rural Appalachia followed suit. The practice is illegal in some states and has caused at least 50 deaths in the U.S., including that of the first serpent handler, George Hensley. In 2012, Mack Wolford, a West Virginia pastor, died of a rattlesnake bite, just as his father had in 1983.

Snake handlers who succumb to bites are not criticized by the church for a lack of faith; instead, it is believed that it was simply their time to die.

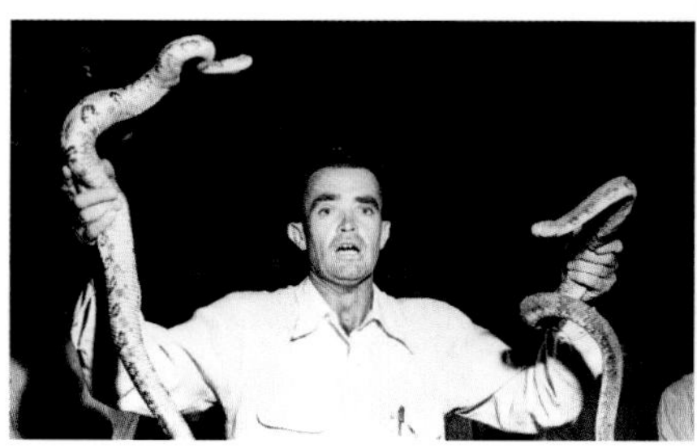

Gordon Millar of Euharlee, Georgia, holds two rattlesnakes during a religious service in Atlanta in 1972.

T.L. Osborn ministers to a crowd in France in 2006.

WHAT IS PENTACOSTAL CHRISTIANITY?

A faith based on a passage in the Gospel of Mark has more than 100 million members.

Pentecostals are evangelical Protestants who abide by a passage in Mark that states that a believer may be given gifts such as the ability to heal and cast out demons. Pentecostal leaders have included:

→ **William Seymour (1870–1922).** In April 1906, a local newspaper published an article mocking this preacher, who rejected racial barriers in favor of "unity in Christ." That same day, the Great San Francisco Earthquake struck. Many terrified Californians ended up joining Seymour's growing flock.

→ **John G. Lake (1870–1935)** was responsible for so many faith healings that his congregants called him "Doctor." "I could lay hands on any man, or woman, and tell what organ was diseased, and to what extent," Lake claimed.

→ **William Branham (1909–65).** In the 1950s, Branham claimed to have cured King George VI of England of multiple sclerosis through prayer.

→ **T.L. Osborn (1923–2013).** Osborn's sermons attracted audiences of 10,000 and more. His philosophy was simple: "If you are sick, God wants to heal you."

section 2

Miracles of Survival and Healing

CHAPTER 10

Incredible Recoveries

Whether one believes they reveal the hand of the divine or are testaments to the strength of the human spirit, truly amazing events continue to inspire us.

WHO KNEW?

If there were a medical treatment that could enable you to live to age 120, would you want it? Fifty-six percent of Americans say they would not, according to a 2013 Pew Research Center survey.

Spontaneous healing is a well-documented but still mystifying phenomenon.

Curing the Incurable

ONCE IN A GREAT WHILE, DEFYING EVERY RULE OF MEDICINE, THE HUMAN BODY SEEMS TO HEAL SPONTANEOUSLY. BUT HOW?

She was 19 years old and extraordinarily sick. In 1974, Kristin Killops was living with friends in Hawaii when she noticed a number of unexplained bruises on her body. Medical tests eventually revealed very bad news: Killops was critically ill with aplastic anemia. In this rare and serious condition, the bone marrow somehow gets damaged and ceases to produce red and white blood cells. The cause is often unknown, but Killops blamed the pesticides used to spray the pineapple fields near her home. The ailing teenager was whisked to a Los Angeles hospital for a bone-marrow transplant—her only hope of survival. It failed, as did a second transplant. She was out of options and given just days to live.

But Killops was not out of hope. She found a healer said to be psychic, who prescribed a diet she believed Killops's body needed. After following the no-sugar, no-starch plan for nine months, Killops began to improve. Over time, the healing continued and Killops was able to resume a full life, working and eventually bearing children. Three decades later, she was alive and well.

Modern medicine is amazing. Thanks to decades of rigorous scientific research, many diseases can be cured or at least managed. Still, science can't always explain how some people, seemingly at random, spontaneously rebound from life-threatening conditions.

There is still much we don't know about the remarkable human immune system. Research over the past several years has indicated that certain cancers, including breast, cervical, and testicular tumors, can stop growing or even disappear on their own, perhaps thanks to the body's natural defense against disease. It doesn't happen often, and people diagnosed with cancer or any other serious illness should seek treatment. But there's no question that spontaneous remissions have occurred.

Praying It Away

Appealing to a higher power has been promoted as a pathway to miraculous

Dr. Bernie Siegel is the author of *Love, Medicine, and Miracles* and other books on self-healing.

LET'S GET VISUAL

Some doctors say mental imagery may help conquer illness.

There are no studies that prove that visualizing away a disease really works. On the other hand, it can't hurt and may at least make you feel more relaxed and in control. Here are several suggestions from Bernie Siegel, an M.D. and author of several books on self-healing.

→ **Draw a picture.** If you dread going to the doctor's office, you might draw a scene from the office. Then cross out or erase anything in the drawing that is frightening and visualize the scene with the negative elements removed.

→ **Sit or lie in a comfortable position.** Become aware of your breathing. Once you are relaxed, visualize your body working with the medical treatment you've been prescribed to clear away the illness.

→ **Use imagery you can relate to.** If you're not a violent person, you may not get much out of an imaginary scenario in which you are attacking the invading disease. Siegel has used the example of a patient who instead imagined his white blood cells carrying his cancer away.

A shaman seeks to deliver healing power to a devotee of the Guatemalan folkloric saint San Simon.

healing, although research into prayer's effect on illness has led to mixed conclusions. A scientifically rigorous years-long study published in 2006 found that patients who underwent heart surgery were not helped by prayers from strangers. In fact, the rate of complications was higher for patients who knew that strangers were praying for them—perhaps a reflection of anxiety among the ill about letting down their spiritual benefactors.

But other studies have found that a patient's religious faith can have a positive effect on his or her health. The rate of strokes among older people who go to church regularly is half that of older people who seldom or never attend. A study in Israel found that religious people had a 40 percent lower rate of death from cancer and heart disease. It's possible that religious people live healthier lives overall, abstaining, for example, from smoking or excessive drinking. But they also benefit from a sense of purpose and optimism—the idea that there are mostly positive things in store for them in the future.

Mental Awareness

You don't need to participate in mainstream Western religion to have a spiritual-healing miracle. In 2003, a Tibetan Buddhist lama in the United States claimed to have cured himself of a case of gangrene so advanced that doctors in New York City had said amputation was his only hope of survival. Instead, Phakyab Rinpoche, 37, consulted the Dalai Lama, who wrote urging him to meditate. Rinpoche later explained why the advice made sense to him: Buddhists believe in reincarnation, so he was not afraid of

ARE YOU POSITIVE?

Research shows that optimists may heal more readily than pessimists.

Spontaneous remission from severe illness is rare and extraordinary, and people with serious health problems should never be made to feel responsible for "curing themselves," experts say. Still, optimism can be powerful medicine.

In a study published in 2010, researchers tracked down 534 lung-cancer patients who, many years before their diagnoses, had taken personality tests designed to assess whether they had an optimistic or pessimistic outlook on life. Those patients who'd been found to be optimists lived an average of six months longer than those found to be pessimists. A third of the optimists hit the five-year survival mark, compared to a little over a fifth of the pessimists.

Other studies have discovered that a sunny disposition correlates with a lower risk of stroke and a more robust immune system. The findings suggest that cultivating optimism, even if that's not a person's natural mindset, could be a helpful way to cope with a tough diagnosis.

One warning: Beware of what psychologists call the "optimism bias." That's the unrealistic belief that everything will somehow turn out okay despite all evidence to the contrary. This attitude can lead to foolish decisions, such as gambling on risky financial investments or ignoring troubling health symptoms. Healthy optimism means believing, for the most part, in a bright future, and planning for it accordingly.

death. But it seemed foolish in his present life not to try to save his leg.

For the next year, Rinpoche spent 12 hours a day practicing a deep meditation technique called Tsa Lung, imagining life-giving wind moving through his body, clearing out impurities. He didn't take medicine. A year later, the gangrene had gone away on its own.

Rinpoche later agreed to let doctors at New York University scan his brain while he meditated, and as of 2014 the research was ongoing. Experts theorize that meditation and breathing may send extra blood and oxygen through the body, helping fight off infection.

Although it may not be practical for most people to meditate this intensely, shorter bouts of mindfulness practice—simply focusing on the present moment—can have health benefits, experts say. There doesn't even need to be a religious component. In a study published in 2011, researchers at the University of Wisconsin trained a group of adults in Mindfulness Based Stress Reduction, a secular technique that involves lying quietly and focusing attention on various areas of one's body, as well as doing some simple yoga poses. The volunteers practiced the technique for 45 minutes a day. The study then tracked their instances of colds and flu over the next several months. The meditators got sick less often than a control group, and when they did catch a bug, it was less severe and they recovered sooner.

In one study, adults who practiced a daily form of meditation got sick less often than the control group.

Heavy Lifting

WHEN THE NEED ARISES FOR EXTRAORDINARY STRENGTH, REGULAR PEOPLE CAN SOMETIMES TRANSFORM INTO SUPERHEROES.

It was a December morning in 2009, and Nick Harris was getting ready to drop off his young daughter at school when he witnessed the unthinkable. A neighbor was backing her Mercury sedan out of her driveway, unaware that she had run over a 6-year-old girl from down the block. The first-grader was pinned under the vehicle. What Harris did next was nothing short of astonishing.

"I didn't even think," the 32-year-old dad from Ottawa, Kansas, later told the Associated Press. "I ran over there as fast as I could, grabbed the rear end of the car, and lifted and pushed as hard as I could."

At 5'7" tall and 185 pounds, Harris wasn't a particularly big man. Still, he was able to lift the car off of the terrified girl. She had a concussion and some scrapes, but Harris's quick rescue saved her from any lasting damage.

In retrospect, and after trying and failing to lift other cars later in the day, Harris admitted that he didn't know how he had done it. He attributed his temporary might to "adrenaline, hand of God, whatever you want to call it."

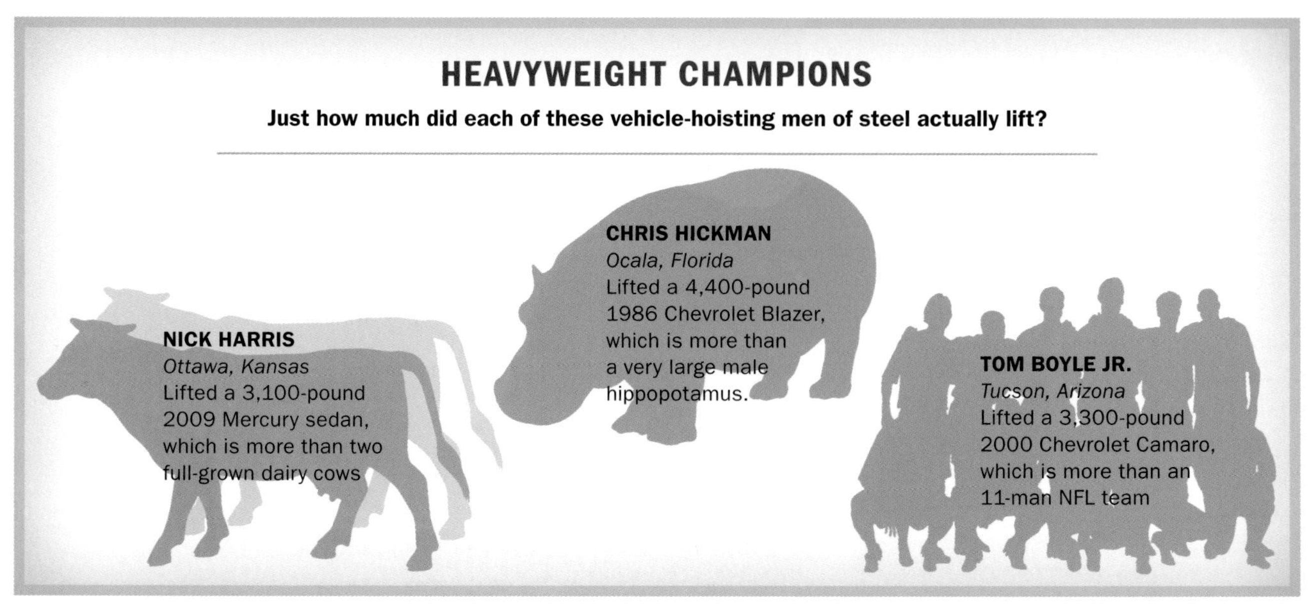

Jeff Smith and his teenage daughters: Hannah, left, and Haylee, right.

The Strength Within

Such feats don't happen every day, but they're more common than you might think. At the scene of an accident in 2008, Ocala, Florida, firefighter Chris Hickman hoisted an SUV a foot off the ground to free a woman whose arm was trapped beneath it. In July 2006, Tom Boyle Jr. of Tucson, Arizona, lifted the front end of a Chevrolet Camaro for at least 45 seconds, while instructing the car's shocked driver to pull an 18-year-old bicyclist out from under the chassis. Afterward, Boyle had no idea how he managed the feat. "There's no way I could lift that car right now," Boyle told Jeff Wise, the author of *Extreme Fear: The Science of Your Mind in Danger.*

In 2011, University of Southern Florida football player Danous Estenor heard screams from across a campus cafeteria parking lot. Pedro Arzola, a local tow truck driver, had been pinned beneath a 3,500-pound Cadillac Seville. Estenor, a 6'3, 295-pound offensive lineman for the Bulls, ran to the scene. Crediting a burst of strange energy, he lifted the car while another witness pulled Arzola to safety. Arzola sustained only minor injuries: bruises, cuts, and a dislocated shoulder.

But if you think these everyday heroes are superhuman, you may not be giving enough credit to humans. Acting on impulse, these rescuers tapped into strength they didn't know they had. They reacted swiftly and appropriately, thanks to physiological responses that can kick in automatically when our bodies shift into emergency mode.

Girl Power

Momentarily enhanced strength isn't the sole province of men, or even of adults. In 2013, Lebanon, Oregon, sisters Hannah and Haylee Smith heard their father screaming for help and found him pinned under a tractor after a freak accident. After unsuccessfully trying to dig him out, Hannah, 16, and Haylee, 13, followed his suggestion to lift the 3,000-pound tractor off of his chest. They did so not once but twice, first to allow breath into his crushed body, and a second time to allow him to wriggle his torso free, leaving only his arm caught. Jeff Smith suffered a broken wrist but was otherwise unharmed. Had it not been for the girls, he said later, "I wouldn't be here."

All Clear

AS SOME CANCER PATIENTS FOCUS HARD ON THEIR REASONS TO LIVE, THEY FIND THEIR BODIES GETTING HEALTHY AGAIN.

Psychotherapist Kelly Turner found similar elements in miraculous cancer survival.

COMMON CORE

These top nine behaviors and attitudes may have helped save lives.

Kelly Turner, a psychotherapist who has interviewed many patients whose cancer went into remission, reports many of the survivors had these factors in common.

1. Radically changing diet
2. Taking control of health
3. Following intuition
4. Using herbs and supplements
5. Releasing suppressed emotions
6. Increasing positive emotions
7. Embracing social support
8. Deepening spiritual connection
9. Having strong reasons for living

Sharyn Mackay was terminal. Diagnosed in April 2003 with a rare form of kidney cancer, the young married mother of four was told that she had only a year to live. By 2004, the cancer had spread to her lungs. Chemotherapy couldn't save her, nor could surgery. "I was absolutely terrified," Mackay, from Northern Ireland, told a British newspaper.

Like most everyone in her position, Mackay did not want to die. Her youngest daughter was only eight—too small, Mackay felt, to be without a mother. Not knowing what else to do, she gave her health over to a higher power. She joined a healing ministry and prayed. Three months later, when Mackay went in for a checkup, her cancer had vanished. Doctors again sent her home—this time not to die, but to live a full, healthy life.

Was it prayer that cured her? Was it luck? Or was there something special about Mackay's immune system? The medical community is considering the third

LUCKY STARS

Some celebrities are as notable for claiming to have cured their own cancer as they are for the talent that brought them their fame.

CELEBRITY SURVIVOR	THE CLAIM	EXPERTS SAY
Suzanne Somers	The *Three's Company* actress and health author beat breast cancer in 2001 with alternative medicine.	Somers also had a lumpectomy and radiation.
David Seidler	After a 2005 diagnosis of bladder cancer, the writer of *The King's Speech* repeatedly imagined "a nice, cream-colored... bladder lining." His cancer vanished without chemo.	Being constantly told to think positive and "will" away their cancer puts an unfair burden on patients.
Kris Carr	The aspiring actress-turned-best-selling author of *Crazy Sexy Life*, diagnosed in 2003 with a rare late-stage cancer, keeps it at bay through clean living.	The vast majority of people with cancer need other interventions.

WHO KNEW?
The results of a Norwegian study published in 2009 suggest that about a fifth of undiagnosed breast cancers go away on their own.

Spiritual connection is often cited as one of the keys to miraculous recovery from cancer.

possibility, researching treatments that harness the body's own power to defend itself from cancer the way Mackay's did. In the United States, two available vaccines can help prevent cancers of the liver and cervix by boosting immunity to Hepatitis B and HPV, infectious diseases that each play a role in causing cancer. There are also vaccines in the works to treat existing tumors, including one approved in 2010 for men with late-stage prostate cancer. Vaccines are currently being tested for leukemia, breast cancer, pancreatic cancer, brain tumors, and several other malignancies.

Life's Purpose

Some experts are also studying how our attitudes and states of mind can affect our immune systems. As psychotherapist Kelly Turner researched nearly a thousand cases like Mackay's, she found similarities in the miracle survivors' stories. Nearly all of them mentioned some or most of nine specific behaviors or attitudes, according to Turner, who turned her findings into a book, *Radical Remission: Surviving Cancer Against All Odds*. The patients' behaviors included expressing emotions they had previously kept to themselves, taking control of their own health, and being strongly motivated to continue living.

It is not hard to find anecdotal evidence that seems to support Turner's thesis. Greg Thomas, for example, was diagnosed with Stage IV head and neck cancer in 2009. A propane deliveryman from Montgomery, Minnesota, Thomas, 57, soon lost his job. He began taking long walks with his dog. After passing St. John's Chapel, an abandoned 160-year-old church, Thomas was drawn to the building and volunteered to fix it up. In painting and restoring the modest little church, Thomas found his purpose. By 2012, his cancer was in remission and the church was gleaming white.

A mosaic of St. Peregrine, the patron saint of cancer.

HISTORY REPEATS ITSELF

Seven centuries apart, two surprisingly similar cancer miracles point to the power of prayer.

In 1325, Peregrine Lazosi, an Italian Catholic priest in his 60s, developed cancer in his right leg. The night before the leg was to be amputated, Lazosi had a vision in which Jesus descended from a crucifix and touched his limb. The following morning, all traces of the tumor had vanished. Peregrine, who became the patron saint of those with cancer and incurable diseases, lived 20 more years.

Around 2013, Therese Daoud, a high school science teacher from Usfiya, an area of Israel associated with the Druze religious sect, was diagnosed with cancer in her leg. She, too, was told the leg would have to be amputated. Instead of going through with the procedure, she prayed. Several months later, Daoud returned to her doctor, who discovered that the orange-size tumor had vanished. A biopsy revealed no sign of disease. "Every time I prayed I felt peaceful and secure," Daoud said. "I had fear, but I had tranquility as well."

Instrument of Peace

A PIANIST WITH TOURETTE'S SYNDROME FINDS A REPRIEVE IN THE KEYS.

In the early 1970s in London, England, seven-year-old Nick van Bloss seemed overnight to develop the odd habit of shaking his head. That bizarre behavior was quickly followed by others, including eye-rolling, jerking, and twitching. He would yelp uncontrollably and punch himself. He felt compelled to touch things. Doctors told van Bloss's parents that he had a case of nerves or was just trying to get attention. It wasn't until van Bloss reached 21 that he was correctly diagnosed with Tourette's Syndrome.

Until then, van Bloss found comfort in only one activity: playing the piano. After discovering the instrument at age 11, van Bloss found that putting his hands on the keys satisfied his urge to touch, and becoming absorbed in the music and rhythm helped calm his tics. "Finding solace in my music, I practiced every moment I could, the beauty of the sounds acting as a panacea to the ugly ills I faced in the outside world," van Bloss wrote in his 2006 memoir *Busy Body: My Life with Tourette's Syndrome.*

People with this neurological disorder are plagued by uncontrollable, repetitive movements or vocalizations. The motions can be simple tics such as grimacing, shrugging motions, blinking, and twitching, or complex patterns of several different actions combined. About 10 to 15 percent of people with the syndrome uncontrollably utter curse words or insults they don't really mean. Symptoms usually appear in childhood, and though people

HITS THAT HEAL

What songs motivate and uplift you? Though music is a matter of taste, these popular tunes top many "most inspiring" lists. Take a listen the next time you feel under the weather.

Somewhere Over the Rainbow
Judy Garland (1939)

What a Wonderful World
Louis Armstrong (1967)

Lean On Me
Bill Withers (1972)

I Will Survive
Gloria Gaynor (1978)

Chariots of Fire
Vangelis (1981)

Don't Stop Believin'
Journey (1981)

Eye of the Tiger
Survivor (1982)

I Believe I Can Fly
R. Kelly (1997)

You Raise Me Up
Josh Groban (2003)

Let it Go
Idina Menzel (2013)

Nick van Bloss was able to calm his Tourette's symptoms by playing piano.

WHO KNEW?
An estimated 200,000 Americans have severe Tourette's syndrome; about 1 in 100 have milder cases.

can grow out of Tourette's, not all do. Medication may control symptoms, but there's no single drug that works for everybody, and there are side effects.

A Body in Motion

For van Bloss, Tourette's meant experiencing more than 35,000 tics a day—approximately one every couple of seconds. In most cases, he was trying to suppress them, a trick he learned as a schoolboy when he was spat on, mocked, and shunned by bullies. "You try and hide everything," he told a British newspaper in 2009.

Eventually van Bloss went on to study at the Royal College of Music in London and seemed to be headed toward a career as a pianist when his Tourette's ambushed him. Performing in a piano competition around 1994, the 27-year-old had an attack onstage and his arms became rigid. He withdrew from the contest, retired from music, and got rid of his piano. And that's how things remained for 15 years, until he had an epiphany: The Tourette's wasn't going away, so it was time he stopped fighting it.

He began to play again, wrote a memoir, and in 2009 was invited to record a CD. Since then he has played and recorded works by Bach and Chopin and has even returned to live performances. "As I looked out at the Steinway on stage," he said of his first concert, "it felt like a homecoming, and I felt at peace."

SOUND MEDICINE

According to a growing body of research, music has a place in all sorts of medical settings.

→ **Premature babies** exposed to live music, whether played to them or sung to them, had slower heartbeats and calmer breathing. The music improved their eating and sleeping habits and helped them achieve states of quiet alertness, according to a study published in 2013.

→ **Elderly people with Alzheimer's** can sometimes remember songs from their childhood or youth long after they've lost other memories. Nursing-home residents with dementia who participate in music programs are less likely to wander or behave disruptively.

→ **Recovering stroke patients** who listened to music for two hours a day had more improvement in memory and mental focus than those who didn't, according to a Finnish study done in the early 2000s.

Cured by the Pope

A NUN'S HEARTFELT PRAYER SEEMINGLY SAVED HER FROM A DREADED DISEASE—AND PAVED THE WAY FOR JOHN PAUL II'S SAINTHOOD.

"I knew he could understand what I was experiencing."

At 4:30 AM, I wake up stupefied that I had slept. I jump out of bed. My body is not painful anymore. There is no stiffness, and my body feels very light. . . . A great peace, a sensation of well-being, envelops me, something very big, a great mystery . . .

This is what the first day of a miracle feels like.

On a June night in 2005, a nun named Sister Marie Simon-Pierre went to sleep suffering from Parkinson's disease, barely able to walk and in agonizing pain. The following morning, she awoke to find that her illness had vanished, she later testified. "This is like a second birth, a new life," the French maternity nurse told an American audience several years later. It was also a bona fide miracle, as defined by the Catholic Church: The nun had prayed for relief to the late Pope John Paul II, and he had answered her prayers from heaven.

Parkinson's disease is a disorder of the central nervous system, thought to be caused by a combination of genetic and environmental factors. It affects about five million people worldwide; most are over age 60. People who have it experience changes in their brain that affect their ability to control their movements. They often develop problems walking, speaking, and swallowing; suffer involuntary tremors; and move increasingly slowly. Symptoms usually worsen over time, and there's no cure. Though Parkinson's itself isn't fatal, it can lead to death from falls or choking.

John Paul II, who was pope from 1978 until his death in April 2005, was himself a sufferer of Parkinson's. And it was to him that Sister Marie Simon-Pierre looked for inspiration after her own diagnosis at age 40 in 2001. "I knew he could understand what I was experiencing," she said. After the pope died, the nun's health deteriorated rapidly, and on a June evening, she went to speak with her superior, Sister Marie Thomas, to resign from her nursing duties.

"Wait a little longer," Sister Marie Thomas told her, and handed her a pen. She asked Sister Marie Simon-Pierre to write the name "John Paul II." Though barely able to control her hand, Sister Marie Simon-Pierre did as she was told.

"Looking at this writing," the nun later recounted, "Sister Marie Thomas holds her breath and says nothing. Silence reigns. After a few moments, with an encouraging smile and confidence, she calmly tells me: 'John Paul II has not had his last word.'"

Now relieved from her symptoms, Sister Marie Simon-Pierre credits the late pope for her miraculous recovery, as does the Church. On April 27, 2014, in recognition of this and a second miracle, the Vatican conferred sainthood on John Paul II.

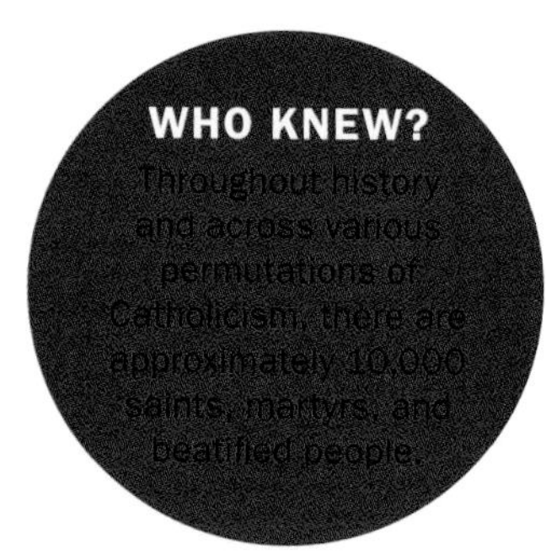

Sister Marie Simon-Pierre holds a glass reliquary containing the blood of the late Pope John Paul II during his beatification mass.

FIVE STEPS TO SAINTHOOD

To be recognized as a Catholic saint, otherwise known as being canonized, is very difficult.

Once the Church confers its highest designation on someone, there are no take-backs, so the process is rigorous and can take hundreds of years. Among other requirements, the potential saint must have performed two proven miracles—after death.

Step One: Live a holy life. Be recognized as extraordinary by lots of people, including your local bishop.

Step Two: Once you've died, your bishop will "open the cause," or recommend that you be considered for sainthood. An appointed advocate will carefully research your writings, teachings, and good deeds. During this process, you will be called "Servant of God."

Step Three: A Vatican panel called the Congregation for Causes of Saints will review the evidence presented on your behalf. If it approves you, the Pope will designate you as "Venerable."

Step Four: You must perform a verifiable miracle, intervening posthumously on someone's behalf (for example, after he or she prays to you). These days, miracles often involve curing an incurable illness. The miracle needs to be witnessed, must not be explainable by any other cause, and must be lasting. If your miracle passes this test, you will be beatified, or "Blessed."

Step Five: You must perform a second, verifiable miracle after you are beatified. This could take hundreds of years. But if you succeed, congratulations: You're a saint!

Floribeth Mora Diaz during a Mass in St. Stanislaus Polish Church in Rome

THE SECOND MIRACLE OF JOHN PAUL II

A Costa Rican woman who prayed to the late pope got the healing she needed.

Like Sister Marie Simon-Pierre, Floribeth Mora Diaz says Pope John Paul II saved her life. A doctor discovered that Diaz, who lived in Peru, had an inoperable aneurysm—a damaged artery in her brain that would eventually burst, leading to a stroke. She was given a month to live. Unable to afford to go abroad to a more modern hospital, Diaz took to her bed and prayed for her children.

Meanwhile, on May 1, 2011, the Vatican recognized the late pope's first miracle, the healing of Sister Marie Simon-Pierre. As Diaz lay in bed, she spotted a magazine announcing the news, with a photograph of the pope. She heard his voice tell her, "Get up and don't be afraid."

Knowing she had been cured, Diaz agreed to thorough testing by her doctor and, eventually, the Vatican. They confirmed that the aneurysm was gone. The late pope had performed his second posthumous miracle. In 2014, a healthy Diaz traveled to Vatican City for the ceremony canonizing John Paul II.

The Cause That Cures

THE SAME VIRUS THAT BRINGS ON PARALYSIS IN POLIO PATIENTS MAY HAVE THE POWER TO SHRINK CANCEROUS BRAIN TUMORS.

Stephanie Lipscomb was only 20 in 2010 when she began to suffer excruciating headaches. For a while, the college student blamed them on the stress of studying and working as a waitress, but eventually, the headaches became so painful that it hurt for her to move. "I couldn't bathe myself, dress myself," she remembered. "All I could do was just lie there in pain." When Lipscomb finally visited the emergency room, doctors told her that her brain scans revealed a tumor the size of a tennis ball behind her right eye.

Nursing student Stephanie Lipscomb was diagnosed with a rare brain tumor.

It was a glioblastoma, the most aggressive kind of brain cancer. The condition affects roughly 10,000 people each year, about half of whom die within 15 months of diagnosis. Lipscomb underwent emergency surgery to remove the tumor, followed by chemotherapy and radiation. The treatment was relatively successful, but two years later, the tumor returned. Doctors believed she only had six months to live, even with more chemotherapy.

Saved by a Virus

Lipscomb was so committed to fighting the disease that she agreed to take part in an unusual experiment at Duke University in May 2012. In the trial, a genetically modified version of the poliovirus was injected directly into her brain tumor. The procedure had been approved only two weeks earlier by the U.S. Food and Drug Administration, and Lipscomb would be the first human to undergo treatment in a clinical trial.

The procedure itself was amazingly quick, especially compared to the many long weeks required for standard radiation and chemotherapy. Lipscomb was wide awake for the entire six-and-a-half-hour operation, which involved drilling a small hole in her skull and inserting a catheter. Doctors then injected the poliovirus through the catheter directly to the location of the Lipscomb's tumor, hoping that the poliovirus could kill cancer cells without damaging the surrounding healthy brain cells.

It took several months before the virus started working, but then it rapidly reduced Lipscomb's symptoms. Incredibly, a year after the procedure, Lipscomb's tumor had disappeared, with only scar tissue remaining, and she was considered in excellent health. As of 2014, Lipscomb had survived cancer for two and a half years. This was more than four times longer than most people with a glioblastoma, although she will need to be monitored for many years before doctors can be sure that the technique is a permanent cure.

Results with other patients have been mixed, and research is ongoing. Doctors hope that the strain of the poliovirus can eventually be used against pancreatic, prostate, lung, colon, and many other types of cancer.

"I was a little crazy to do this," Lipscomb said, "but I feel grateful to be alive and give others hope." Her mother put it more simply: "She's amazing. She's our miracle child."

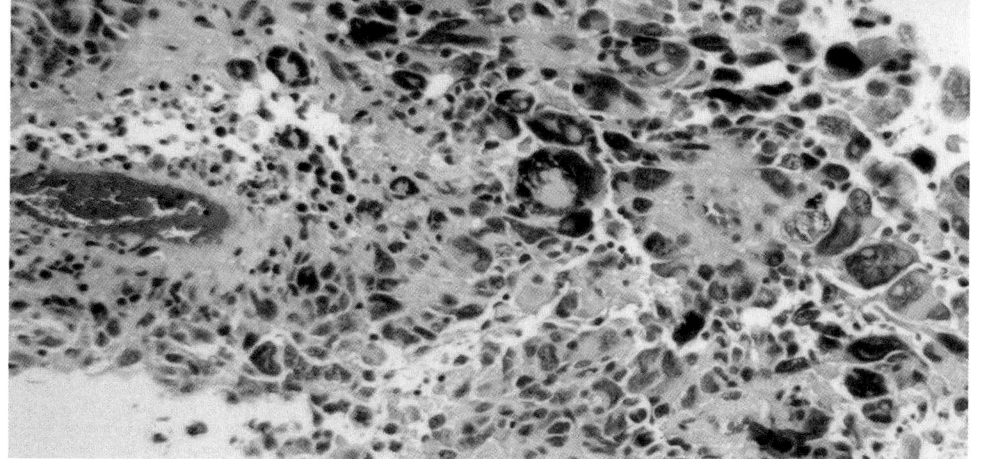

A brain biopsy shows a crowd of malignant cells in a condition known as giant cell glioblastoma.

KILLING CANCER FROM WITHIN

How can something as lethal as a poliovirus help us fight our most insidious diseases?

As early as the 1950s, doctors noticed that cancer patients who got vaccinated for polio showed signs of improvement, but research at the time was focused on developing chemotherapy and radiotherapy.

In the past few years, the medical community has begun again to explore cancer treatments using viruses, and several—including those that cause measles, herpes simplex, and polio—have been tried as possible cancer killers. In 2005, China approved the world's first virus therapy for the treatment of head and neck cancer. The diagram below shows how the virus attacks cancer cells without harming normal ones.

The poliovirus uses a receptor molecule to "unlock" the brain cell and enter it. The modified version of polio currently under study has been spliced with the rhinovirus that causes the common cold. Because cancer cells have a different biochemical makeup than regular brain cells, the modified virus can enter a cancerous cell and replicate until the cell dies, but it cannot replicate inside of a healthy cell.

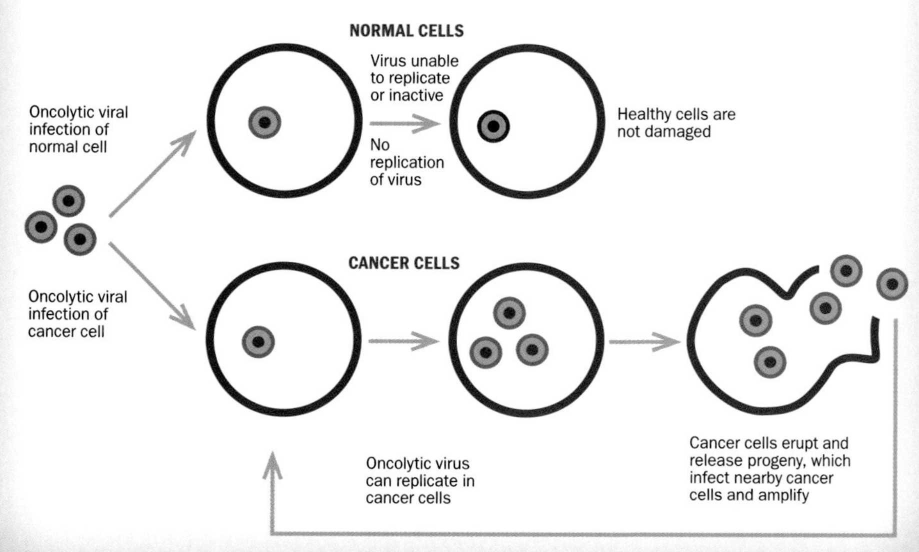

MIRACLE CURE OR QUACKERY?

When mainstream medicine fails to cure, some patients seek out other alternatives.

One 2012 study reported that about 40 percent of brain tumor patients tried alternative medical treatments like homeopathy, and suggested the real number could be even higher. The mainstream medical community tends to dismiss such therapies, and typically there is little or no clinical research to back them up.

→ **Ruta graveolens** commonly known as rue, is an herb that thrives throughout the world. Some patients say their tumors shrank after taking a *ruta*-based medication.

→ **Goji berries** are the fruit of boxthorn shrubs. Since 2000, the berries and their juice have been marketed as healthful and effective in slowing the aging process. Some brain cancer patients claim that drinking goji juice caused their tumors to stop growing or even shrink.

→ **Shiitake mushrooms** have long been used in Japan to treat all sorts of ailments. Recent research in both Japan and the U.S. also suggests that the mushrooms may contain compounds that are useful against cancer.

I Believe I Can Fly

PEOPLE WHO PRACTICE MIND OVER MATTER SAY THEY CAN WALK OVER HOT COALS, ENDURE PAIN, AND EVEN LEVITATE.

Dan Meyer, sword swallower

Deliberately sticking a sharp object down your throat is foolish. Deliberately sticking 21 sharp objects down your throat at once might be considered lunacy. But Dan Meyer, who holds numerous Guinness World Records for sword swallowing, insists that he is not out of his mind. Quite the opposite: "The mind can push the body past previous limitations," Meyer told an Australian newspaper in 2012. "Swallowing a sword always seemed 99 percent impossible, until I changed my focus to the 1 percent that was possible."

Are our own self-doubts and negative beliefs the only obstacles preventing us from achieving the impossible? Proponents of mind over matter say yes. Spiritual and religious teachings attest to at least some people's ability to master their thoughts and overcome physical limits. Buddha, Jesus, and various Catholic saints are said to have walked on water and performed other physics-defying feats. Other saints have supposedly levitated, as have some Hindu gurus and practitioners of transcendental meditation. Some yogis and mystics are rumored to be able to withstand being buried alive, at least for a few hours, and to raise their body temperatures just by willing it to happen.

The Mind-Body Connection

Though some, if not all, of these reports are surely mythology, people can do amazing things if they set their minds to it. In the 1980s, fire walking—a ritual in which participants stride barefoot over hot coals—became a trendy confidence-building exercise among corporate executives. Studies have shown that people who practice yoga can learn to consciously and voluntarily slow their pulse rates. And martial artists break boards with their bare hands by

THINK YOURSELF THIN

According to a 2007 Harvard University study, simply believing you are getting lots of exercise can help you drop pounds.

To test the extent to which a person's mindset can affect his or her health, researchers from Harvard in 2007 recruited hotel maids who believed that they did not get enough exercise. Half of the group was told that scrubbing, vacuuming, and doing other cleaning chores for many hours a day was sufficient exercise; they were also given information on how many calories each activity burned. The other group of housekeepers were not coached in any way.

A month later, the maids who had been informed that they were getting enough exercise had lost an average of two pounds, with no change to their behavior besides seeing themselves as exercisers.

While the findings don't mean we should all sit around and eat pizza while thinking about jogging, they do suggest that it's important to give ourselves credit for our healthy habits.

WHO KNEW?
More than 25 percent of Americans think it is possible to "influence the world with the mind alone," according to a 2005 Gallup/Baylor University poll.

Tony Robbins, self-help writer and speaker, firewalking

striking them correctly, but also, equally importantly, by conquering their fear.

In truth, not all of these activities depend on superior mental powers. Walking over hot coals is relatively easy, scientists point out, because practitioners move quickly, and coal isn't a great conductor of heat. At the same time, believing that you can will yourself through certain situations can be dangerous. In 2012, at least 21 participants at a San Jose, California, "Unleash the Power Within" seminar run by motivational speaker Tony Robbins suffered serious burns while fire walking. "I heard wails of pain, screams of agony," one participant later told the *San Jose Mercury News*. Another observer wondered if the people who got burned hadn't been focused enough.

Are our own self-doubts and negative beliefs preventing us from achieving the impossible?

But the true reason may have had nothing to do with their state of mind: The firewalk was so crowded with participants that the victims may simply have been forced to remain too long on the coals.

A yogi appears to levitate during transcendental meditation.

NOT GONNA HAPPEN

Concentrate, meditate, and think all you want, scientists say; some feats are not humanly possible.

→ **Walking on water.** This one is theoretically achievable. All you have to do is zip across that lake at about 67 miles per hour—almost three times as fast as the world's fastest human, Usain Bolt.

→ **Teleportation.** Sorry, Scotty, you won't be beaming us up any time soon. Successful teleportation would not only require disassembling and then correctly reassembling the trillions of atoms in a human body, but also moving them at the speed of light, which defies the known laws of physics.

→ **Flying or levitation.** According to Rhett Allain, an associate professor of physics at Southeastern Louisiana University, to get airborne, a 150-pound person would need to have a pair of wings 22 feet across.

The Big Sleep

SOME PEOPLE IN COMAS NEVER AGAIN EMERGE FROM A MYSTERIOUS TWILIGHT ZONE OF CONSCIOUSNESS. OTHERS, INEXPLICABLY, DO.

When Ben McMahon, an Australian teenager, lapsed into a coma after a devastating car crash in 2012, he was a speaker of English. When he awoke, he was fluent in Mandarin, writing and talking like a native Chinese.

Though McMahon had studied the language in high school, he never spoke it well, and doctors were unsure what mysterious process had occurred in the teen's brain. One neuroscientist theorizes that the accident engaged certain unused language connections. Two years later, McMahon was studying business in Shanghai and considered himself "so fortunate" for this linguistic gift.

A comatose person is not simply asleep; he is deeply unconscious

Not Simply Asleep

McMahon's story is remarkable, but the fact that anyone in a coma wakes up at all is itself miraculous. A comatose person is not simply asleep; he is so deeply unconscious that noise, bright light, movement, and even pain won't rouse him. A coma can be caused by a drug or alcohol overdose, diabetes complications, stroke, or head trauma. In some cases it may be the brain's way of protecting itself by shifting into a low-energy state.

Unfortunately, patients don't always wake up, especially from comas caused by a loss of blood or oxygen to the brain. Some of these patients recover only to a vegetative state, in which they look awake and make some involuntary movements but have very limited brain function. Others enter into a minimally conscious state, in which they can respond to some things using subtle eye movements or gestures. The longer a patient remains vegetative or minimally conscious, the less likely he is to regain full awareness. After four months in a coma, only about 15 percent of brain-damaged patients will make even a partial recovery, and very few will heal completely.

A Slow Process

Although comatose movie or television characters often seem to pop awake exactly as they were before, recovery from a lengthy coma is usually a slow process. Patients tend to regain awareness briefly at first, then for longer stretches.

The experience isn't necessarily easy; patients can be confused or agitated, with little or no memory of how or why they've been hospitalized. They may need to relearn how to talk, eat, and walk. As extraordinary as it is for victims of serious brain trauma to regain consciousness, it is really just the first step on a long path back to a normal life.

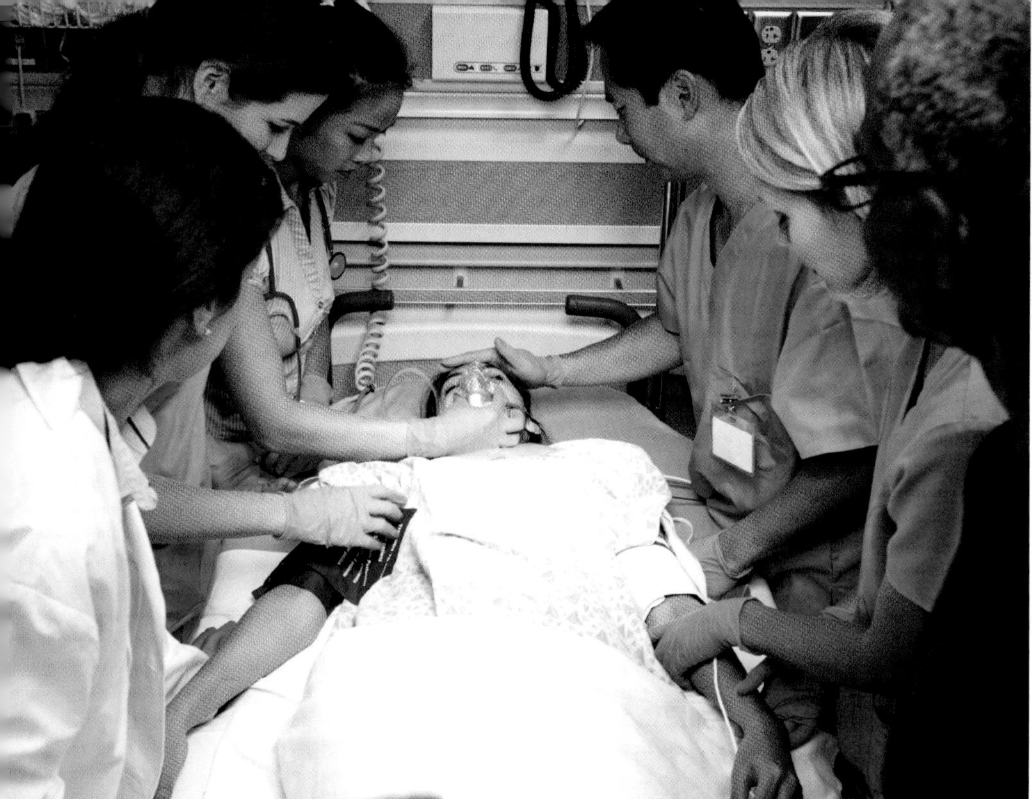

Doctors can induce a coma in cases where the brain needs to be completely at rest in order to repair itself.

DO NOT DISTURB

A neurologist succeeded in waking patients thought to be permanently "asleep." Some of them were unhappy about it.

In the 1920s, a worldwide epidemic of a form of encephalitis killed five million people and left some survivors in a permanent coma-like state. Barely conscious and considered hopeless, some of these patients languished in a New York hospital until the late 1960s, when neurologist Oliver Sacks treated them with L-DOPA, a then-experimental drug.

The results were astounding: Men and women who had been uncommunicative for 40 years "awoke" with revelations about what they had been experiencing, from hazy dreams to exasperating, endlessly repetitive thoughts. When the medicine wore off, they reverted again to their trancelike condition.

Sacks found that four doses of the drug a day could give patients back their waking lives, but there were side effects. Sacks's patients suffered erratic spasms and jerking, insatiable appetites, uncontrollable libidos, and other problems. Many elected to stop taking the medication, voluntarily disappearing back into the darkness.

Dr. Oliver Sacks's 1973 account of treating coma patients with L-DOPA, *Awakenings*, was made into a movie starring Robin Williams and Robert DeNiro.

Nicola Watson, a locked-in syndrome sufferer, at home with her husband, Neil, in Cumbria, England

THE CONSCIOUSNESS CONTINUUM

Sufferers of "locked-in" syndrome, often quadriplegics with serious damage to the brain stem, are fully conscious. The intellect is intact, but they can neither move nor speak.

Levels of brain injury include the following:

→ **Catatonic.** This state is most often associated with psychiatric disorders rather than brain injuries. Sufferers are conscious but do not move, speak, or make eye contact. If a caregiver moves a patient's arm or leg into a fixed position, it remains that way.

→ **Stupor.** Here, an otherwise unresponsive patient can be aroused by something forceful, such as a slap.

→ **Coma.** The patient is completely unresponsive for a period of six hours or more.

→ **Brain dead.** The patient has a heartbeat but cannot breathe or digest food on his own and does not respond to stimuli.

The Healer

WITH DETERMINATION AND PROPER TREATMENT, A LIBERIAN DOCTOR SURVIVED EBOLA—AND CONTINUED TO HELP OTHERS.

In July 2014, a woman suffering gastrointestinal distress came into Phebe Hospital in Liberia's Bong County. She told the staff that she was from Bangha. By the time the woman died, three days later, hospital workers had learned that she was actually from nearby Lofa, a northern county bordered by Sierra Leone and Guinea, where Ebola was wreaking havoc.

As the Ebola virus is transmitted through close contact with an infected individual's bodily fluids, Phebe Hospital's medical workers were at especially high risk. Soon, the nurses who had been treating the woman developed high fevers and were placed in isolation. All five tested positive for the disease.

The next to contract Ebola was Dr. Melvin Korkor, 42, who had also treated the Ebola patient. Korkor knew that while the deadly virus can kill as many as 90 percent of people infected, early treatment would provide the best chance of survival. He and the five nurses were transferred to Elwa Hospital's hermetically sealed isolation unit in Monrovia. Korkor asked his anxious wife to bring him his Bible. "I told her, 'No crying. I am coming back,'" Korkor later told a reporter. "My heart became hardened and I said to myself I was going to make it."

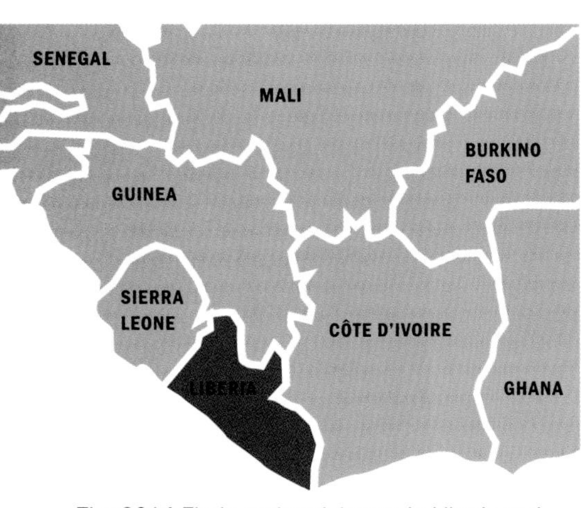

The 2014 Ebola outbreak began in Liberia and spread to neighboring countries.

Sustained by Faith

Facing death, Korkor forced himself to stay focused and eat even though he had no appetite. He watched helplessly as each of his stricken colleagues succumbed to the disease. To stay strong, he prayed and read his Bible, especially Psalm 91, which promises that God will protect the faithful from "the pestilence that walketh in darkness" and "the destruction that wasteth at noonday." After four days of spiritual meditation, Korkor tested negative for the virus. "It was like being reborn," he said.

Most of the 200 remaining staff at Phebe Hospital left after their colleagues fell ill. By August the hospital had fewer than 25 staffers, and only one of its four wards remained open. More than 240 West African health-care workers developed Ebola by the end of the month, and more than 120 died.

Fighting Superstition

Korkor, fully recovered and back at work, cautioned that ignorance would lead to more devastation. Despite Ebola's high fatality rate and the local belief in the involvement of witchcraft, he wanted people in the region to know that the disease is survivable if treated early. Speaking at his local church, Korkor thanked God for saving his life, and added, "If you start to feel ill, please get tested straightaway."

Dr. Melvin Korkor credits his survival of Ebola to early treatment and his faith in God.

WHO KNEW?

Nearly all of the Ebola cases recorded in 2014 resulted from human-to-human transmission, according to the World Health Organization. The incubation period from infection to symptoms is 2 to 21 days.

SAINT DAMIEN OF MOLOKAI

A heroic priest devoted his life to treating "untouchables."

For thousands of years, few diseases carried the stigma that leprosy did. The chronic ailment, which causes increasing disfigurement over decades of suffering, was feared as highly contagious, and those afflicted were shunned. That attitude continued even into the 19th century. As late as 1873, the government of the Sandwich Islands—today Hawaii—deported hundreds of lepers to isolated Kalaupapa Peninsula on Molokai Island.

But one Catholic priest from Belgium, who was living in the area, was touched by the plight of the patients and volunteered to oversee the colony. For the next 16 years, Father Damien transformed the peninsula from a place to die into a place to live. He learned the Hawaiian language, coordinated funding and medical care, improved food supplies and housing, constructed a water system, planted trees, and founded schools, orphanages, bands, and choirs. His demands for assistance from the Roman Catholic Church and the Hawaiian government helped raise global awareness of the disease.

After a decade of dressing leprous skin ulcers and burying the dead, Father Damien was diagnosed with the disease himself in 1884. Because treatment would have meant leaving Kalaupapa, he refused it and died there in 1889. Hawaii erected a statue of the missionary in the Capitol building in Washington, D.C., in 1965. Father Damien was beatified by Pope John Paul II based on two claims of miraculous cures; he was canonized by Pope Benedict XVI in 2009.

Father Damien

Dr. Kent Brantly (right), with his wife, Amber, during a press conference announcing his release from Emory Hospital in Atlanta, Georgia.

TWO WHO SURVIVED

Did experimental treatment save the lives of two Americans who contracted Ebola?

In July 2014, physician Kent Brantly, 33, of Fort Worth, Texas, and missionary Nancy Writebol, 59, of Charlotte, North Carolina, were both working at Elwa Hospital in Monrovia, Liberia. When the two Americans were diagnosed with Ebola, they were airlifted to Atlanta's Emory University Hospital, where their medical team included five doctors, 21 nurses, and hundreds of support personnel. In late August 2014, Brantly and Writebol were pronounced recovered and were released.

Both received the experimental drug ZMapp, a combination of three engineered immune-system compounds. In addition, Brantly received a blood transfusion from a recovered Ebola patient while in Liberia.

"Today is a miraculous day," Brantly said upon his release. He urged those who had prayed for his recovery to continue to pray for all Ebola sufferers.

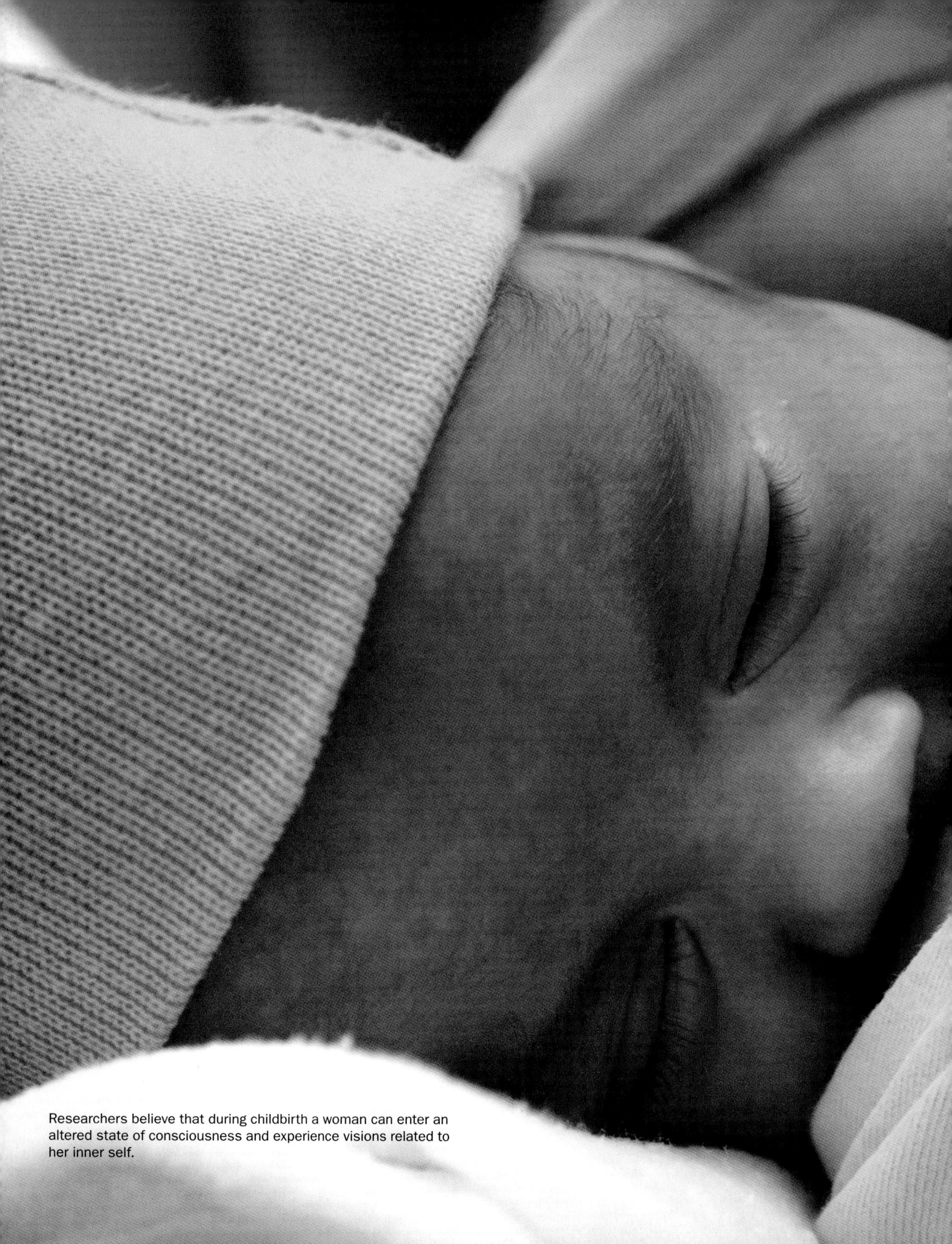

Researchers believe that during childbirth a woman can enter an altered state of consciousness and experience visions related to her inner self.

CHAPTER 11

The Wonder of Children

When mothers and babies survive premature birth and other life-threatening conditions, it often feels like divine intervention.

Birth, Death, Rebirth

A THIRD OF WOMEN WHO COME CLOSE TO DYING WHILE IN LABOR SAY THEY'VE HAD A MYSTICAL EXPERIENCE.

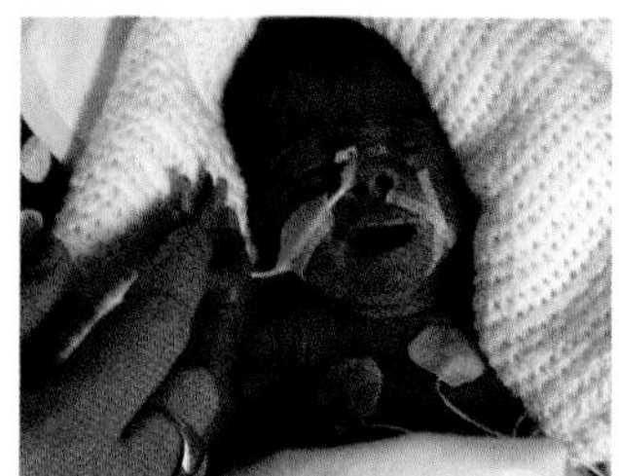

Giving birth prematurely can be associated with near-death experiences.

"I was in the abundant brilliant light far away in the universe. It vibrated and moved. Galaxies and stars gleamed in brilliant colors against the darker space, and at the same time there was that mist-like, exquisitely beautiful, non-dazzling light all around me.... It was a light of unconditional love.... It was the purpose and meaning of all life.... But all the time I knew that I had to go back."

THIS ONE'S FOR THE GIRLS

Do laboring mothers' near-death experiences differ from all others?

Researchers believe that during childbirth a woman can enter an altered state of consciousness or expanded state of mind, experiencing visions related to her inner self or to an "activated collective unconscious" shared by all people.

Those who have near-death experiences share particular visions. Some mothers report having received advice and psychic strength from their long-dead grandmothers, who encouraged them to return to life. Occasionally, a woman reports having witnessed her baby's spirit entering its body. These mothers report that they understand the suffering that babies endure as they enter the world, according to New Zealand anthropologist Gregg Lahood and midwifery educator Judy Cottrell.

This extraordinary story was recorded by Kersti Wistrand, a Swedish psychologist who interviewed hundreds of new mothers in the 1980s and 1990s. The narrator nearly died during a difficult 35-hour labor, and her experience is more common than one might expect: Wistrand found that women who suffer complicated childbirths often have such visions. Around the same time she was conducting her study, Russian psychiatrists identified the same phenomenon, discovering that women who underwent dangerous deliveries reported near-death experiences approximately three times as often as the general population.

Crisis in Childbirth

Despite modern medical advances, childbirth can be life threatening. Each year in the United States, about 52,000 laboring mothers face serious medical emergencies, and 34,000 go through acute crises that nearly kill them. During such moments, a woman may experience the sensation of separating from her body, passing through a dark tunnel toward a bright light, and feeling surrounded by peace and well-be-

Near-death experiences often include the sensation of passing through a dark tunnel toward a bright light.

ing. Many describe reunions with deceased loved ones; most say they realized during the near-death experience that they had to return to life.

"Excited and Terrified"

Most near-death experiences are blissful, or at least enjoyable, but they can also be confusing or frightening. A woman may take years to process the experience fully, and some never do. Others feel insane, embarrassed, or misunderstood.

Christina Grof, a practitioner of transpersonal psychology, documented her own 1973 experience in her book *The Stormy Search for the Self*: "As the people around me encouraged me to 'push...push...nice and hard, remember to breathe...,' I felt an abrupt snap somewhere inside of me as powerful and unfamiliar energies were released.... Brilliant mosaics of white light exploded in my head, and...I felt strange, involuntary breathing rhythms taking over. It was as though I had just been hit by some miraculous but frightening force, and I was both excited and terrified."

After her son was born, Grof was given morphine for her pain, and the vision wore off. "And I became embarrassed and fearful," she said. "I had completely lost control. Very quickly, I pulled myself together."

Born Again

But a mother who embraces her near-death experience can find it wonderfully transformational. One American woman who participated in a study and chose to remain anonymous gave birth in India in 1973. She decided after her near-death experience to help other people facing adversity. Her vision changed her life for the better.

"I would never be the same again," she wrote in 2013. "One of the most important things I gained was the feeling that there is a greater spirit of unconditional love to which we can turn continually for wisdom, comfort, and guidance through life's challenges." It taught her, she said, "to learn greater self-acceptance, nonjudgment, forgiveness, and compassion; and to seek and find the joy that comes from being connected to the Light."

NEAR-DEATH EXPERIENCES EXPLAINED

Scientists and mystics have different answers to the riddle of mothers' mysterious visions.

Why do so many women in labor report near-death experiences, even some who never actually come near clinical death? Scientists generally point toward biology and psychology:

➔ The extreme pain of labor triggers a sensory or emotional overload, leaving the woman disoriented.

➔ Anesthesia, medication, and the overproduction of endorphins or other natural chemicals affect the woman's brain.

➔ Blood loss can lead to shock and/or oxygen deprivation, triggering hallucinations.

New Agers credit something more mystical:

➔ The woman undergoes a "physiological transformation" as she becomes a mother.

➔ The newborn gives off intense energy vibrations, which the mother picks up.

Father's Day

A MEDICAL MIRACLE PROVIDED THE ULTIMATE GIFT TO A PARALYZED NEWLYWED DESPERATE TO BE A DAD.

Paul D'Alessandro would never walk again. That's what doctors told the Elmont, New York, construction worker after he fractured his spine in a 1983 building collapse that left him a paraplegic. But there was more: It would likely be impossible for him to become a father.

D'Alessandro and his schoolteacher wife, Anna, had been married for just 18 months. They were devastated. The two could trace their intertwined ancestral roots back to Cassino, Italy, where in World War II their families had hidden together during bombing raids. Anna's parents and Paul's grandparents had even immigrated to America on the same boat. The couple had their hearts set on continuing that history with children of their own.

As they began to consult fertility experts, however, the D'Alessandros were discouraged. To conceive a child together, Paul would have to be able to produce a sperm sample, they were told.

Medical Breakthrough

In the years following the accident, the D'Alessandros put the issue of childbearing on the back burner as they focused on Paul's rehabilitation. Then, in 1986, Paul came across an article in *Paraplegia News* about Dr. Carol Bennett, a University of Michigan urologist. The doctor had adapted for humans a procedure used in zoos to help perpetuate endangered species, such as giant pandas. Using a mild, painless electrical current from equipment designed by a professor of veterinary medicine, Bennett had successfully retrieved vi-

LIFE AFTER DEATH

After her husband passed away, his grieving wife conceived his son.

When Scott Martin, of Geelong, Australia, was diagnosed with fast-moving esophageal cancer in 2011, he and his pregnant wife, Lyn, had a decision to make. The two had had fertility problems and had opted to store Scott's sperm. By the time Scott died, just two months after his cancer diagnosis, Lyn had suffered a miscarriage. The double tragedy was overwhelming. "I felt so isolated," Lyn told a local reporter. "I was in a big dark hole."

So Lyn opted to try again to become a mother. This time it was successful. Through in vitro fertilization, she gave birth to her husband's child, a boy named Reilly, in January 2013. Ten months later, Reilly was a healthy, happy, blue-eyed toddler with an unexpected gift: "When Reilly smiles, he's just like his dad," Lyn said.

Miracle baby Reilly Martin with his mom, Lyn Martin

WHO KNEW?

About 1.3 million Americans, 61 percent of them male, are paralyzed from spinal-cord injuries.

During in vitro fertilization, sperm is injected into a harvested egg cell to create an embryo.

able sperm samples from paralyzed men, enabling them to become fathers.

The D'Alessandros began traveling to Michigan, carrying a statue of Saint Gerard, the patron of expectant mothers, for good luck. On the fifth visit, Bennett's team had a viable sperm sample. Through in vitro fertilization, doctors mixed Anna's eggs with Paul's sperm in a petri dish.

Bennett later told *People* that the successful result "was one of the nicest things to happen to me in my medical career." In December 1987, the ecstatic D'Alessandros became parents of a healthy baby boy. Tipping the scales at 7 lbs. 10½ oz., Paul D'Alessandro, Jr., was the fourth child in the U.S. born as a result of this medical breakthrough.

SCIENCE IN THE BEDROOM

In recent decades, medical advancements have brought millions of people new hope for parenthood.

➔ Louise Joy Brown, born July 25, 1978, in Lancashire, England, was the first human conceived using in vitro fertilization, a novel process at the time that involved combining Brown's mother's eggs with her father's sperm in a petri dish. Brown was dubbed the "test tube baby," and her birth was a landmark moment in infertility treatment.

➔ After learning that her chances of conceiving were less than 20 percent, Becki Dilley of Berne, Indiana, tried fertility treatments. On Thanksgiving Day 1992, Becki and her husband, Keith, got the happy news that Becki was pregnant. But another surprise was in store. In May 1993, Becki, 27, and Keith, 30, became the proud parents of sextuplets, the first set born in 20th-century America.

➔ While women in their 40s have given birth through IVF using frozen embryos or donor eggs, dental hygienist Belinda Slaughter of Orlando, Florida, became the oldest woman to conceive through IVF using her own undoctored eggs. In May 2014, 46-year-old Slaughter defied her doctors' calculations that she had only a 1 percent chance of conceiving, and gave birth to a boy, Jackson.

Spontaneous Recovery

AN INFANT DEFIES DEATH AND REBOUNDS FROM LEUKEMIA.

WHAT HAPPENED? EVEN MEDICAL EXPERTS AREN'T SURE.

Two days after Ethan Jacob Stacy was born in Nashville, Tennessee, in 2003, his parents were given devastating news: Their son had acute myeloid leukemia (AML), a virulent blood cancer that is rare in newborns. Oncologist Melissa Rhodes, one of Ethan's physicians at Vanderbilt Children's Hospital, warned the Stacys that infants born with leukemia rarely thrive. The best she could offer was to put Ethan through rounds of chemotherapy, but she could not guarantee he would make it. The chemo alone could be lethal for a newborn.

Death's Door

Chad and Mandy Stacy had an excruciating decision to make: Should they subject Ethan to the myriad risks? "We came home, and I remember lying in bed and praying…God, give us an answer," Mandy recounted on the television show *The 700 Club*. "And we both woke up the next morning, and we said, 'We're not going to put him through it.'"

Two weeks later, Ethan's parents took him home to die. Within days, the baby developed tumors all over his body, including his calf, feet, and forearms. "He actually had leukemia in his skin, in his hands, his feet, and his legs, as well as in his liver and spleen," Dr. Rhodes said. "He was showing that he had a very advanced disease at that point."

At three weeks old, Ethan stopped eating and exhibited other signs consistent with the end of life.

The Power of Prayer

The Stacys' faith remained strong, and even in their darkest hour they continued to pray. "I remember rocking him hard and singing, 'Open the eyes of my heart, Lord, I want to see you,'" Mandy said. "I knew that if I just focused my mind on Christ, that's the only way that I could make it through." Then, suddenly, Ethan started feeding again. Over the next few days, he gradually started getting better. Sitting at the kitchen table, Mandy told herself that the Lord had intervened. "I can see God working," she said.

As the weeks passed, Ethan's tumors disappeared, and when the Stacys took their son back to Vanderbilt, his platelet count had rebounded from a low of 39,000 to 415,000. There was no medical explanation. "Ethan had gotten about as sick as a baby could possibly get, and then spontaneously got better," Dr. Rhodes marveled. "We did the bone marrow test, which showed no evidence of leukemia. For him to have gotten as absolutely sick as he did, and then just turn around spontaneously overnight, that's a miracle."

In June 2011, Ethan, by then a healthy, happy eight-year-old, and his parents, Mandy and Chad, made their appearance on television. Their smiles said it all.

Ethan Stacy with his parents on *The 700 Club* television program in June 2011

THE ULTIMATE CUDDLE THERAPY

An Australian mother strokes and soothes her baby back to life.

On March 25, 2010, just 20 minutes after giving premature birth to twins at a hospital in Sydney, Australia, Kate Ogg was told by nurses that her son, Jamie, had died. The health care workers gently placed the tiny boy—born at just 27 weeks along with his twin, Emily—across Kate's chest. Although Emily survived the premature birth, the doctors were unable to find a heartbeat in Jamie.

Ogg took off her gown and arranged her son with his head over her arm. "If he was on his way out of this world, we wanted for him to know who his parents were and to know that we loved him before he died," Kate said.

After five minutes, Jamie starting making quick, startled movements, first small and then more pronounced. Though the Oggs were told that they were merely seeing reflexive post-mortem movements, Kate continued to caress and speak to Jamie for nearly two hours. Soon, he grabbed Kate's finger. In a little while, he accepted breast milk. The Oggs tried to summon the doctor several times, but hospital staff repeated that Jamie's motions were normal reflexes and not signs of life. Finally, the doctor returned, put a stethoscope to Jamie's chest, and said, "I don't believe it. I don't believe it." In 2014, Jamie and Emily celebrated their fourth birthdays.

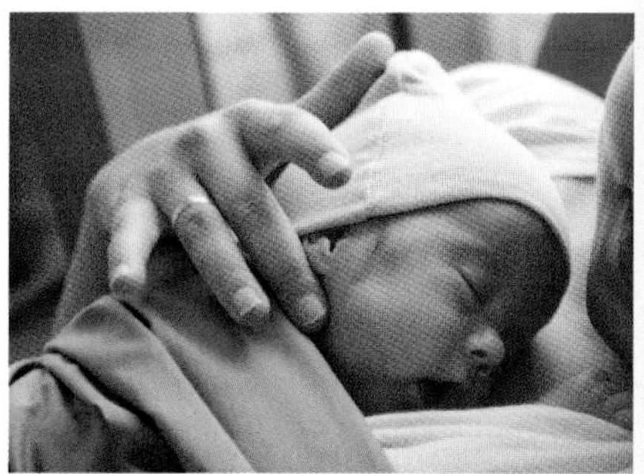

A mother's urge to keep her newborn close can have life-saving consequences.

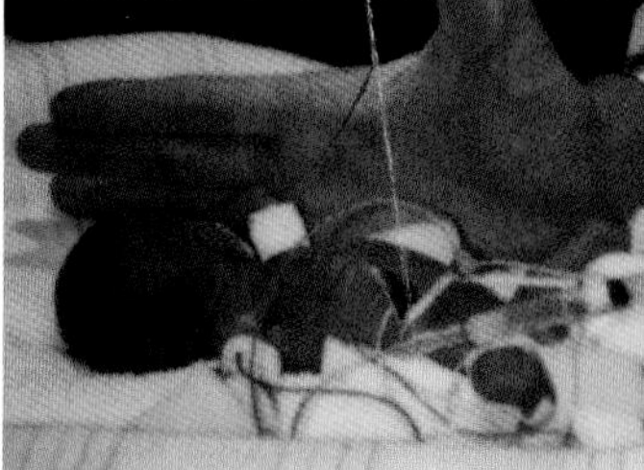

Rumaisa Rahman, with the hand of her neonatologist, one day after birth.

SMALL WONDERS

These three newborns beat the odds and broke records.

→ When Nicky Soto found out she was carrying a baby in 2010, her doctors advised her to terminate the pregnancy because the child was growing outside of her uterus. Nevertheless, the Arizona woman and her husband proceeded, and in May 2011, with the help of a team of 20 doctors and staff, Azelan Perfecto was born. He was the first baby known to have survived an ectopic pregnancy.

→ In 2012, Latonya Bowman, a pregnant Detroit woman, was abducted, doused with lighter fluid, set on fire, and shot in the back. Three days later, after going into early labor, she gave birth to a baby boy via C-section.

→ In 2004, Rumaisa Rahman and her twin sister, Hiba, were delivered at 25½ weeks at Loyola University Medical Center in Maywood, Illinois. Hiba weighed 1 lb. 4 oz., while Rumaisa was just 8.6 oz. A decade later, Rumaisa held the record as the world's smallest surviving premature baby. She was smaller than other kids her age and has some minor motor delays, but was otherwise a healthy little girl.

Lightning strike after dark, Sedona, Arizona

CHAPTER 12

Beating the Elements

The will to live, plus spiritual and physical strength, helps some people overcome truly daunting circumstances.

WHO KNEW?

In 2001, Dr. Jerri Nielsen published *Ice Bound*, about her voyage of self-discovery battling breast cancer in the Antarctic. Susan Sarandon starred in a 2003 television-movie version.

When There's No Doctor in the House

ISOLATED IN THE ANTARCTIC, JERRI NIELSEN BATTLED HER OWN AGGRESSIVE BREAST CANCER WHILE CONTINUING TO WORK AS A RESEARCH PHYSICIAN.

In March 1999, Jerri Nielsen, a 47-year-old emergency-room doctor from Cleveland, Ohio, was working as the sole physician at the National Science Foundation's Antarctic South Pole research outpost when she discovered an unsettling lump in her right breast. With winter, subzero temperatures, and total darkness having already set in, the doctor knew an airlift out would be impossible.

The polar station's two-bed hospital was nicknamed the Hard Truth Medical Centre, and many of its supplies dated from the 1950s. There were no nurses or assistants, and Nielsen served not only as the 42-person station's one doctor but also as its dentist, storekeeper, and postmaster. She would have to fight the disease with only the help of her untrained colleagues.

Under Nielsen's tutelage, a welder on the team learned to perform a biopsy by

BEYOND THE CALL OF DUTY

One wounded Revolutionary War soldier had good reason to avoid doctors. "He" had a secret.

When Continental Army enlistee Deborah Sampson was injured during a skirmish near West Point in 1787, she was as afraid of the doctors as she was of her wounds. Sampson had joined the fight for independence by disguising herself as a man, and she feared that if her identity was discovered she would no longer be allowed to fight. Instead, Sampson operated on herself, extracting a musket ball from her thigh with a penknife and sewing needle.

Her cover was blown the following year when she fell sick with fever and lost consciousness in a Philadelphia hospital. Given an honorable discharge, Sampson soon married and had three children. Eleven years after Sampson died in 1827, Congress approved a military pension for her widowed husband, referring to Sampson's "female heroism."

practicing needle techniques on potatoes and thawed chicken. The two worked together, using ice as an anesthetic, and successfully harvested tissue. When they transmitted images of it to the United States via computer, Nielsen's fears were confirmed: She was suffering from an aggressive form of cancer.

"There is no end of life until your last breath. We can all do something to help someone."

As the U.S. Air Force was unable to transfer Nielsen out of the research facility, it parachuted chemotherapy drugs and other supplies to a fire-lit field near her outpost. The dangerous airdrop succeeded, with only an ultrasound device being destroyed in the process.

Self-Treatment and a Perilous Rescue

Nielsen began treating herself with hormone injections and intravenous chemotherapy, guided by cancer specialists via e-mail and video. Although Nielsen continued her medical duties at the 41-person research center, she soon developed infections requiring more aggressive treatment, and the Air Force decided to evacuate her from the station. On October 16, when South Pole temperatures had risen to around 58 degrees below zero, Operation Deep Freeze went into action. Two Air National Guard planes set off for

Staff members of the National Science Foundation's Antarctic South Pole station examine bundles of emergency medical supplies dropped by the U.S. Air Force, 1999.

Antarctica to airlift Nielsen to America and deliver a replacement doctor.

After multiple surgeries and a mastectomy, Nielsen's cancer went into remission. She published a best-selling account of her courageous endeavor, married, and embarked on a motivational-speaking career. She participated in benefits for cancer organizations and returned to the Antarctic several times.

In 2005, Nielsen's doctors discovered that her cancer had returned, and had spread to her liver, bones, and brain. Nevertheless, she continued to inspire others.

"My experience at the pole had to do with accepting things that most people fear most deeply," Nielsen told *Psychology Today* in 2006. "It certainly had far more to do with peace and surrender than it did with courage."

In a 2008 talk at the University of Toledo, where she herself had studied medicine, Nielsen removed her wig, revealed her bald skull, and told students: "There is no end of life until your last breath. We can all do something to help someone." Nielsen died in June 2009, at the age of 57.

A C-17 dropping its cargo over the South Pole; a similar plane airdropped supplies to help Jerri Nielsen treat her cancer.

STAYING ALIVE AT ALL COSTS

Many of us never know how capable we are until tested. Facing death, these extraordinary individuals drew on almost superhuman reserves of strength and stamina.

Crawling Through the Andes

In 1985, Joe Simpson, 25, and Simon Yates, 21, were descending a peak in the Andes when Simpson fell, driving his tibia through his knee joint and breaking his ankle. As a blizzard raged, Yates struggled to lower Simpson to safety, but finally cut the rope to save himself and returned to base camp. Miraculously, Simpson survived; he crawled for four days through the Andes. Five years later, despite doctors' prognoses that he'd never walk again, Simpson climbed Nepal's Ama Dablam peak.

In a Boulder's Path

In 1993, Bill Jeracki, a 38-year-old anesthetist, was fishing alone near St. Mary's Glacier outside Denver, when a falling boulder crushed his left leg. With snow forecast, Jeracki created a tourniquet from fishing line and a flannel shirt, severed his lower leg with a pocketknife, and clamped bleeding arteries with fishing hemostats. He then crawled to his truck, drove half a mile, and was airlifted to the University of Colorado Hospital. Jeracki subsequently founded a prosthetics company.

127 Hours

Aron Ralston, a 27-year-old outdoorsman, was rock-climbing alone in southeastern Utah in 2003 when a dislodged boulder pinned him by his right arm in a three-foot-wide space. After spending five days attempting to free himself, Ralston broke his own forearm, then amputated it with a dull pocketknife, created a makeshift tourniquet, and used his other arm to rappel 65 feet to the canyon floor. Bleeding profusely, he hiked seven miles before encountering other hikers, who alerted rescuers.

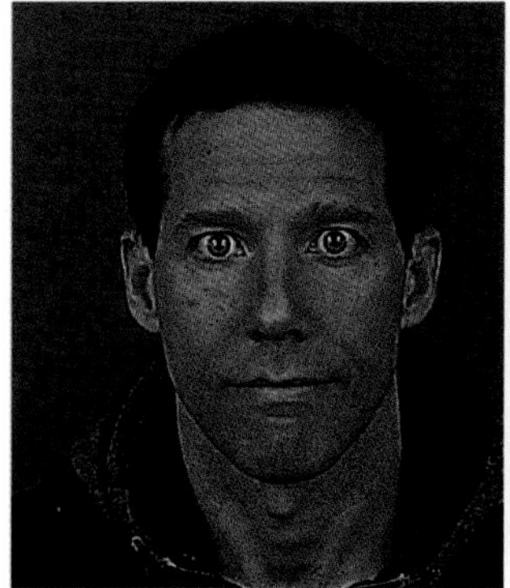

Aron Ralston's ordeal was turned into the movie *127 Hours*.

Nightmare in the Desert

A DISTANCE RUNNER SURVIVED 10 DAYS WITH ALMOST NO FOOD OR WATER IN THE BURNING SAHARA, OVERCOMING EVEN HIS IMPULSE TO TAKE HIS OWN LIFE.

"I had once heard that dying of thirst was the worst possible fate," recalled Italian pentathlete Mauro Prosperi after being lost in the Moroccan Sahara for 10 days. The 39-year-old father of three and former policeman had been competing in the 1994 Marathon des Sables, a six-day, 145-mile endurance run across the famous desert.

Prosperi was in seventh place when a blustery windstorm blew up massive sand clouds, obscuring the course. Disoriented, he pressed on, wrapping his face in a scarf, determined to maintain his position. Finally Prosperi sought shelter under a bush, but by the time the eight-hour storm passed, he was hopelessly lost. He had a compass, but no reference points. With temperatures climbing above 100 degrees, Prosperi followed desert-survival protocol, walking only in the morning and evening. When his food and water ran out after 36 hours, he began drinking his own urine and killing and eating lizards and snakes.

Mauro Prosperi, Italian pentathlete and police officer

Hope Lost and Regained

On the third day, Prosperi found shelter in a small, deserted Muslim shrine and affixed his Italian flag to its tent pole. He killed bats by twisting their necks, then drank their blood to quench his thirst, but he suspected he was suffering from severe dehydration. Seeking to avoid a slow, agonizing death, Prosperi reluctantly scratched a goodbye note to his wife with a piece of charcoal, then slashed his wrist with a penknife.

But he didn't die. Lack of water had caused his blood to thicken and clot, which Prosperi saw as a sign that he was meant to live. With renewed hope, he stumbled across the desert toward a distant mountain range. After nine days in burning isolation, he finally encountered Tuareg nomads, who brought him on camelback to a nearby village in Algeria, about 186 miles off-course to the west. Prosperi was then taken to a hospital, 30 pounds lighter and on the verge of liver failure.

"I learned how important it is to live your life fully," Prosperi said of his experience, "and cherish it." He has since competed in the same race six more times.

With less than 20 millimeters of annual rainfall, the Sahara is the driest place on Earth.

The Sahara desert covers some three and a half million square miles—bigger than the continental U.S.

Only 500 species of plants are found in the entire Sahara; tropical rainforests can have more than 2,000 species in a four-square-mile radius.

Nearly 25 percent of the desert is covered with 500-foot-high sand dunes—the height of a 50-story building.

Temperatures in the Sahara average 86°F, but during the hottest months can soar to 122°F.

Mauro Prosperi survived 10 days in the Sahara wasteland.

William LaFever survived in the desert with only his clothing and a lighter.

ENDURANCE AS ENLIGHTENMENT

For some, near-death experiences in the desert lead to an awakening.

→ In 2012, William LaFever, an autistic 28-year-old from Colorado Springs, Colorado, planned a trek from Boulder, Utah, to Page, Arizona, through the Escalante Desert. But the experienced outdoorsman got lost, and his gear was stolen. After three weeks he was found sitting in a river near Lake Powell, on the Utah–Arizona border. Emaciated and near death, he had been unable to move for several days, and had eaten only frogs and plants since leaving Boulder. He said facing death alone in the desert was "a spiritual experience."

→ In 1999, Robert Bogucki, a 33-year-old Alaskan, survived 43 days in western Australia's Great Sandy Desert. Bogucki, who planned to fast in the wilderness, began his trek by bicycle. When tourists found his bike two weeks later, police launched a search. They called it off after 12 days, believing Bogucki had perished or gotten a ride back to civilization. Bogucki was finally found by a news helicopter, 248 miles from his departure point. He'd survived on plants for 12 days and lost 44 pounds. He had wanted, he later said, to "just make peace with God."

It's Electrifying!

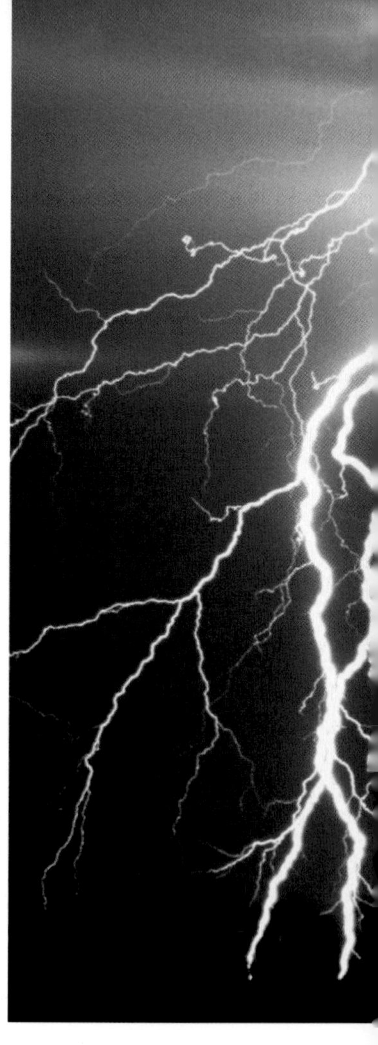

GETTING HIT BY LIGHTNING IS RARE. SURVIVING THE EXPERIENCE UNSCATHED IS MORE UNUSUAL STILL.

William Moseley, lightning strike survivor

STRIKE...TEN?

A single bolt of lightning can affect many people at once.

When the war drama *The Silent Mountain* was filming in Italy in 2012, actor William Moseley got the shock of his life. He and nine crewmembers were in a hut during a storm when a bolt came through the roof and slammed them. Amazingly, all 10 people were fine. "It was a freak of nature," Moseley told *The Hollywood Reporter*.

When Robb Montejano spotted lightning in the sky over Seattle, Washington, during a freak storm in August 2014, he made an all-too-common mistake. Instead of heading for cover, Montejano decided to record the experience, and in the process turned himself into a human lightning rod. "I just felt this surge of electricity go 'boom' through my body," Montejano said later. The encounter earned him a new nickname, "The Flash." Luckily, the moniker was his only lasting souvenir of the experience.

About 25 million bolts of lightning reach the Earth each year, or about 100 zaps of lightning per second for every thunderstorm, and it's not unusual for humans to get in the way. Some 240,000 people are hit annually. While some escape unscathed, a tenth of strike victims die and close to three quarters are seriously debilitated. They can suffer brain injuries, nerve problems, cardiac arrest, and even personality changes.

Survival depends on getting immediate treatment, especially for acute effects such as cardiac arrest, according to Mary Ann Cooper, professor emeritus of emergency medicine at the University of Illinois at Chicago, who has studied lightning victims for over 30 years. Among other issues, strikes can cause symptoms similar to post-concussion syndrome, in which survivors are no longer able to ignore distractions as well as most people can. "That ability is scraped off," Cooper told the *Washington Post*.

Repeat Survivors

Even more amazing than managing to come through unscathed is being able to so more than once. That has been the case with lifestyle guru Martha Stewart, who has lived through three lightning strikes, all of which happened indoors. Once, Stewart was struck while washing dishes, a second time she was talking on the tele-

WHO KNEW?

Do you think lightning never strikes twice? Have a chat with the Empire State Building: It gets hit about 25 times a year.

Lightning strikes after dark in Sedona, Arizona.

phone, and the third time she was touching metal when lightning came inside and zapped her. She has said she thinks she has a bizarre ability to attract electricity.

The first time Shenandoah National Park ranger Roy Cleveland Sullivan was hit by lightning was in April 1942. The zap left him with a gouge down his right leg and a destroyed toenail, but he lived to tell the tale—and to get struck six more times over the course of his life.

> About 25 million bolts of lightning reach Earth each year.

In 1969, Sullivan was driving when a bolt took out three trees along the road and hit him through an open window of his truck. A year later, Sullivan was knocked off his feet in his own front yard, and two years after that, his hair was set on fire by a strike at a campground guardhouse. By this point, the *Guinness Book of World Records* had taken notice. But Sullivan's stats had to be updated in 1973, when a fourth strike set his hair on fire again, and blew off one of his shoes. He was zapped a fifth time in 1976, and once more in 1977.

No one knows why or how Sullivan was hit—and lived—so many times. He suspected that "some chemical, some mineral" in his body was an attractant, but his outdoorsy line of work undoubtedly increased the odds.

Rubber boots won't protect against lightning strikes.

DON'T GET SHOCKED

Follow this advice during a lightning storm to avoid becoming a statistic.

→ **Neither rubber-soled shoes nor the rubber tires of a car protect against lightning strikes.** If you are sitting in a car, don't lean against the metal frame.

→ **If you're outdoors, get inside as quickly as possible.** If you can't do that, avoid taking shelter under trees and high objects. Do not lie flat, because lightning can create a deadly ground current. Instead, curl up into a ball under low bushes.

→ **Swimming during a storm can be deadly:** Water conducts electricity, and a head protruding from a pool or lake makes a good target.

→ **If you are indoors, unplug everything you can before a storm hits.** Avoid touching anything electrical once the storm is overhead.

The South Seas and their islands may look idyllic, but they have been the site of many amazing lost-at-sea stories.

CHAPTER 13

Saved from the Sea

Sailors and fisherman lost on open waters relate harrowing brushes with death: Dehydration, fatigue, and circling sharks are just a few of the dangers.

When frozen seas began to squeeze the *Endurance* to its breaking point, the men and dogs set up camp on the ice.

WHO KNEW?

Antarctica has no permanent residents, though it is home to a rotating group of scientific researchers from various countries.

Epic on Ice

ERNEST SHACKLETON'S WORLD WAR I–ERA JOURNEY TO ANTARCTICA MADE HISTORY, JUST NOT IN THE WAY THE EXPLORER HAD IMAGINED.

Endurance was the name of their ship. It also turned out to describe the experience of explorer Ernest Shackleton and his intrepid crew, who managed to survive for more than a year in the Antarctic after disaster struck their South Pole expedition.

Born in 1874, Shackleton was a restless British adventurer determined to be the first person to reach the South Pole. When another man beat him to it in 1911, Shackleton set a new goal: to sail to Antarctica and cross the continent by foot and dogsled.

On August 1, 1914, Shackleton and his crew of 27, plus 69 dogs, left England. They planned to stop at Buenos Aires, Argentina, to restock the ship, proceed to South Georgia Island off the southernmost tip of South America, and then sail to Antarctica.

Endurance reached South Georgia Island by late fall and was restocked and ready to take up anchor on December 5. Shackleton and his men didn't know it, but they would not touch land again for 497 days.

After his ship sank in the frigid Antarctic, Sir Ernest Henry Shackleton managed to get his entire crew safely home to England.

On January 18, 1915, *Endurance* became trapped in ice off the coast of Antarctica. Shackleton decided to wait for the frozen slabs to break. In May—the beginning of winter in the Southern Hemisphere—the sun rose over the horizon for the last time until spring. In September, the water began to thaw and move, but this only increased the pressure on *Endurance*'s hull. Remaining hopeful, Shackleton ordered everyone to abandon ship to camp on the ice. On November 21, squeezed past its breaking point, *Endurance* sank.

By March 1916, the men were forced to kill and eat the dogs. Shackleton's new plan was to reach Elephant Island, an uninhabited outcropping 350 miles away from where the boat sank. The men took three lifeboats and, after a week on the water, reached the 215-square-mile island around April 14.

Shackleton soon realized that because Elephant Island was not on shipping routes, the group was unlikely be rescued. He chose five of his crew to accompany him to South Georgia Island, 800 miles away, to bring in a rescue team; the rest stayed behind on Elephant Island. The six men reached land after 17 days in a lifeboat on stormy seas; it took another 36 hours for Shackleton and two of the men to slog across glacial mountains to reach a whaling station.

From there, the men failed three times to get back to Elephant Island to retrieve the crew left behind; finally, Shackleton convinced Chilean naval authorities to provide a tug boat for the harrowing trip back. On August 30, Shackleton returned to Elephant Island and rescued the 22 remaining members of the group. Miraculously, the entire team eventually returned to England alive—a clear testament to Shackleton's leadership skills and ingenuity, and the fortitude of the team.

The green line shows the *Endurance*'s journey from England to Antarctica; blue, the expedition's travels across the pack ice; and red, the team's route back home.

WHO KNEW?

The same day Ernest Shackleton began his voyage in 1914, Germany declared war on Russia. The explorer offered his ship to the British government, but was turned down and instead cleared to proceed with his expedition.

Shackleton's men on Elephant Island

Survivors of the yacht Lucette, visible in foreground, talk to newsmen, in Panama, July 25, 1972, aboard Toka Maru No. 1, the Japanese tuna fishing boat that rescued them.

tear. He was awarded a prestigious British Empire Medal, then emigrated to the United States. He died in 1991 at age 72 in Brooklyn, New York.

Scottish Family Robertson

In 1970, Scottish couple Dougal and Lyn Robertson and their children set out to sail around the world. Seventeen months later, the Robertsons' boat was attacked and sunk by killer whales near the Galapagos Islands. The Robertsons, with their sons, 18-year-old Douglas and nine-year-old twins Neil and Sandy, as well as a family friend, stayed alive on a 10-foot dinghy for 38 days. They drank rainwater and sea turtle blood and caught food with a spear made from an oar. A fishing trawler finally rescued them.

Years later, a grown Douglas Robertson told the BBC, "In a funny kind of way life had a quality to it—the quality of survival, the reward of seeing another sunset, another sunrise. We felt like wildlife must feel in the jungle; to live another day was our only goal."

Dougal J. Robertson waves goodby to the Japanese tuna fishing boat that rescued him and his family.

Not-So-Pleasurable Cruise

Tami Oldham Ashcraft had only a little more to work with than Lim. In 1983, Ashcraft and her fiancé, both experienced sailors, were delivering a yacht from Tahiti to San Diego when Hurricane Raymond hit. Ashcraft, 23, was thrown against a cabin wall and lost consciousness. She came to a day later to find her fiancé gone—presumably swept overboard in the storm—and the cabin half full of water. Its masts had snapped and every electronic device had been destroyed. Ashcraft managed to pump out the water, fashion a mast and sail, and reach Hawaii, 1,500 miles away, using an old-fashioned navigation tool called a sextant. The journey took her 41 days. She later wrote about the terrifying experience in *Red Sky in Mourning: A True Story of Love, Loss and Survival at Sea.*

DESPERATE MEASURES

The unappetizing practice of drinking urine often factors into survival stories. Is it safe?

Some people who have survived disasters at sea say they avoided dehydration by drinking their own urine—an indication of how thirsty a few days adrift can be. But is the practice safe?

Survivalists and the U.S. Army warn against it.

While the urine of a properly hydrated person has a high enough percentage of water that it can be safe to consume, a dehydrated person's urine can be dangerous. It has a lower percentage of water and carries dehydrating salt and waste products the body is trying to get rid of, including nitrogen and calcium.

Still, for those who are completely out of options, urine beats seawater—which is so salty and dehydrating that it's almost guaranteed to kill you faster than not drinking anything.

Trouble in Paradise

THESE 20TH-CENTURY CASTAWAYS CHOSE THEIR SOLITUDE, BUT THEY ENDED UP INCREDIBLY LUCKY TO BE ALIVE.

DON'T LEAVE HOME WITHOUT IT

In case of emergency, there's one tool you'll really want to have with you.

Survivalists have a long list of items they would take with them into the wilderness, including water purification tablets, matches, rope, a compass, and a whistle or other signaling tool. But there is one thing everyone seems to agree is number one: a good field knife. A sturdy, fixed-blade (non-folding), seven-inch model can chop wood, skin game, or cut bandages for a field dressing. You can use it to create a fire-starting tool called a bow drill. You can even use it to whittle if you're bored.

The blissful solitude of a tropical island might sound alluring, but once there the seclusion can turn oppressive. That's what Gerald Kingsland and Lucy Irvine discovered when the two complete strangers headed for a remote island off the coast of Australia.

In 1982, Kingsland, a 49-year-old English journalist down on his luck, planned to spend a year living with a woman away from civilization and to write a book about the experience. He recruited Irvine, 25, a Scottish free spirit who responded to his want ad for a wife to accompany him.

The couple's adventure together was rocky. Irvine was an organized go-getter, while Kingsland was laid back and liked to take naps.

The two struggled to get by on seafood and coconuts, plus scarce rations of rice, beans, and tea. They lost weight, grew weak, and were plagued by cuts that wouldn't heal. A drought thwarted their efforts to grow a garden. After a year, Kingsland and Irvine nearly starved to death before they were rescued by natives from a nearby island.

Upon their return, Kingsland finished his book, *The Islander*, and Irvine wrote one, too. Her account of the experience, *Castaway*, was made into a movie starring Amanda Donohoe as Irvine and Oliver Reed as Kirkland.

Stroke of Luck

After retiring from the navy in his native New Zealand in 1952, 50-year-old Tom Neale, enchanted by the idea of living in pristine beauty, retreated to an atoll in the Cook Islands to live alone.

Two years out of the gate, he had a brush with death that was almost laughably pedestrian: While tossing an iron weight to anchor his small boat, Neale wrenched his back, leaving himself barely able to struggle to his shack, where he lay essentially paralyzed, drifting in and out of consciousness for four days.

"The possibility of rescue never for a moment entered my mind," Neale later wrote in an autobiography, *An Island to Oneself: The Story of Six Years On a Desert Island*. "The chance was too remote and absurd. I would just have to stick it out and hope the jammed muscles would

When English journalist Gerald Kingsland and a companion spent a year on Tuin Island, in the Torres Strait just north of the Great Barrier Reef off the coast of Australia, the two almost died of starvation.

unlock. That was as near to a miracle as I could expect."

But the miracle happened. As Neale lay helpless and immobile, two American sailors happened ashore. They administered food and "a stiff tot of rum," and stayed with the ailing Neale for several days before leaving to get help. A rescue ship arrived two weeks later to bring Neale to Rarotonga, the most populous of the Cook Islands, for medical treatment.

Although it would be six years before Neale would return to his atoll, he did go back in 1967 and remained there for a decade.

CAST AWAY IN POPULAR CULTURE

Harrowing survival stories are a mainstay in literature and film.

Lord of the Flies

William Golding's classic 1954 novel, which has twice been adapted for the big screen, revolves around a group of British schoolboys evacuated from England during wartime. When their plane is shot down and they are stranded on an island without adults, their makeshift civilization disintegrates into violence and chaos.

Life of Pi

The 2012 movie based on Yann Martel's surrealistic novel explores the spiritual awakening of a young boy who is shipwrecked during what was to be his zoo-owning family's emigration from India to Canada. Stuck on a lifeboat with a Bengal tiger, he tames his inner demons—and the tiger—over 227 days at sea. Shipwreck survivor Steve Callahan, who was adrift for more than two months in the 1980s, served as an advisor on the movie.

Girl Versus Shark

THIRTEEN-YEAR-OLD BETHANY HAMILTON WAS ON TRACK TO BE A WORLD-CLASS SURFER—AND SHE WASN'T ABOUT TO LET ANYTHING GET IN THE WAY OF THAT.

STRIKING DISTANCE

According to Oceana, an international conservation organization, the risk of a fatal shark attack is extremely small.

→ Number of shark attacks in the U.S. between 2006 and 2010: **179**

→ Number of shark-related fatalities during those years: **3**

→ Number of people who need to be rescued from surfing accidents annually: **30,000**

→ Depth of water for the majority of unprovoked shark attacks: **1 to 3 feet**

It was like the opening scene in a horror movie. In October 2003, Bethany Hamilton, 13, was with her best friend, Alana Blanchard, and Alana's father and brother in Kauai, Hawaii. All four were relaxing on their surfboards in the sun, their limbs dangling in the water. Seemingly out of nowhere, a 14-foot tiger shark emerged from the deep, biting off Hamilton's left arm just below the shoulder and tearing a wide gash in her surfboard.

The Blanchards knew they had to act quickly. They helped Hamilton back to shore and then used a surfboard leash as a tourniquet around what was left of her arm. By the time she arrived at the hospital, the young surfer had lost 60 percent of her blood and was in shock.

But Hamilton was a fighter. After a series of surgeries without infection, she made a full recovery. In spite of an understandable fear of sharks, within a month of the attack she was back on her board, teaching herself to surf "single-handedly." In January 2004, only three months after the incident, she entered a major competition, placing fifth.

For Hamilton, who was born into a family of surfers and who had been competing since she was eight years old, returning to the ocean was almost a physical necessity. "All my friends surfed, and my whole family surfed," she said. "It was almost getting back to normal life."

Only a year after the attack, Hamilton took first place in a division of the 2005 National Scholastic Surfing Association championships. In 2007, she achieved her childhood dream of becoming a professional surfer, competing for cash prizes in numerous Association of Surfing Professionals events. "Make a plan to overcome that obstacle, a way to swim out of that current, a plan with all intention to reach your goals!" she told interviewers.

More recently, after Hamilton turned 25, she told an interviewer that she was less competitive than she had been in the past, but was "still driven to always get better and better at surfing." Her technique

WHO KNEW?
The broken surfboard that Bethany Hamilton was using during the shark attack is on display at the California Surf Museum in Oceanside, California.

Inspirational surfer Bethany Hamilton performs a cutback on a wave in California.

seemed to work: After not winning a competition for almost a decade, she placed first in the 2014 Surf-N-Sea Pipeline Women's Pro.

Soul Surfer

Hamilton has also become a media star. In 2004, she wrote about her experiences in *Soul Surfer: A True Story of Faith, Family, and Fighting to Get Back on the Board*. In 2011, *Soul Surfer*, a movie based on the book, was released. The film was a hit among audiences and grossed more than $45 million in box office tickets and almost $20 million in video sales.

In 2014 Hamilton wrote *Body and Soul*, a fitness guide for teenage girls to encourage them make healthy decisions, get active, and find the things that they have fun doing.

"We all go through rough times. We have those obstacles that seem too large to overcome or that current that you never seem to swim out of. We have to decide what matters most to us—our passions," she wrote.

Hamilton, 14, holds a copy of her book *Soul Surfer*.

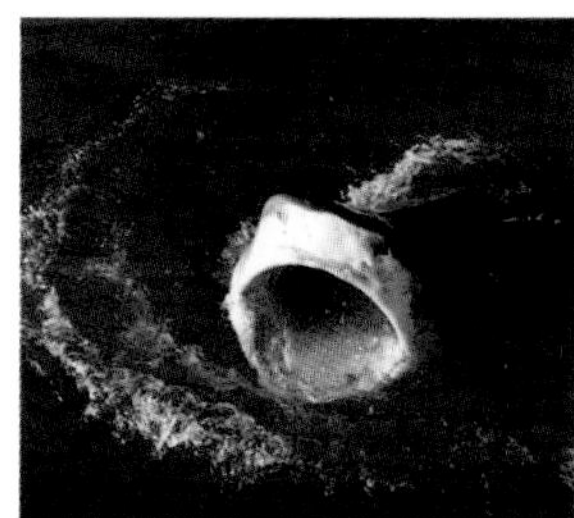

A tiger shark can saw easily through flesh, bone, and other tough material.

THE "GARBAGE EATERS"

Bethany Hamilton was bitten by a tiger shark, a predator with a reputation for devouring just about anything.

This "hyena of the sea" is often found close to the coast, mainly in tropical and subtropical waters. Its jaws are broad and powerful and its serrated teeth can saw easily through flesh, bone, and the shells of sea turtles. Hamilton's arm was removed so cleanly and with such precision that the operating doctor, upon first seeing the wound, thought someone had amputated her arm without his permission.

Tiger shark attacks are a relatively rare phenomenon around the world. For example, only about three occur each year in Hawaii. Most are not fatal. Like most sharks, the tiger shark has far more to fear from humans than vice versa. It is killed in large numbers for its fins, flesh, and liver, and is considered a near-threatened species.

Alone and Adrift

A ROUTINE SHARK-HUNTING EXPEDITION TURNED INTO A YEARLONG ODYSSEY AT SEA FOR A SOFT-SPOKEN MEXICAN FISHERMAN.

When José Salvador Alvarenga landed in the Marshall Islands in the northern Pacific Ocean in January 2014, he was weak and disoriented, wearing only rags. His shaggy hair had been bleached orange in the sun, and his beard was overgrown and unkempt. Unable to walk, he crawled up the beach toward a house, calling for help in his native Spanish. After a time, using hand gestures and drawings, he would share an incredible story: He had been adrift in the water, mostly alone, for more than a year.

Alvarenga's tale started in late December 2012. A soft-spoken professional fisherman in his mid-30s, Alvarenga had set out on a routine shark-hunting expedition from Tapachula, Mexico, with just one crew member, the 23-year-old Ezequiel Cordoba. It was meant to be a one-day trip. But after a few hours, the men's engine failed. Then strong winds blew the 24-foot vessel off course, leaving Alvarenga and Cordoba helplessly adrift.

OK, REALLY?

When Alvarenga was rescued, skeptics raised a number of doubts about his story. But experts responded with plausible explanations.

COULDN'T HAVE HAPPENED!	SURE IT COULD HAVE!
If he was so hungry, why wasn't he thinner when he finally washed ashore?	His internal organs were swollen, a result of long-term exposure to the elements.
Wouldn't he have scurvy? The disease, caused by a vitamin C deficiency, was common among sailors of yore who spent months at sea.	The meat of turtles and birds has enough natural vitamin C to stave off scurvy.
How could he get all the way from Mexico to the Marshall Islands in just 13 months?	Ocean currents could have carried him there in that amount of time.

Survival Skills

Hours turned into days, and days turned into weeks. Alvarenga and Cordoba had no emergency rations and had to eat what they caught: fish, birds, and sea turtles. They collected rainwater to drink, but when there was no rain they were forced to drink their own urine.

After some weeks, it was clear that Cordoba was in trouble. "He couldn't keep the raw food down," said Alvarenga, who held his own nose in order to stomach the uncooked meat. He coaxed his companion to do the same, but to no avail. The young Mexican died of starvation, and Alvarenga had to push his body overboard.

Eventually, Alvarenga gave up trying to keep track of time. He contemplated suicide, but said he was too afraid to go through with it. He thought about his parents and fantasized about his favorite foods. He thought about God, and prayed. In late January 2014, those prayers were answered: His boat washed up on an atoll in the Marshall Islands.

Alvarenga was reunited with his mother, father, and teenage daughter in his native El Salvador in early February. In March, he traveled to visit Cordoba's family in Mexico; the two had vowed that if either of them survived, he would tell the other's loved ones what had happened.

Far from reveling in the limelight, Alvarenga insisted that he wanted to stop talking and thinking about his ordeal and wished the media would leave him alone. The stress of his months on the water and the constant specter of death had taken its toll, and he had developed a phobia of the sea.

"He does not want to hear about the ocean," his doctor in El Salvador told reporters a couple of weeks after his rescue. "His symptoms are truly post-traumatic."

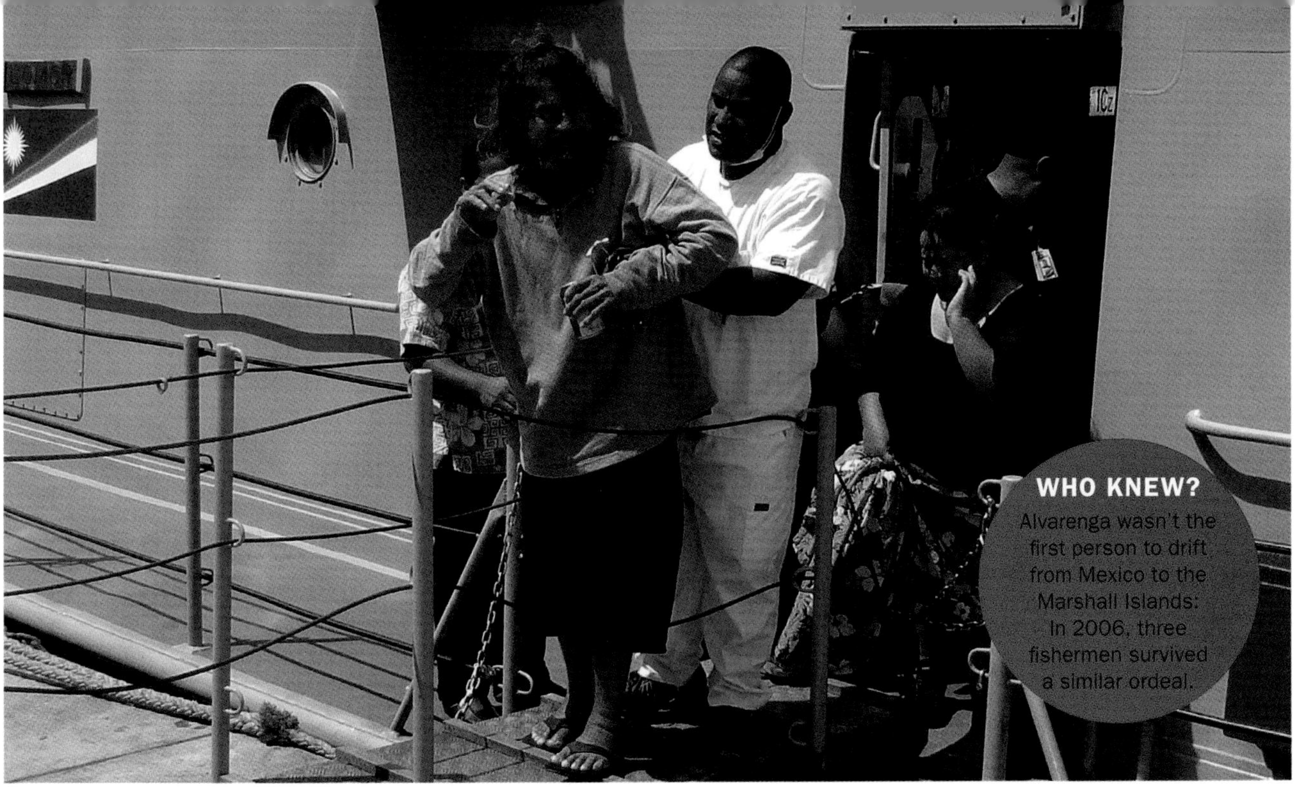

WHO KNEW?
Alvarenga wasn't the first person to drift from Mexico to the Marshall Islands: In 2006, three fishermen survived a similar ordeal.

Jose Salvador Alvarenga walks with the help of a Majuro Hospital nurse in Majuro after a 22-hour boat ride from isolated Ebon Atoll on February 3, 2014.

SMALL VESSEL, BIG OCEAN

The approximately 6,000 miles Alvarenga traveled from the southwest coast of Mexico to the Marshall Islands is almost twice the length of the United States from Maine to California. He made the journey across open water in a boat that was smaller than a school bus.

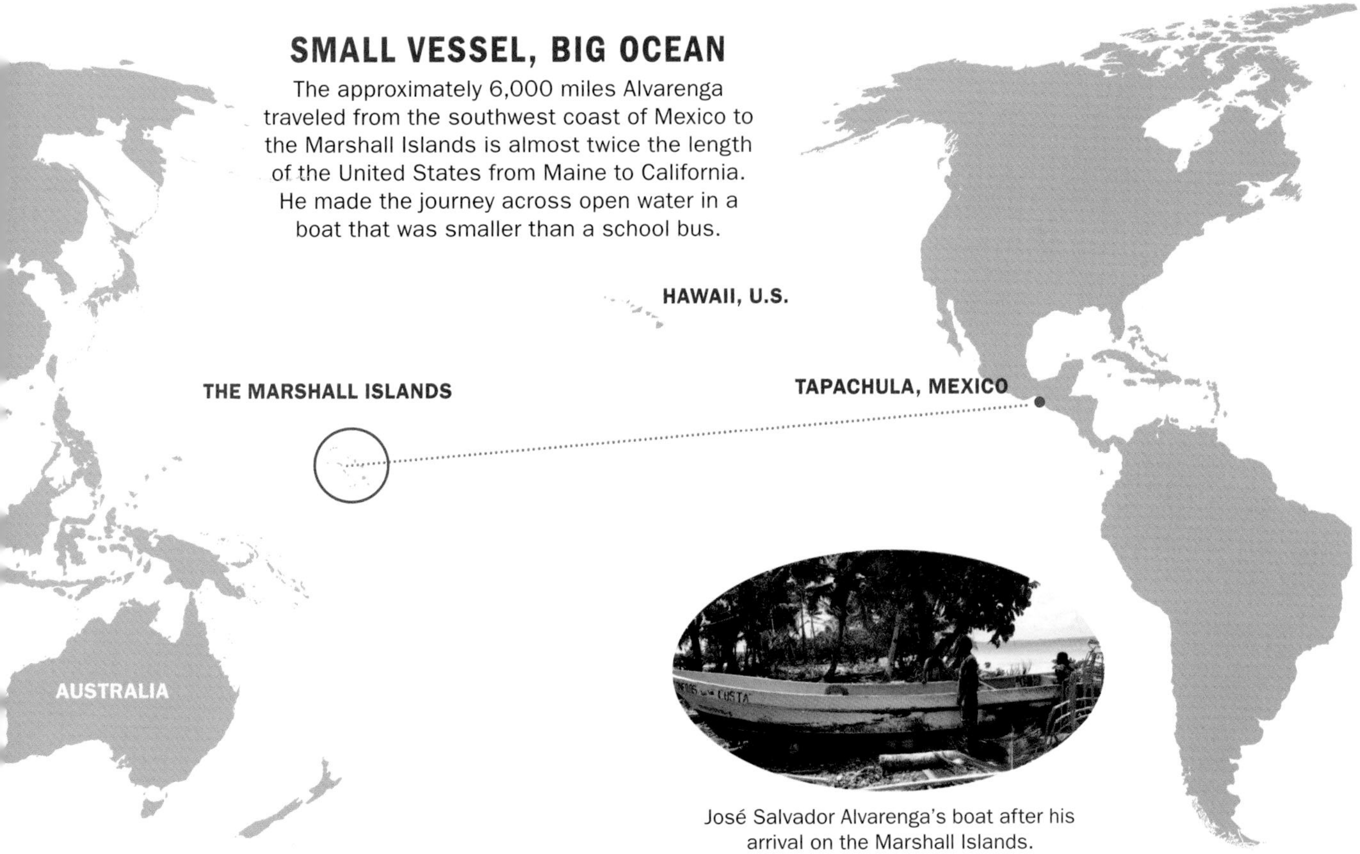

José Salvador Alvarenga's boat after his arrival on the Marshall Islands.

In Deep Water

TRAPPED INSIDE A SUNKEN TUGBOAT, HARRISON OKENE SURVIVED THREE DAYS AT THE BOTTOM OF THE ATLANTIC OCEAN.

Harrison Okene was the only survivor in a crew of 12 on the tugboat *Jascon 4*.

He prayed for a miracle. He recited a psalm. He bargained. "When I was under the water," Harrison Okene later told the *Associated Press*, "I told God, 'If you rescue me, I will never go back to the sea again, never.' " On the third day, just as Okene, a 29-year-old tugboat cook, had given up hope and accepted that he would die, the miracle happened.

Few experiences sound as terrifying as being trapped in chest-high water in a sunken boat 100 feet below the surface of the ocean. But that's exactly what happened to Okene in May 2013.

His ordeal began in the Atlantic about 20 miles off the coast of Nigeria, as the tugboat he worked on was towing an oil tanker. At 4:30 AM Okene was awake and preparing to start the day when the tug lurched and suddenly capsized, tossing Okene across the cabin. As the boat went dark and sank, Okene was able to collect a life vest, a few tools, and flashlights. He waited inside a tiny compartment, shutting the door and perching on a pile of mattresses to stay above the rising water. He had already spotted the bodies of three of his fellow crewmembers.

Dwindling Hope

Alone in the dark, half-submerged in freezing water, Okene thought about his 27-year-old wife and prayed repeatedly; memories of his dead colleagues filled his head and he worried about the rest of the 12-man crew. He lost his sense of time. Eventually, the young cook heard an engine and the sound of a dropping anchor nearby, but he was sure the rescuers wouldn't know to look for him. When a diver entered his compartment, Okene had to swim over, tap the man, and grab his hand to get his attention. The startled emergency worker called, "He's alive! He's alive! He's alive!" Okene was the only member of the crew to survive.

Seven months later, Okene was still feeling the effects of his experience, waking from nightmares in which he was back in the sinking tugboat. He wondered why he was the only one of his friends to make it out alive. "Why me?" he asked. "Why did my colleagues have to die?"

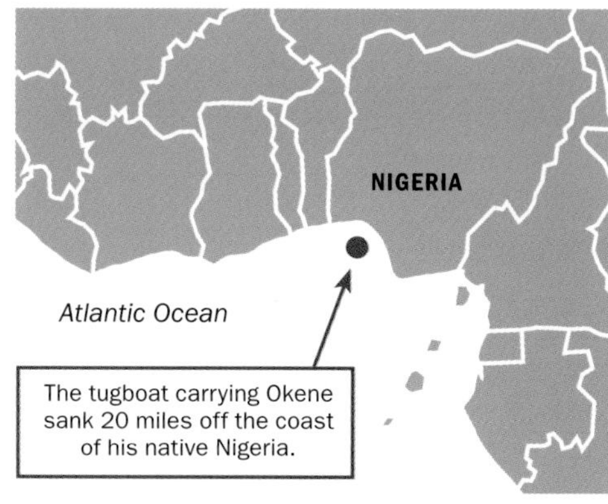

The tugboat carrying Okene sank 20 miles off the coast of his native Nigeria.

WHO KNEW?
The United States Coast Guard has saved more than one million lives since its formation in 1790.

Those who survive being stranded at sea often suffer from dehydration, but drinking salt water can be fatal.

Water, Water Everywhere

Survivors at sea overcome attacks by jellyfish and sharks, dehydration, and hallucinations.

HEATHER BARNES, 2013 **16 HOURS**

In July 2013, **Heather Barnes,** a 20-year-old marine biology major, was vacationing in Honduras when she went snorkeling by herself one morning. After a bout of stomach and leg cramps, Barnes was carried out to the open ocean by a strong current. At first she thought she should remain in place. But after two hours of treading water, Barnes opted to try and swim back to the resort on Cayo Grande, where she and her friends were staying. After 16 hours, Barnes made land at another spot on the island, Lion's Head, where she was found by locals.

BRETT ARCHIBALD, 2013 **27 HOURS**

Brett Archibald, a South African surfer, was on an Indonesian tour boat to the Mentawai Islands in April 2013 when the water got choppy and he leaned over the water to be sick. Archibald believes he passed out and fell overboard, coming to from water splashing on his face. He had no life jacket and was besieged by jellyfish, pecking seagulls, and a circling shark. As Archibald treaded water and floated for 27 hours, he was sustained by thoughts of his wife and two young children. He was rescued by a cruise boat that had joined search efforts.

RICHARD NEELY AND ALLYSON DALTON, 2008 **19 HOURS**

British dive instructor **Richard Neely** and American pub owner **Allyson Dalton** were on a diving trip along Australia's Great Barrier Reef in May 2008 when they came up from a routine dive and found themselves 200 yards from the tour boat. No one noticed the two were missing, and they were left adrift in the waters off the Great Barrier Reef. To stay warm, Neely and Dalton strapped themselves together with their weight belts and a rope from a buoy, which may well have saved their lives until a rescue helicopter finally spotted them after they had been in the water for 19 hours.

Man Overboard!

A COOL HEAD AND A PAIR OF GREEN RUBBER BOOTS TURNED TRAGEDY TO TRIUMPH FOR A FISHERMAN WHO LOST HIS FOOTING ON A DARK NIGHT AT SEA.

What does it take to survive 12 hours adrift in the Atlantic Ocean? For Montauk, New York, lobsterman John Aldridge, the answer was close at hand.

On July 24, 2013, Aldridge was nearing the end of an 18-hour workday on his boat, the *Anna Mary*, while his fishing partner, Anthony Sosinski, slept below. At about 3:30 AM, as Aldridge was working on deck, a piece of equipment malfunctioned, knocking him off balance and over the edge of the boat. The 45-year-old resurfaced just in time to see the boat speeding away from him on autopilot. He was 40 miles offshore.

When Sosinski awoke to find the boat empty, he sent out a man-overboard SOS. But Aldridge had been in the water for nearly three hours at that point, and the Coast Guard faced a 60-mile search radius. The prospect of locating a lone man in the roiling expanse was a daunting one.

"Death was not an option."

Aldridge was a fisherman with two decades of experience; he knew that the odds were against him and that survival depended on a clear mind, quick action, and perhaps a small miracle. As he later told *CBS News*, "[It was] positive thinking the whole time. Death was not an option."

Aldridge's miracle came in the unlikely form of his favorite fishing boots.

SEARCHING THE WRONG SEA

John Aldridge's rescue required the perfect combination of cutting-edge technology and human ingenuity.

When the Montauk Coast Guard team responded to Anthony Sosinski's SOS, it relied on a state-of-the-art computer program known as Sarops, which uses currents and wind measurements to identify a likely search zone.

The challenge in the case was that it was unclear when and where Aldridge had gone overboard. All the team knew was that Aldridge was supposed to have woken Sosinski at 11:30 PM. Based on that piece of information, the drift analysis generated by Sarops suggested sending rescue crews to a radius 30 miles north of where Aldridge was actually afloat on his boots. Instead, veteran search-and-rescue coordinator Pete Winters followed his instincts and reasoned that the lobsterman might have chosen to finish the night's work on his own. Operating under the assumption that Aldridge fell overboard early in the morning, Sarops redrew the search zone and ended up much closer to the correct location.

But in the end, it wasn't intuition or technology but chance that saved the day: A helicopter crew veered slightly outside the Sarops grid to maximize their final fuel time, and spotted Aldridge just before heading back to their base.

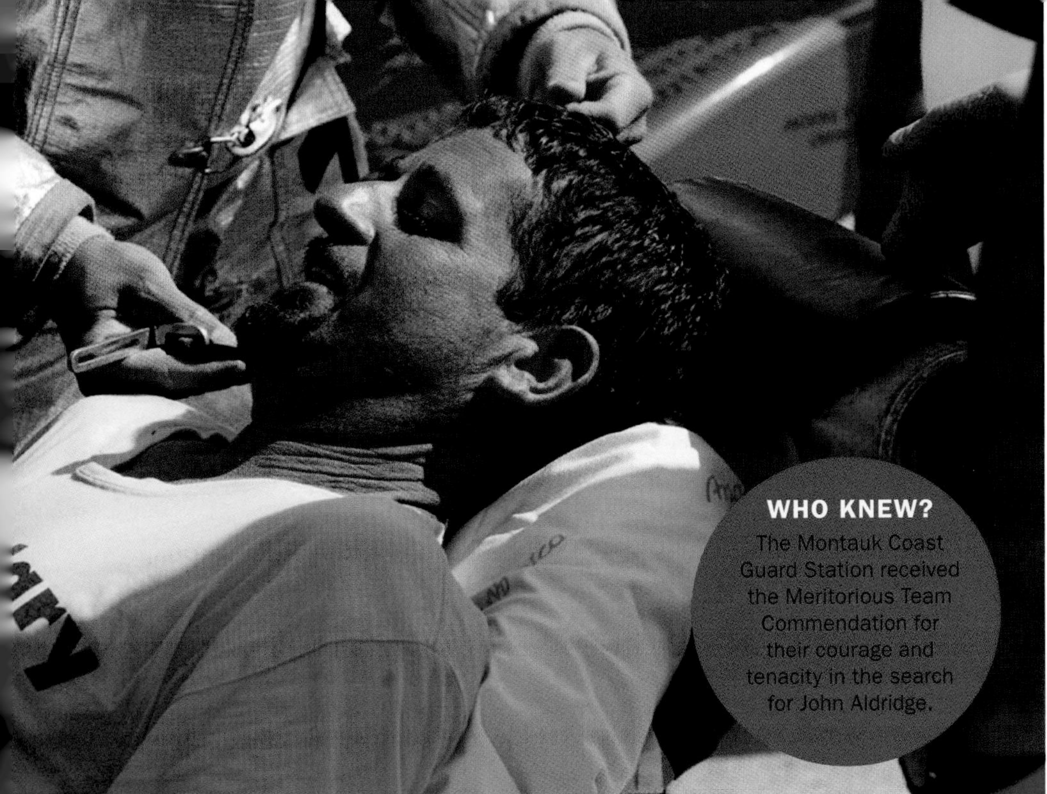

WHO KNEW? The Montauk Coast Guard Station received the Meritorious Team Commendation for their courage and tenacity in the search for John Aldridge.

Lobsterman John Aldridge lies on a stretcher after being rescued by a Coast Guard helicopter.

Designed to withstand subzero temperatures, the green rubber footwear was sturdy, well-insulated, and had prompted many a ribbing from Aldridge's fellow seamen. Now, as he treaded water, Aldridge noticed that the boots were pulling his feet up to the surface. He tugged first one and then the other boot off and plunged them upside down into the water, trapping air inside to maximize buoyancy. He then hooked his arms over the boots as if they were crutches and—sure enough—they helped him stay afloat.

John Aldridge holding one of his fishing boots. His father got a tattoo of the green boots and the GPS coordinates where John was found.

Dawn brought a welcome sight: a line of lobster trap buoys. Still hugging the boots under his arms, Aldridge paddled through a mile of ocean swells to reach the buoys. He secured himself to one of them with a fisherman's knot and for the next several hours fought exhaustion, sunburn, and panic about the ominous fins circling nearby.

Around midafternoon, as a helicopter search crew made its final sweep of the day, rescuers spotted John bobbing in the waves. "It was pretty miraculous that we found him," Coast Guard Officer Erik Swanson told the *New York Daily News*. Aldridge had survived 12 hours alone in the ocean. As he was lifted toward the helicopter in a rescue basket, the fisherman made sure to hold onto his boots as well.

After treatment for hypothermia and exposure, Aldridge returned to fishing, continuing to wear his green rubber miracles on his feet.

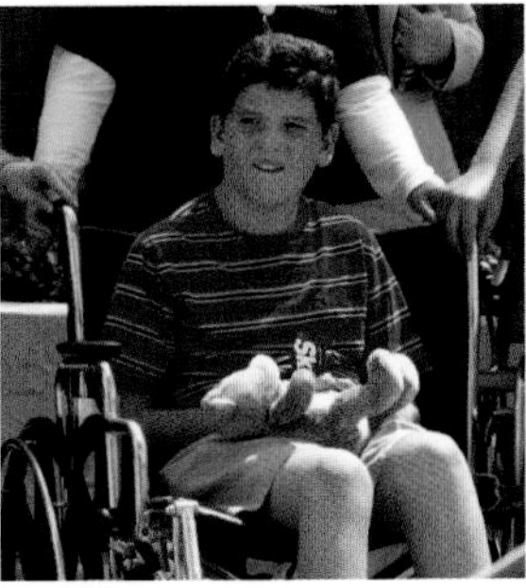

Chris Marino, 12, is released from Halifax Medical Center in Daytona Beach, Florida.

PLUCKED FROM THE WAVES

A number of people thrown into open waters have survived through ingenuity and luck.

→ **2008** Walter Marino and his son Christopher were enjoying the water in an inlet near Daytona Beach, Florida, when a riptide towed the autistic 12-year-old out to sea. Walter swam after the boy but was also caught by the power of the ocean, and the two were swept into the Atlantic. Things got worse in the middle of the night, when waves pulled the Marinos apart. After the pair were rescued by fishermen and the Coast Guard, Marino told CNN his son's attitude is what made the difference between life and death. "It was a big entertainment roller coaster for him, that's what got me through it—because he wasn't freaking out," Marino said.

→ **1982** American naval architect Steven Callahan survived 76 days alone in a life raft after his sailboat sank during a voyage from England to Antigua. He later said he was able to stay alive by maintaining normal sailing routines such as exercise and navigation drills.

The devastated island of Bhola, in Banladesh, after a cyclone and tidal waves struck the area in November 1970

CHAPTER 14

Coming Through Disaster

They are the lucky ones, the brave and resilient survivors of Mother Nature's wrath and man-made mayhem. How did they do it?

Under the Volcano

WHEN THE LONG-DORMANT MOUNT ST. HELENS ERUPTED IN 1980, IT RAINED DOWN BOULDERS AND ASH.

WHO KNEW?
In all, Mount St. Helens ejected some 540 million tons of ash. Its 9,677-foot peak was replaced by an 8,363-foot-high crater.

On the morning of May 18, 1980, Bruce Nelson and Sue Ruff, two 22-year-olds from Kelso, Washington, were enjoying a camping and fishing getaway with four friends along the Green River. As the couple began quietly toasting breakfast marshmallows, Mount St. Helens, 14 miles away, was exploding into life. The eruption and earthquakes associated with it would quickly trigger the largest landslide in U.S. history. The mountain's weakened north flank was dislodged, and a wave of earth and ice, tumbling at speeds reaching 180 miles per hour, was set in motion. By the time the landslide came to a halt several hours later, it had demolished 24 square miles of forest and taken the lives of 57 people and thousands of animals, most of whom suffocated on hot ash.

Protected

Nelson, Ruff, and their friends remained oblivious as the deadly surge neared the Green River campsite. There were no rumblings, no warning signs at all that a cloud of landslide debris was fast approaching. "The cloud was so dense with sand and debris that it absorbed all the sound," geologist Richard Waitt later explained. In a whoosh, the gritty gusts knocked the couple into a deep, dark hole created when two huge trees were ripped from the ground. While waves of red-hot lava rushed overhead, Nelson and Ruff crouched in the hole, terrified but miraculously protected from the volcanic expulsion. They emerged a short time later, unharmed except for singed hair. Debris and huge ice chunks rained down from above.

Two hours later, as Nelson and Ruff searched for their friends, they heard the cries of Brian Thomas, 22, and Dan Balch, 20, whom they found lodged on top of a pile of debris. Thomas had been hit by a tree and had a broken hip, while ash, mud, and ice had pinned Balch flat as the heat blast melted the skin off his arms and hands. He had crawled into a muddy river to seek relief. There were no signs of the other two campers, Terry Crall and Karen Varner. Nelson and Ruff carried Thomas to a ruined cabin, walked Balch back to the river, then began wading through knee-deep hot ash to find assistance.

Rescue

As night fell, rescuers in emergency helicopters saw and evacuated the exhausted couple, who helped them find Thomas. The severely burned Balch hiked out on his own, mostly barefoot, over the next 11 hours. On May 23, Nelson insisted on returning to the camp with authorities to look for Crall and Varner, who were still missing. Their corpses were discovered in their tent, Crall's arm encircling Varner.

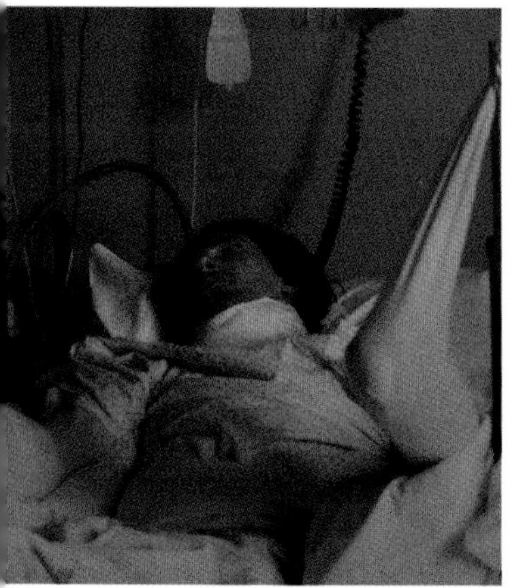

Camper Dan Balch was badly burned, but hiked to safety.

The eruption of Mount St. Helens, viewed from West Point Peak, Washington, on May 18, 1980

WARNING SIGNS

Starting in 1978, a series of increasingly frequent earthquakes suggested the disaster to come.

Before Mount St. Helens, in Washington's Cascade range, erupted in May 1980, it had been dormant since 1857. But that didn't mean the volcano was wasn't explosive. In 1978, U.S. Geological Survey scientists issued a report identifying increasing activity over four-and-a-half millennia.

Mid-March 1980 geologists recorded 100 earthquakes.

March 25 After five strong quakes occurred in an hour and a large snow fissure appeared, Forest Service officials limited mountain access and the Federal Aviation Administration restricted flights over the area.

March 27 a magnitude 4.7 earthquake spewed a 7,000-foot-tall black plume, creating a 200-foot-wide crater. Loggers, forest employees, residents, and campers within a 1.5-mile radius were evacuated.

March 30 Ninety-three explosions occurred.

March 31 Officials declared a state of emergency, although some local cabin owners complained the government was exaggerating.

April 1 Steam-and-ash plumes reached 20,000 feet.

Mid-April Scientists observed a bulge on the peak's north flank.

May 18 A lateral blast reached 660°F, spewing superheated ash clouds and stone at least 300 miles per hour for some 15 miles. Central Montana, to the east, was hit with a 16-mile-high gas-and-ash column. Spokane, about 250 miles northeast, was shrouded in darkness as ash filled the sky. Some 200 square miles of trees were flattened.

Professor Stanley Williams

IN THE BELLY OF THE BEAST

A professor studying a volcano in Colombia lived through a horrific eruption.

In 1993, Arizona State University volcanology professor Stanley Williams and an international team of scientists were inside the 14,029-foot-high Galeras Volcano, above Pasto, a 16th-century city in Nariño, Colombia. Their expedition was part of a decade-long effort to pinpoint signs of impending explosions at the world's most dangerous peaks.

Recent tremors and gaseous emissions had subsided, and the group mistakenly assumed the dangerous giant was sleeping. Suddenly, the ground trembled violently, and the volcano exploded. Boulders crushed Williams's legs and fractured his skull. Hot gases burned his body extensively. Williams dragged himself out of the crater, crawled down the mountainside, and sought shelter from the fiery debris behind a large rock. His six colleagues and three tourists died.

After recovering, Williams continued his work collecting data in the mouths of volcanoes. His goal is to help geologists predict eruptions the way meteorologists forecast weather.

Crushing Snow, Soaring Spirit

THE LONE SURVIVOR OF AN ALASKAN AVALANCHE CREDITS BLIND FAITH AND DETERMINATION WITH KEEPING HIM ALIVE.

AVALANCHE TIMES TWO

Ken Jones nearly died in the Transylvanian Alps. But after being told he'd never walk again, he went on to inspire others.

In January 2003, Ken Jones, a 26-year-old from Shropshire, England, was caught in two avalanches near the summit of Romania's Moldoveanu Peak. Hurled from a cliff, he regained consciousness in darkness, alone in the frozen wilderness with a broken leg and shattered pelvis. For four days, Jones, frostbitten and bleeding internally, limped and crawled for 10 miles to a village, where doctors saved his leg but predicted that he would be confined to a wheelchair for the rest of his life. Instead, Jones applied the same iron will that had saved his life to recuperating and learning to walk again. Today, he is an avid outdoorsman and motivational speaker. His company, Avalanche Endurance Events, trains aspirants to elite army branches. He published a memoir, *Darkness Descending*, in 2014.

Colby Coombs was just 18 years old when he first climbed Alaska's Mount McKinley, North America's highest peak, in 1985. The wilderness enthusiast had found his passion and soon began teaching mountaineering courses at Alaska's National Outdoor Leadership School.

Looking for a new challenge, Colby and his friends Ritt Kellogg and Tom Walter decided in June 1992 to attempt a steep new variation of the route up Mount Foraker, the state's second highest peak, just southwest of McKinley. On day three of the expedition, the trio had neared the summit when a storm gathered, compromising their visibility. They initially attempted to reverse course and descend, but were unable to navigate the porous ice. With no other option, the trio tied themselves together and continued the climb up the 50-degree slope.

Suddenly Coombs's rope went slack. He glanced up just as an avalanche propelled the three men 800 feet down the mountainside.

When Coombs regained consciousness six hours later, it was morning. He was dangling from his rope near the top of a rock buttress, wracked with excruciating pain and freezing, his pack and gloves gone. He later learned he had a concussion, two fractured neck vertebrae, a broken shoulder blade, and a fractured ankle. Walter's body dangled lifelessly on the other end of the rope, an eerie counterweight, his face a frozen mask of snow. The rope to Kellogg was limp.

Devastated, Coombs crawled to a small ledge and fell into a fitful sleep, still wearing his shattered helmet. After waking, he rappelled down and found Kellogg's dead body, the rope still encircling it.

"I just had to keep my eyes open and ignore the pain."

Perilous Descent

Emotionally and physically numb but determined to return to the base camp, Coombs assembled the gear and food he needed. Over the next four days, he painstakingly picked his way down the mountain's face, dragging his fractured foot behind. His badly frayed rope kept catching on rocks. He encountered a steep snowfield and was forced to alter his course. He later said that he survived by summoning an "unstoppable mentality" and drawing on a deep well of faith: "I just had to keep my eyes open and ignore

WHO KNEW?

A slab avalanche carries torrents of snow at speeds of up to 80 miles per hour and can destroy forests and small villages.

At least 45 climbers have died in avalanches in Denali National Park in Alaska.

the pain." After finally reaching base, Coombs navigated another perilous five miles across the gaping crevasses of Kahiltna Glacier, then finally stumbled onto an airstrip camp.

In the search that followed, aerial recovery teams located Walter's icepick near the ridgetop, but neither Walter nor Kellogg's bodies were ever recovered. After surgery, Coombs spent three months in a wheelchair. He then graduated to crutches and after another three months, took his first unassisted step.

A Career Devoted to Climbing Safety

Undaunted by his near-death experience, Coombs guided his first McKinley climb the following year. He and his wife, Caitlin Palmer, founded Alaska Mountaineering School in Talkeetna, in 1996, guiding climbs emphasizing safety. The following year, he published an account of his experiences.

"If you do get in trouble, anything that gets in the way of success has to be eliminated—emotion, fear, pain... will impede your survival," said Coombs.

A digital avalanche beacon can help find people or equipment buried under snow.

WHAT TO DO

Avalanches kill about 150 people annually in North America and Europe. Remaining calm and taking quick action can help prevent calamity.

➔ Carry a snow shovel, a beacon to connect to others in your party, and a high-tech probe to find victims and dig lifesaving air holes.

➔ Thrash your arms and legs, or "swim," to stay on top of sliding snow.

➔ Create an air pocket in front of your face with your hand, so you can breathe until help comes.

➔ If you've lost your sense of direction, spit. Gravity will show you which way to dig.

➔ Wear a helmet. Roughly one-third of avalanche fatalities are caused by head trauma.

➔ If traveling with others in an avalanche-prone area, allow some space between each person. If sudden disaster occurs, those unaffected can guide rescuers to victims.

The wreckage of the Alfred P. Murrah Federal Building

OK in Oklahoma

THE YOUNGEST SURVIVORS OF THE AMERICA'S WORST ACT OF DOMESTIC TERRORISM BROUGHT HOPE TO OKLAHOMA CITY— AND THE WHOLE COUNTRY.

At 9:02 AM on April 19, 1995, militia movement sympathizer and Gulf War veteran Timothy McVeigh detonated a truck bomb that tore through the Alfred P. Murrah Federal Building in Oklahoma City, Oklahoma. It was the deadliest act of terrorism on U.S. soil prior to the September 11 attacks. It took the lives of 168 people, including 19 children who attended the same second-floor daycare center, and injured over 600. Miraculously, six little ones who attended America's Kids Daycare survived the bombing.

P.J. Allen

When the 5,000-pound bomb went off, 18-month-old P.J. Allen was thrown dozens of feet from the burning building. He had burns over 55 percent of his body, a ruptured eardrum, a fractured arm, and badly damaged lungs from inhaling the fiery smoke. But it never occurred to his family that the toddler would not pull through the ordeal. "It was a grueling time," said relative Lois Felder-Jones. "We held the family together by praying."

Nearly 20 years after the bombing, Allen was a student at Oklahoma State University. Though his weakened lungs prevent him from competing in sports and the smoke damage affects the way he speaks, P.J. has said that he has never asked, *Why me?* "because this to me this to me is normal. As far as I can remember, this has been what my life is like." In the years after the explosion, Allen "felt as though God was watching over me, and that he kept me alive for a special purpose. I myself don't know what that is yet," Allen told his college newspaper in 2014.

Brandon and Rebecca Denny

For Jim Denny, having two children survive the bombing was like winning the lottery five days in a row. His daughter, Rebecca was just two, and son Brandon was three. Both were seriously wounded in the attack, especially Brandon. He sustained a life-threatening brain injuries that required four major surgeries, and it was feared he would never be able to walk or talk again. In the years since, Brandon

Timothy McVeigh (in orange) after being charged in the bombing of the Alfred P. Murrah Federal Building

P.J. Allen (left), Rebecca Denny (second from left), Brandon Denny, and Christopher Nguyen (right), survivors of the 1995 bombing of the Alfred P. Murrah Federal Building. Together they read the Oklahoma City National Memorial mission statement in 2005.

P.J. Allen (left), Brandon Denny (standing left), Christopher Nguyen, Nekia McCloud (standing right), Rebecca Denny (front), and Joe Webber (right), 2005.

has suffered seizures and has been through extensive speech and physical therapies, eventually regaining the use of his legs and voice.

Both Rebecca and Brandon graduated from high school in 2011. Rebecca went on to study psychology at Oklahoma State, while Brandon took a part-time job at a thrift store. "You have to go into every day knowing that those other people didn't make it. You have to go into every day knowing that you have to do the best with what you have because they don't have it," Rebecca told an interviewer in 2011.

Christopher Nguyen

Four years old the day of the blast, Christopher Nguyen was one of the oldest of the child survivors. He had been inside a bathroom when the bomb exploded, and he suffered a broken jaw, internal bruising, and cuts and burns all over his body. His father, Thu Nguyen, was sure his son had been killed in the blast, and didn't see him until he had been admitted to the hospital. "It's just really something of a miracle and we couldn't explain that. Nobody can," said Thu. "I never forget that day—that feeling of a father, helpless."

Though Christopher struggled with regular nightmares for a few years after the bombing, today he has no memory of the event. "I didn't let the bombing control me," he said in 2010. "It is a part of me... but it doesn't control who I am." In 2012, Christopher graduated from the University of Oklahoma Price College of Business with a degree in marketing and finance.

Nekia McCloud

Nekia McCloud, also four years old at the time of the attack, suffered ruptured eardrums, a broken leg, a skull fracture, and brain trauma so severe she had to relearn to walk and talk. Her mother has shielded her from the media over the years, focusing instead on living as normal a life as possible. The family has not attended anniversary ceremonies, and they try not to talk about the bombing. "We try to get on with our lives. How are you going to forget if they keep bringing it up?" Lavern McCloud said in 2001.

Joseph Webber

Eighteen-month-old Joseph Webber wasn't breathing when Oklahoma City Police Inspector Don Hull came upon his body amid the rubble and repeatedly performed CPR to get him breathing again. When doctors examined the toddler, they found he had two ruptured eardrums, a broken jaw and arm, and a concussion.

Today, Webber has no memory of the event, which left him with a long scar reaching from his left eye to his jawbone. "I'm glad I don't remember it," he has said. Webber graduated from Oklahoma City's Bishop McGuinness High School in 2012 and enrolled at Oklahoma State.

"A LIVE ONE"

A 15-year-old rescued 12 hours after the blast was the last person to be pulled from the rubble of the federal building alive.

At around 7 PM the night of the bombing, when almost all signs of life had faded, a firefighter exclaimed, "We've got a live one!"

A member of Search and Rescue Dogs of Oklahoma had discovered 15-year-old Brandy Liggons, a student who had been visiting the Social Security offices when the fertilizer-and-fuel bomb hit. She was completely covered in rubble, twisted metal framing, and thick electrical conduit. Liggons seemed to be wrapped around a metal chair, said Rick Nelson, a surgeon from Muskogee, Oklahoma, who was volunteering in the rescue effort. The process of extricating her was "like pick-up sticks," he said. "If you moved one piece the wrong way the whole thing could come crashing down."

Nelson held Liggons' hand, administered oxygen, and talked with her throughout her rescue, which took 3 hours. "I told her she was being treated by the best-looking surgeon in Oklahoma—stuff like that," said Nelson, who later started a trust fund for Liggons. "That girl's a miracle."

Mary Liggons sits at the bedside of her 15-year-old daughter, Brandy, the last survivor pulled from the wreckage of the terrorist-bombed Alfred P. Murrah Federal Building, in ICU at Children's Hospital, on April 22, 1995.

The remains of the YMCA behind a field of grass where the Murrah Federal Building once stood.

CLOSE CALL

A nearby YMCA daycare center was also damaged in the blast, but all of the 52 children and nine staff members lived.

More than 300 buildings were damaged when Timothy McVeigh detonated his bomb in 1995, including an adjacent YMCA that also housed a daycare center. "It was really terrible," recalled state representative Kevin Cox, who was half a block away when the bomb went off, "Babies were crying and screaming, with blood and plaster and insulation on their bodies." Jordan Matli was only three years old at the time, but she remembers it vividly: "At first there was a huge boom sound and parts of the ceiling fell in. There were kids screaming and glass shattering." Luckily, everyone was inside when the blast occurred. "If [the teacher] had taken them outside, there would have been fatalities," said Betty Morrow, mother of two children who were at the YMCA daycare that day.

WHO KNEW?

Banker Stanley Praimnath, whose South Tower office was on the 81st floor, saw United Airlines flight 175 coming toward him as it crashed between the 77th and 85th floors. The tower fell five minutes after he got out.

Hijacked United Airlines flight 175 from Boston crashes into the South Tower of the World Trade Center and explodes at 9:03 AM on September 11, 2001, in New York City.

The Heart of the Towers

AS THE WORLD TRADE CENTER COLLAPSED AROUND THEM, A GROUP OF RESCUERS MADE A NOBLE AND LUCKY CHOICE.

By 9:10 AM, September 11, 2001, seven minutes after the second plane hit the World Trade Center, fire chiefs were directing operations from the lobby of the North Tower. Captain John Jonas of Ladder Six in Chinatown received his orders, and they sounded dire: "Boys, they're trying to kill us. Let's go." The squad of firemen headed up into the North Tower via Stairwell B, located in the center of the structure, against droves of evacuating people coming down the stairs.

Stopping to Help

At 9:59 AM, there was a thunderous sound. The North Tower shook and the lights flickered; it was the South Tower, which had been hit first, collapsing. Having made it up as far as the 27th floor, Captain Jonas ordered his men to evacuate, barking: "If that one can go, this one can go." But the men couldn't quite follow his orders. At around the 20th floor, the rescuers came upon Josephine Harris, 59, a Port Authority bookkeeper who had limped down from the 73rd floor. They couldn't leave her. Billy Butler, Ladder Six's strong man, began helping Harris

New York firefighters, from left, Matt Komorowski, Billy Butler, John Jonas, and Sal D'Agostino, survived the collapse inside a stairwell.

A firefighter walks through the rubble of the World Trade Center after it was struck.

navigate the stairs, and the crew's pace slowed until the fifth floor, when the bookkeeper stopped, exhausted. Port Authority canine officer David Lim, also working his way to the street, soon came upon the group and offered to help carry Harris down to the next floor.

"No one realizes about the wind."

The first thing the group felt was the gale-force rush of air coming down the stairwell. The North Tower was collapsing above them, one floor into another, getting louder as it got closer. Fireman Matt Komorowksi was blown right over Lim, who fell next to Harris, who clung to Butler's boot. Below them were Battalion Chief Richie Picciotto, covered in debris, lieutenant Mickey Kross, stuck alone on a broken ledge, and lieutenant Jim McGlynn, with a few from his crew.

The men sounded off one by one, acknowledging they were alive. "The

THE EXTRA MAN

One firefighter will be forever grateful for a last-minute assignment.

On the morning of the September 11 attacks, Bronx firefighter Steve Sullivan received a call to cover for a member of Squad 288 in Queens. As Sullivan drove to the assignment listening to the radio, the music was interrupted by reports that a plane had hit one of the World Trade Center towers. Unable to reach his own squadron, Sullivan continued to Squad 288, but the crew he had been assigned to had already left. He rode into Manhattan instead with other 288 firefighters who arrived after the collapse of the second tower. All of the men from his Bronx firehouse died that day, as did all of the first crew from Squad 288, except for the man Sullivan was sent to cover. "It has always been some consolation to me that he did not die waiting for me to arrive. I still can't believe what happened that day. I am so grateful," said Sullivan.

tower came down like a peeling banana," Jonas later recalled. The exterior fell faster than the interior, leaving a stump in the middle surrounded by 16 acres of debris, with Harris and the men buried under the rubble.

After three hours, a ray of sunlight hit the floor inside as rescuers dislodged debris. "It was the most beautiful sight in the world," recalled Kross. The men made their way up the staircase, right out into the middle of the destruction, and a rescue team led by Lieutenant Glenn Rohan of Ladder 43 lifted out Harris and McGlynn's three men from Engine 39.

Later, the seven men would all credit Harris with saving their lives, for if they had moved any faster or slower, they certainly would not have made it out of the tower. "If she wasn't there, God knows where we would have been," Captain Jonas said.

WHO KNEW?

Ron DiFrancesco, a money-market broker, is the last known survivor to make it out of the South Tower. As he exited, a fireball hit him. He woke up in the hospital.

OTHER REMARKABLE TALES

How an engineer, a bank employee, a finance executive, and a policeman escaped the nightmare.

Pasquale Buzzelli

A 34-year-old structural engineer for the Port Authority, Buzelli took the stairs down from his office on the 64th floor of the North Tower. He was at the 22nd floor when the building shook and crashing sounds thundered above him. Buzzelli dove into a corner, and felt the walls crack and fall away. He woke up two hours later, seated on a hunk of concrete atop a pile of wreckage 180 feet farther down.

Tom Canavan

Taking the stairs down from his 47th-floor office at First Union Bank, Canavan had gotten as far as the lobby of the North Tower when the South Tower fell. Knocked down and covered by debris, he and another man managed to crawl through rubble in the dark for some 20 minutes until they found a small hole and pushed themselves out to freedom. Walking across wreckage that melted the soles of his shoes, he witnessed the fall of the North Tower just minutes later.

Lauren Manning

An executive at Cantor-Fitzgerald in the North Tower, Manning had just entered the lobby when the second plane struck. Burning jet fuel rushed down the elevator shaft and exploded out into the lobby, covering her in flames. She ran out to roll in the grass as a man pulled off his jacket and smothered the flames. With burns over 82 percent of her body, Manning endured a two-month medically induced coma and 25 skin graft surgeries.

Rich Jimeno

A police officer who volunteered for a North Tower rescue team, Jimeno was in the mall below the buildings when the South Tower fell. Pinned by a wall, he managed to survive through the collapse of the North Tower, too. At 10:30 PM—12 hours later—a Marine heard him banging on a pipe and appeared in a hole 20 feet above him. The rescue took three hours, plus another eight to free Sergeant John McLoughlin, the only other survivor from Jimeno's rescue team.

Lost, Then Found

IT TOOK 10 YEARS, BUT TRAGEDY TURNED TO JOY FOR ONE FAMILY DEVASTATED BY THE INDIAN OCEAN TSUNAMI.

WHO KNEW?
After the earthquake and tsunami, countries and humanitarian organizations worldwide donated a reported $14 billion to the region.

On December 26, 2004, a historic tsunami killed over a quarter of a million people in more than a dozen countries, including Indonesia, Sri Lanka, India, and Thailand. The Rangkuti family from the Indonesian province of Aceh, Sumatra, was just one of many to whom the unthinkable happened. As Septi Rangkuti watched helplessly, the tremendous wave swept his daughter Raudhatul Jannah, four, and her brother, Arif Pratama, seven, out to sea. When the water finally receded, Septi and his wife, Jamaliah, began the devastating task of searching for their children.

"We looked for them among piles of bodies, but we didn't find them," Septi told a German news service in 2014. "After one month we resigned ourselves to the thought that they had probably died."

But a decade later, something astonishing occurred. Raudhatul Jannah's uncle spotted a girl in a nearby village who bore a striking resemblance to his long-lost niece. Septi and Jamaliah paid a visit to the girl, by then 14, and knew immediately that she was their daughter. "God has given us a miracle," Jamaliah said.

The Rangkutis' tale has an even happier ending. After media reported the girl's reunion with her family, her brother, Arif Pratama, was also found. The boy, by then 17, had been homeless for many years. "It's true," Septi said, "he's our son."

Ten years after the 2004 Indian Ocean tsunami, Indonesian teenager Raudhatul Jannah (second from left) was reunited with her mother, Jamaliah (left); her father, Septi Rangkuti (right); and her younger brother in Banda Aceh.

Against All Odds

The Rangkutis were not the only family from Aceh with a miraculous survival tale in the wake of the tsunami, which followed the third largest earthquake ever recorded.

Among those who fought for their lives was Ari Afrizal, 21, who was working on a construction site when he was swept out to sea. He held on to debris for two weeks, subsisting on coconuts that floated by, and was on the verge of starvation when a passing boat rescued him. Rizal Shahputra, 23, also of Aceh, spent nine days at sea clinging to a floating tree branch before a container ship picked him up. An-

On the island of Sumatra in Indonesia, the area near the Baiturrahman mosque was devastated by the tsunami in 2004.

other survivor, a 23-year-old pregnant woman, persevered in the water for five days by clinging to a palm tree and eating its fruit and bark. She saw sharks all around her, but none attacked.

The Youngest Survivors

Even more inspiring are the children who lived, including Yeh Chia-ni, six, of Taiwan, who was flung into a coconut tree when the wave hit the Thai resort where she and her family were on holiday. The child hung on for 22 hours before she was rescued. An 18-month-old Swedish boy, deposited by the wave in a pile of rubble, was spotted by a Thai princess who had him airlifted to a hospital. The toddler was eventually reunited with his father. And Suppiah Tulasi was sleeping at her parents' restaurant on the Malaysian island of Penang when the wave struck. Her father later clawed his way back to the badly damaged building, where he found the 20-day-old infant alive on a mattress in five feet of water.

FOREWARNED IS FOREARMED

Recognizing natural cues helped these survivors save themselves—and those around them.

→ Ten-year-old Tilly Smith, who had just studied tsunamis during geography at school in England, was on the beach in Thailand with her family in 2004 when she recognized the warning signs: a receding ocean and frothing bubbles. According to Smith's mother, "She was screaming at us to get off the beach." The girl and her parents warned others, saving many lives.

→ John Chroston, a biology teacher visiting Thailand from Scotland, also recognized the tsunami warning signs. He persuaded the driver of a van to take his family and some others to higher ground, thereby saving the lives of his wife, 11-year-old daughter, and 15 other tourists.

→ On some Indonesian islands, tales of previous natural disasters passed down from earlier generations served as alerts. Many had heard that when the ground shakes and the water recedes, it's time to flee to higher ground. That is what they did on the Indonesian island of Simeulue, where the death toll was surprisingly low, even though the island was extremely close to the earthquake's epicenter.

WHO KNEW?
In Sri Lanka and Thailand, elephants ran for higher ground up to an hour before the tsunami hit.

The Day the Earth Shook

AMID THE DEVASTATION WREAKED BY THE JANUARY 12, 2010, HAITI EARTHQUAKE WERE SOME REMARKABLE DISPLAYS OF HUMAN RESILIENCE.

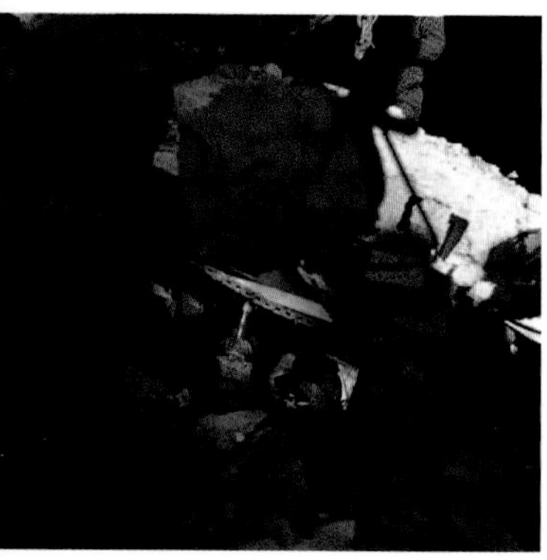

Haitians rescuers dig to free an unidentified man trapped in rubble after the January 2010 earthquake in Port-au-Prince, Haiti.

Babies resting in a bucket in Port-au-Prince, Haiti, following the earthquake.

A 7.0-magnitude earthquake struck Haiti in January 2010, destroying its capital, Port-au-Prince, and killing an estimated 150,000 to 316,000 people in the city of about 900,000. But amid the horror, there was amazing resilience.

A Staggering 27 Days

"I still don't understand how I'm here," said 27-year-old Evans Monsignac, as he recuperated in the Intensive Care Unit at Tampa General Hospital in Florida. Monsignac had survived a staggering 27 days beneath the rubble and was the last person to be pulled from the ruins. The father of two had been at work in a market stall when the quake hit. "Suddenly things were just flying all over and flattening me," he told the *Telegraph* the following March. "I tried to turn to the right, but I was pinned down by rock, I tried to turn to the left, I was pinned down with rock."

Though some speculate that, at the very least, Monsignac must have had access to food and clean water, the peddler has insisted he subsisted on small sips of sewage water that leaked through the wreckage around him. "I was resigned to death. But God gave me life," Monsignac said. "It's a miracle, I can't explain it."

Miracle Babies

Elisabeth Joassaint was just 15 days old when the earthquake struck, but a week later the infant was found in the same bed where she had been sleeping during the disaster. She was uninjured and essentially healthy. "This wasn't the way Jesus wanted the baby to die," said Joassaint's grandfather.

Joassaint was among the handful of miracle survivors from the earthquake, helped by the fact she was so young: Babies are born with extra energy stores they can mobilize if the mother's milk does not start immediately. One 18-month-old girl survived six days buried under the debris, and was uninjured when discovered.

Two-month-old Jenny Alexis, trapped for five days, suffered broken ribs, crushed arms, and a skull fracture. But she survived, too, after being rushed to a makeshift hospital and then airlifted to a Miami hospital.

"She's a miracle baby," said Dr. Karen Schneider, who treated Jenny in Haiti. "For almost four days, she had almost no fluid, and yet I've always said God has a special plan for her."

Sherider Anilus, 28, and her daughter sit on the spot where their home collapsed during the earthquake in Port-au-Prince, Haiti.

I HAVE AN APP FOR THAT

Technology came to the rescue of a trapped Colorado aid worker.

Dan Woolley, an aid worker for Compassion International who had been making a film about poverty in Haiti, was staying at Port-au-Prince's Hotel Montana when the 2010 quake struck. He was heading to the lobby elevator when "all of a sudden just all craziness broke loose," he said. "Convulsions of the ground around us, the walls started rippling and then falling on us." When the tremors stopped, Woolley used the camera he was wearing around his neck to light his way to the elevator.

After realizing that he was bleeding from his head and leg, he remembered that he had an app—Pocket First Aid & CPR—that could help. He told CNN that his phone was "like a high-tech version of a Swiss Army knife that enabled me to treat my own injuries, track time, stay awake, and stay alive." He used a sock to stop the bleeding on his head and bandaged his leg with his shirt, then secured it with his belt.

Woolley also used the app to determine what he needed to do for shock. It advised him to avoid sleeping, so he set his phone alarm to go off every 20 minutes. Woolley was rescued after 60 hours.

Dan Wooley recounting his ordeal

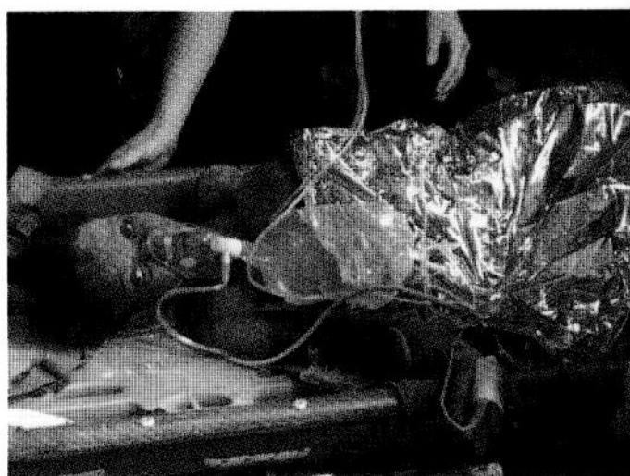

Darlene Etienne, being treated at a field hospital after being pulled out of the rubble

MANNA FROM HEAVEN?

These foods and drinks may have helped Haitian earthquake survivors stay alive.

→ **Bathwater**. Rescuers pulled 16-year-old Darlene Etienne from the wreckage in Port-au-Prince 15 days after the quake. Etienne had been trapped in the bathroom, giving her access to the bathwater that may have kept her alive.

→ **Beer, cookies, Coca-Cola, and whisky**. Twenty-four-year-old Wismond Exantus lived for 11 days on cookies, beer, Coca-Cola, and other items in the rubble of the grocery store he was working in when the quake hit. To help him sleep, he drank a bit of whisky.

→ **Dried fruit rolls**. A seven-year-old who was rescued after being trapped in a collapsed grocery store for four days said that she had eaten dried fruit rolls for sustenance.

→ **Urine**. With no food or water nearby for the 10 days he was trapped in the rubble of his house, 21-year-old Emmannuel Buso turned to his own urine to stay hydrated. "I am here today because God wants it," he said.

WHO KNEW?

Despite the history of safety problems at the San José Mine in Chile, its owners were never held responsible for the collapse that trapped 33 miners.

Chilean miner Juan Illanes celebrates after being brought to the surface.

Buried Alive

TRAPPED FOR 69 DAYS IN A HOT, SMELLY SHAFT 2,300 FEET BELOW GROUND, 33 CHILEAN MINERS SURVIVED AN UNIMAGINABLE HELL.

The new One World Trade Center in New York is the tallest building in the Western Hemisphere at 1,776 feet. Imagine that skyscraper descending down into the earth instead of ascending above it. Now make it 2,300 feet. That's how far belowground some workers were trapped when the San José Mine in Chile collapsed in 2010.

Over its 120-year existence, the notoriously dangerous gold and copper mine had grown into a sprawling subterranean city, with multiple levels and rooms for storing excavation equipment and machines. The mine was so huge that it took 40 minutes by truck, up a zigzagging road called the Ramp, to get back to the surface. The conditions were brutal. The deeper one went, the hotter it got—sometimes over 100 degrees.

On August 5, 2010, workers deep inside San Jose's center heard a deafening noise. A slab of rock had come loose and plunged down through the mine, triggering a thundering roar. The slab was so huge that it blocked the entire mineshaft, trapping 33 miners below. There was no way out.

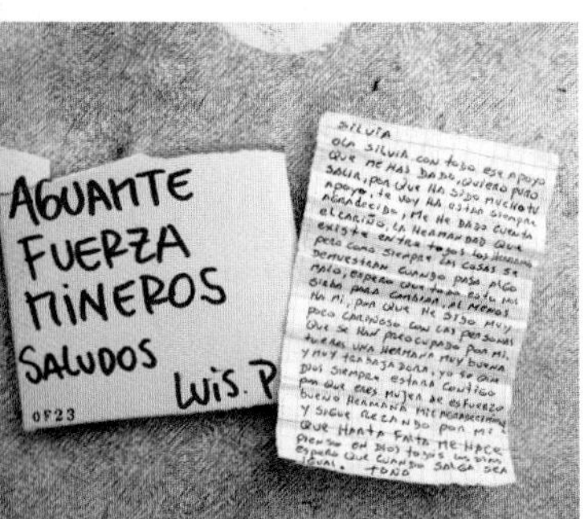

A message written by a trapped miner and a letter written to a trapped miner by a relative at Campamento Esperanza.

Huddled together in a room dubbed the Refuge, the men assessed their situation. The collapse had knocked out the mine's electricity, running water, and air circulation, but the workers had a first aid kit and a few provisions: some canned tuna, a few gallons of water, and cookies. Not realizing how dire their predicament was, a few of the hungry miners gobbled down some of the food.

Hoping for Rescue

On the third day after the accident, the men were heartened by the faraway sound of exploratory drilling and imagined help was on its way. They calculated that it would take the rescue crew about a week to reach them. But the week came and went without contact with the surface, and the miners realized the drill had bypassed the Refuge.

As time went on, the men grew filthier, hungrier, and weaker. Each reacted differently to the situation. Some became so depressed they wouldn't get up. Others got angry. Though not all the men were religious, they began to gather for daily prayer sessions. They wrote diaries on scraps of paper, took videos with cellphone cameras, and worked hard to keep up morale. But their good spirits waned as they began to starve. Some considered suicide.

And then, 17 days after the cave-in, a drill pierced the ceiling in a passageway near the Refuge. The men rushed to the massive tool and began to hit it with a wrench, signaling to rescuers that they were alive. The ground crew responded with signals of their own. The miners tied notes to the bottom of the drill, and as it inched back up to the surface over the next few hours, they began to sing the Chilean national anthem.

> "We are well in the Refuge. The 33."
>
> —note from the miners

On the surface, the rescuers found the messages. When they read that all 33 miners were still alive, they burst out in cheers and hugs. Some began to cry.

On October 12th, the rescuers finished building the exit shaft and began to haul up the miners one by one. The men credited their survival to teamwork, their democratic decision-making, and a sense of brotherhood. As each miner was lifted to the surface, the crowd chanted, "Chi Chi Chi! Le Le Le! We are the miners of Chile!"

THE DEADLIEST JOBS IN AMERICA

What's more dangerous than mining? In the United States, the highest-fatality occupations in 2012 ranged from pilot to logger.

JOB	FATALITIES PER 100,000	CAUSED BY...	AVERAGE ANNUAL PAY
Steelworker	37	Falls, heavy materials	$50,700
Roofer	41	Falls, heat stroke	$38,800
Pilot	53	Crashes, turbulence	$128,800
Fisherman	117	Storms, drowning	$36,900
Logger	128	Falling trees, dangerous equipment	$34,600

Chilean miner Juan Illanes as he comes out of the Fenix capsule after being brought to the surface following a 10-week ordeal in the collapsed San José mine, near Copiapo, Santiago, Chile.

Jessica McClure's rescue

"BABY JESSICA" GROWS UP

Whatever happened to the famous toddler rescued from a well?

When Jessica McClure got stuck 22 feet below the ground in October 1987, the whole world, it seemed, held its breath. The Midland, Texas, 18-month-old had been playing near an open well when she accidentally fell in and got wedged into an eight-inch-wide space with one leg above her head. Rescuers worked around the clock to free her, and at the end of her two-day ordeal, the millions who had watched on live television breathed a collective sigh of relief.

After the rescue, the McClure family retreated from public view and Jessica grew up locally famous but out of the national limelight. In 2011, married and a mother of two, she agreed to a rare interview with the *Dallas Morning News*. She told the paper she had no memory of the accident and had only learned about it when she was five or six, watching television with her stepmother. She saw an old news segment about an infant who'd fallen into a well, and her stepmother told McClure she was that baby. "I was stunned," McClure said.

Devastation in Japan

AN EARTHQUAKE, TSUNAMIS, NUCLEAR MELTDOWN— AN UNPRECEDENTED DISASTER CAUSED COUNTLESS TRAGEDIES, BUT THERE WERE ALSO A FEW TRIUMPHS.

When the tsunami arrived in Emiko Chiba's hometown, she was in her car, which was lifted like a surfboard.

It was the most powerful earthquake that had ever struck Japan, and, at a magnitude of 9.0, the fifth strongest ever recorded in the world. The 2011 Tōhoku quake began at 2:46 PM on March 11 in the Pacific Ocean about 45 miles off the country's northwest coast, and thundered for six devastating minutes. It jiggled the Earth's axis by at least four inches and shifted Japan's main island, Honshu, eight feet to the east. It collapsed a dam and destroyed or damaged over a million buildings.

And that was just the beginning. The quake triggered ocean waves as high as a 13-story building and reaching up to six miles inland. The tsunami damaged the coastal Fukushima Daiichi Nuclear Power Plant, causing a large-scale radioactive meltdown. All told, the quake and its associated disasters killed almost 16,000 people, 10,000 of them in Minami-Sanriku, a coastal town about three hours north of the power plant.

Emiko Chiba was not one of them.

Chiba, 42, was driving her car on the winding roads of Minami-Sanriku when she saw the water surging toward her, leveling everything its path. Before she could formulate any kind of plan, the wave raised her car and carried it along like a surfboard. "She can't remember how long she was in the air," her husband, Kazahiro, later told the *Toronto Star*. "Her memory is all black."

When Chiba's car came to rest, she walked for an hour to the nearest standing house, where Kazahiro eventually found her. Returning to what was left of their hometown, the couple realized just how lucky Chiba had been. The tsunami had swept away vehicles, destroyed highways, and churned mud, debris, cars, and boats into a horrific mess. Almost two-thirds of the residents of Minami-Sanriku had perished.

MIRACLES THAT WEREN'T

After the disaster in Japan, a number of uplifting stories circulated that unfortunately proved to be false.

WHAT SUPPOSEDLY HAPPENED	WHAT REALLY HAPPENED
Despite flooding, fires, and freezing temperatures in the city of Kesennuma, a man was found in his ruined house, having somehow survived it all.	The man had escaped the tsunami, returned to his house, and fallen unconscious.
A photo surfaced of a "miraculous mosque" that remained standing even as the quake and tsunami leveled everything around it.	The mosque in the picture was actually in Indonesia, not Japan.

Fukushima Daiichi Nuclear Power Station after it was hit by a tsunami triggered by the massive Tōhoku earthquake

Swept Away But Safe

There were other survivors as well. Days after the water receded, Japanese soldiers in Ishinomaki, a town on the coast northeast of Sendai, had given up hope of finding anyone else alive when they heard a faint cry coming from a pile of debris. Carefully, they removed layers of wood, slate, and shattered glass, until they uncovered a four-month-old baby girl in a pink woolen bear suit. A wave had hit the baby's home, sweeping her from her parents' arms. Amazingly, the parents also survived and the family was reunited.

Hiromitsu Shinkawa, 60, was swept 10 miles out to sea on what had been the roof of his home in Minami Soma. By his second day in the water, he had given up hope. "No helicopters or boats that came nearby noticed me. I thought that day was going to be the last day of my life," Shinkawa later recounted to a reporter. Still floating on the roof of his house, he spotted a rescue ship and frantically waved a red flag he had made from a scrap of fabric snatched from the water. The ship soon reached him and he lived to tell the story.

So did Jin Abe, 16, and his 80-year-old grandmother, who were found trapped under the rubble of their home in Ishinomaki. For a week after the disaster, the two survived by eating scraps of food salvaged from a refrigerator. Police found them when Abe managed to pull himself through a hole in the wreckage and alert rescue workers. The two had endured a snowstorm and freezing temperatures, but were basically unharmed. "I always believed he was alive," Abe's father later said.

The "miracle pine" tree in the ravaged area of Rikuzentakata, Iwate Prefecture

THE MIRACLE PINE

In a devastated forest, the tsunami left a lone tree standing.

In the days following the twin disasters, many Japanese referred to "the miracle pine" because it was the only tree in the vicinity to survive. The 89-foot, 250-year-old pine was the sole remnant of what had been a forest of 70,000 trees along the coast in Rikuzentakata.

But too much sea salt had soaked into the soil, poisoning the tree's roots. The pine, which had become a symbol of hope for the local community, soon died. It was cut down, but experts preserved it by inserting a metal skeleton into its trunk and adding replica branches and leaves. The reconstructed tree, returned to its original location, now serves as the centerpiece of a memorial park.

Rescue workers take part in the rescue operation on the top of the damaged building at Savar.

Under a Concrete Slab

DEFYING THE ODDS, A YOUNG SEAMSTRESS LIVES 17 DAYS IN THE RUBBLE OF RANA PLAZA, THE COLLAPSED BANGLADESH GARMENT FACTORY.

When the eight-story Rana Plaza manufacturing plant collapsed outside Dhaka, Bangladesh, on April 24, 2013, more than 1,200 garment workers lost their lives.

Reshma Begum was among them, but was one of the lucky ones.

Instead, the 19-year-old seamstress, who had been working at New Wave Bottoms for about $60 a month, remained boxed into a precarious space created by fallen concrete slabs. She survived at first on food she found among the the wreckage, and then just on water. On the outside, workers and Begum's own family had given up hope. Almost two weeks had passed since the last person was pulled alive from the rubble, and the death toll had climbed above 1,000.

Then on May 10, 2013, 17 days after one of the world's worst industrial disasters ever, Begum was found alive.

The Rescue

Army sergeant Abdur Razzaq was the first to suspect someone was alive under the debris when he glimpsed a protruding iron rod that appeared to be moving. As Razzaq bent to check out the rebar, he heard faint tapping sounds. After quickly

Civilians rescue an injured garment worker from the rubble of the collapsed Rana Plaza.

TRUE GRIT

Three female survivors of the Bangladesh factory collapse showed extraordinary strength.

→ Rozina Begum, 26 (no relation to Reshma), who was working on a pair of trousers when the building came down, may have been saved by her own sewing machine, which landed on her. Though the machine lacerated her thigh, it prevented a beam from crushing her entirely. Rescuers tried unsuccessfully to pull her out, then handed her a saw, which she used to cut off her left arm.

→ Trapped for four days, 21-year-old Merina Khatun survived by drinking from a small bottle of water she had with her. "One of my colleagues, who was also trapped and was with me, lost her mind and at one point she started to bite me, saying 'Take me to my son,'" Khatun remembered. The seamstress lost consciousness and woke up in a hospital. "I thought the Almighty Allah had given me my life back when I saw my parents by my bedside."

→ "Seven members of my family worked [at the factory]. Just two of us are alive," 23-year-old Rojina Akter told NPR in the aftermath. She and 15 other workers were stuck in a small space when beams started falling around them. "When a coworker noticed a hole in the debris," Rojina reported, "we made a rope tying our scarves together.... I was numb with pain but I cried out with joy after seeing the sky."

breaking a hole through the rubble, he heard a shout, "Save me!" and saw Begum standing between a concrete slab and a beam. Workers drilled and hammered their way to the young mother and found her in remarkably good condition, wearing a bright pink scarf and purple clothing, her face lightly covered in dust. Her appearance was so good, some reporters suspected the rescue was a hoax, yet as

Survivor Reshma Begum lies on a stretcher after being pulled out from the rubble of the collapsed building in Savar, Bangladesh, May 10, 2013.

the effort was broadcast live on local television, Begum was welcomed with cheers of "God is great" throughout Dhaka.

Luck Meets Pluck

Begum eventually talked to reporters about what happened. The day before the accident, Begum said she and her coworkers had noticed cracks in the building and reported them to a supervisor. The boss, however, was dismissive. "There is no problem. You do your work," the women were told.

Begum was on the job when the factory came crumbling down. She said she at first tried to crawl to safety but couldn't find her way out and instead ended up under an arrangement of fallen beams and slabs. During her initial hours and days underground, Begum heard people screaming and dying around her. As the days wore on and silence fell, she started to lose hope. "No one heard me. It was bad for me. I'd never dreamed I'd see the daylight again."

Luckily, the space she was trapped in was large enough that she could walk around. Begum was able to scrounge through her dead colleagues' belongings for cookies and other food, which lasted for 15 days. For the last 48 hours, she had nothing but water, but remained strong and hydrated. Major Moazzem Hossain, one of the rescue crew who lifted Begum out of the rubble, noted the seamstress's relatively good health.

Recovery and Renewal

After spending nearly a month in the hospital, Begum was discharged in June 2013, a national heroine. Like many other survivors of the collapse, she vowed never to set foot in a garment factory again, and she was offered a number of other jobs. Ultimately, she took a position at Dhaka's Westin, a five-star hotel, where she was assigned to the housekeeping department.

Six months after the collapse, Begum told the BBC that she was learning English and computer skills, but that she was still haunted by her 17 harrowing days in the rubble: "I can't tolerate darkness in my room at night. The light is switched on always. If the light is turned off, I start panicking.... It feels like... I am still there."

Begum also spoke out for the many garment workers still toiling for low pay under unsafe conditions. "Whatever is needed to make their lives safer must be done," Begum said. "They work very hard and suffer a lot." She added, "If I am successful some day, I would like to help them out, too."

WHO KNEW?
Bangladeshi garment workers are the lowest paid in the world.

THE CRUSADING SURVIVOR

Aklina Khanam is raising awareness of the terrible conditions in some of the factories that create the clothes that Americans buy.

Like many of her coworkers, Aklina Khanam was concerned about cracks that had been spotted in the factory walls and was reluctant to go to work on April 24. But the petite 19-year-old needed the money, so she headed to the New Wave Factory in spite of the risk.

When the building crumbled around Khanam, she found herself trapped under a machine, unable to move for 12 hours. In the months that followed, Khanam was unable to work and a year later had received no compensation from the government or her employers. Then the organization United Students Against Sweatshops offered to bring Khanam to the U.S. to share her story of long hours, meager pay, and physical and mental abuse with young people—the target market for most of the brands she worked for.

"If we don't tell them, then how can they understand?" she said. Khanam also worked with the student group to pressure retailers to compensate victims. "They have a responsibility to us," said Khanam. According to the Clean Clothes Campaign, as of April 2014 retailers had contributed $14 million to a fund overseen by the International Labor Organization to compensate survivors.

When it's human versus machine, the machine often wins—but occasionally humans get lucky.

CHAPTER 15

Horror in Motion

In a flash, everything changes. A plane plummets from the sky. An elevator cable snaps. You're swept under a train. Then what?

Race to the Bottom

WHEN A PLANE CAREENED INTO THE EMPIRE STATE BUILDING IN 1945, ONE WOMAN MIRACULOUSLY SURVIVED A 1,000-FOOT FREE FALL IN THE ELEVATOR.

On the morning of July 28, 1945, a B-25 bomber flown by highly decorated Army pilot William F. Smith Jr. left Massachusetts and headed south. The flight plan had called for Smith to land at LaGuardia Airport in New York City, but when he checked in with air traffic control, tower personnel warned Smith about a thick fog enveloping the city. "At the present time, I can't see the top of the Empire State Building," said the controller. "Roger, Tower, thank you," replied Smith, who steered instead toward Newark Airport, about 24 miles away.

As Smith navigated out of Manhattan, he tried to escape the fog, but lost his bearings and dropped to a dangerously low altitude. The maneuver proved fatal. Smith was careening toward the 1,250-foot Empire State Building, at the time the tallest skyscraper in the world. He tried to pull up and bank away, but it was too late—the bomber crashed into the north face of the building between the 78th and 79th floors. The aircraft tore through the walls and girders, ripping an 18-by-20-foot hole in the side of the structure as flaming fuel from the exploded gas tanks poured down and inside.

WHAT ARE THE CHANCES?

It takes more than luck to survive a 1,000-foot elevator plunge.

Betty Lou Oliver

Initial reports of Betty Lou Oliver's wild ride suggested that the elevator's safety brake worked briefly, but then gave way at the seventh floor. This version of events turned out to be false, since the governor cable controlling the car had already been severed in the plane crash. Had the governor cable remained intact, the brake would have kicked in around the 35th floor, where Oliver would have been trapped in an express shaft that had no doorways from the first to 40th floors.

Instead, what seems to have happened is that 1,000 feet of elevator cable piled up at the bottom of the shaft as the car plummeted. The coil miraculously acted as a buffer, cushioning the impact. Additionally, the elevator was "high-pressure" in design, meaning that there was very little clearance between the car and the shaft. As the car fell, the trapped air beneath it had almost nowhere to go and became compressed, creating an air cushion that slowed the elevator's descent.

The scene after an Army B-25 bomber crashed into the 78th and 79th floors of the Empire State Building on July 28, 1945, in New York

One engine hurtled straight through the building and out the other side, landing on the roof of a nearby sculpture studio and igniting a fire. The other engine cut through an elevator shaft, damaging cables and propelling debris down into the shaft. One wing ended up a block away, on Madison Avenue. Smith and his two passengers died instantly; 11 people inside the building were also killed. Betty Lou Oliver, a 20-year-old elevator attendant on the 80th floor, was thrown from her post upon impact and was badly burned—but alive. In an interview with the *Lawrence Journal-World* newspaper, she recalled: "Just then a great block of machinery came spewing, cracking, and burning through the top of my car. Instantly I was covered with hot, black oil. It was...as if hell itself had dropped into my car."

Fast Ride

Unaware that a second elevator bank had sustained major damage in the crash, a rescue team gave Oliver first aid, then transferred her to the waiting lift and sent her down to the ambulance on the street. As the door closed, a sound like a gunshot reverberated through the building, witnesses recalled later: The frayed cable had snapped and the elevator was sent into free fall, plummeting roughly 1,000 feet from the 75th floor to the sub-basement.

At the bottom of the shaft, the smashed car lay amid bricks, steel, and debris from the plane. Oliver was curled up in a corner with burns and a broken pelvis, back, right leg, and neck. Rescuers cut her free and rushed her to the hospital, where she made an astonishing recovery, returning to her job in just five months. Oliver later told an interviewer that she had realized through a haze of semiconsciousness that she had to fight to stay alive. When a Catholic missionary was sent to her bedside to administer the last rites of his church, Oliver looked up at him with her open left eye and said, "But Father, I'm a Protestant—just hold my hand."

The Empire State Building was hit by a plane only once, but is zapped by lightning an average of 25 times a year.

CRASH COURSE

Some little-known facts about the day a B-52 bomber hit the world's tallest building.

➔ When the plane struck, some workers in the building thought the U.S. was under attack by the Japanese.

➔ Damages to the building from the crash were estimated at $1 million—roughly $13 million in 2014 dollars. Despite its location 1,000 feet up—the highest fire in New York City history until September 11, 2001—the four-alarm blaze caused by the crash was quickly managed by the fire department.

➔ Since the plane hit the Empire State Building on a Saturday, only about 1,500 workers were on site. Had it been a typical weekday at the same time, close to 10 times that number would have been present and the crash could have been much worse.

➔ Betty Lou Oliver appears in the *Guinness Book of World Records* for the "longest fall survived in an elevator."

Soft Landing

AFTER A CHRISTMAS EVE FLIGHT TUMBLED 10,000 FEET INTO THE JUNGLE OF PERU, ONE TEENAGER MADE IT OUT ALIVE.

Juliane Koepcke after receiving the Corine Literature Prize for her 2011 autobiography, *When I Fell from the Sky*

It was Christmas Eve 1971, and 17-year-old Juliane Koepcke was traveling with her mother, Maria, from their home in Lima, Peru, to Pucullpa, an hour away by plane. The elder Koepcke had originally planned to leave on December 20th, but postponed the trip so that Juliane could attend her prom and high school graduation. Arriving at the airport, which was especially busy because of the holidays, the Koepckes' only option was Lansa, an airline that had recently lost two commercial flights. As Juliane later remembered, "We desperately wanted to be with my father for Christmas, so we figured it would be alright."

Mother and daughter boarded Lansa flight 508 around 11 AM and took seats in the second row from the back. Twenty-five minutes in, the flight encountered heavy clouds, then rain and thunder. There was a flash of lighting, and the engine howled. Juliane recalled, "We were headed straight down. Christmas presents were flying around the cabin and I could hear people screaming." Her mother said, "That's the end." Suddenly, the deafening noise stopped, and Juliane became aware of wind around her and the green of the forest spinning far below. She was in free fall.

"We were headed straight down . . . I could hear people screaming."

After plummeting nearly two miles to the jungle floor, Juliane regained consciousness under a canopy of trees. She was alone in an intact row of three seats, her seatbelt still around her. She managed to read her watch: It was 9 AM on Christmas day. A part of one of the plane's engines was nearby, but there was no other sign of the wreckage. Suffering from gashes on her arms and legs, a broken collarbone, and a severe concussion, Juliane nearly blacked out trying to stand, but eventually managed to crawl around, looking for her mother or any other survivors. She saw no one.

Lost and Found

Having spent time in the jungle with her parents—both were zoologists—Juliane knew how to get her bearings. She heard the sound of water nearby and pushed herself through thick vegetation to reach a creek and crawled in so she could float downstream and hopefully find other humans. Three days later, she came across a grim reminder of her situation—another block of seats from the plane, face down. She pushed on through clouds of insects, spending much of her time in the creek, and surviving on a bag of candy from the wreckage. Though wary of jaguars, piranha, and crocodiles, Juliane continued. "I knew crocodiles don't tend to attack humans," she said later.

Juliane Koepcke, whose family emigrated to Peru from Germany, arrives at the Frankfurt airport in April 1972, a little more than three months after the crash.

After 10 days of drinking murky river water, Juliane thought she was hallucinating when she spotted a small shelter on the riverbank. But the structure was real, and she was able crawl in. Once inside, she discovered a bottle of kerosene, which she used to douse the gash behind her arm, now brimming with maggots. Eventually, three Peruvian lumberjacks found her there and treated her wounds. A day later, they took her on a seven-hour canoe trip to the nearest town, where Juliane received further treatment. From there, a pilot brought her to a nearby mission, where she recovered and was finally reunited with her father.

SAVING JULIANE

Experts theorized that the canopy of trees in the rainforest helped break the teen's fall and save her life.

Two days before Juliane Koepcke emerged from the jungle, the search teams that had been scouring the rainforest for the missing Lockheed Electra turboprop aircraft called off their mission. But after the rescuers were able to speak with the teen, they started to search again, hoping to trace a path to the wreckage and find other survivors.

Eventually, it was confirmed that all of the other 91 people on board had perished. Investigators blamed the crash on a lightning strike that broke one engine and a wing off the plane.

So, how did Juliane manage to survive the fall? She herself theorized, "Maybe it was the fact that I was still attached to a whole row of seats." Experts agreed, explaining that the spiraling motion must have slowed her descent. Perhaps, too, the height and density of the canopy of trees helped break her fall.

A scene from *I Miracoli Accadono Ancora*, starring Susan Panhaligon as Juliane

STRANGER THAN FICTION

Juliane's unbelievable survival story became an oft-told tale.

→ Called "the miracle girl," Juliane became an instant celebrity in Peru. She received hundreds of letters, some addressed simply to "Juliane—Peru." Overwhelmed, she eventually isolated herself from both journalists and the public.

→ The first publication to report on Juliane's experience was *Stern* magazine in Germany. Her father, who had emigrated to Peru from Germany, had sold them the right to break the story.

→ An account of Juliane's story reached movie audiences with the release of *I Miracoli Accadono Ancora* in 1974. The low-budget film was re-released in English a year later as *Miracles Still Happen*, and sometimes appears as *The Story of Juliane Koepcke*.

→ In 2000, filmmaker Werner Herzog released a made-for-TV documentary about Juliane titled *Wings of Hope*. Herzog took Juliane back into the jungle, to the scene of the crash. The filmmaker had a particular interest in the story because he, too, had been at the Lima airport on December 24, 1971, while working on his film *Aguirre, Wrath of God*, and had nearly taken the same ill-fated flight.

Survival at 12,000 Feet

A PLANE FULL OF YOUNG ATHLETES CRASHED INTO A REMOTE MOUNTAINTOP. WHAT HAPPENED NEXT IS A TESTAMENT TO TOUGH CHOICES AND TEAMWORK.

A Chilean police rescue patrol helps crash survivor Fernando Parrado after his 10-day trek to civilization, December 22, 1972.

They were regular young people—student athletes in their early 20s who had played rugby together at Catholic school in the vibrant city of Montevideo, Uruguay. As alumni, they'd formed a weekend team and wanted to play an exhibition game in Santiago, Chile, a two-hour flight away. The group chartered a 45-seat plane, filling the extra seats with friends, family members, and supporters. The short flight, which was to take them west across Argentina, over the Andes, and into Chile, departed on October 12, 1972. But bad weather forced them to land and stay the night in the Argentine city of Mendoza, just east of the mountain range.

The next afternoon, the team was back in the air, soaring through a cloud-shrouded pass. That's when the pilot made a deadly error. His view obscured, he descended too soon. The plane clipped a mountain, losing its right wing. It clipped a second mountain, losing its left wing. The sheared fuselage crash-landed on a peak that would come to be known as the Glacier of Tears. Eighteen passengers died in the collision and many more would succumb as the days passed. Those who remained would be faced with an unfathomable choice.

Inhospitable Conditions

The section of the Andes where the charter plane crashed was rugged and remote. At an altitude of 11,800 feet, the air was thin, and there were no plants, trees, or animals. The cold was devastating, forcing the passengers to huddle together for warmth in the wrecked fuselage. They rationed what little food they had, which was mostly chocolate and wine. But as time passed, the group became desperate. They heard on a radio salvaged from the wreckage that the search had been called off. Facing starvation, they ripped open the plane's seats, hoping they might find straw; they even tried eating pieces of the leather luggage.

Eventually, the remaining players concluded that their only chance of staying alive was to eat the bodies of their dead classmates, family members, and friends. As Catholics, they tried to think of what they were doing as a kind of Communion.

Two months after the crash, having lost all hope of being rescued, the group elected three members to attempt the treacherous journey down the mountains and back into Argentina. Soon, one of the searchers turned back as it became clear that the

The last survivors of the Uruguayan plane crash in the Andes huddle together in the craft's fuselage on December 22, 1972, the final night before their rescue.

rations were insufficient for three people. Ten days later, the reconnaissance team spotted a man on horseback. Soon rescue helicopters were dispatched to retrieve the 16 remaining survivors. In all, the group had spent 72 days in the mountains.

In 2012, the survivors, by then in their 60s, reunited in Santiago for a rugby match against the team they had been scheduled to play. "At about this time we were falling in the Andes," Pedro Algorta, one of the team members, recalled just before they walked onto the field. "Today we're here to win a game."

"THERE IS ALWAYS A STRENGTH REMAINING SOMEWHERE"

In a 1973 interview, one of the men who endured the Andes crash spoke of how the group came to make its most painful decision.

At the time of the crash, Alfredo Delgado was a 24-year-old law student. After his rescue, he was asked how he and his fellow survivors decided to take the terrible but necessary step of consuming the dead.

"The cold, the anguish, the hunger, [were] successive steps," he said. "The death surrounding us, the hunger, it was one step after the other." By the time the survivors made the choice, they had discussed the idea and were prepared for it as best they could be. Delgado explained that they felt it was important not to wait until they were so weak that they could no longer function. "Each step seemed to be the last, the end, but in each of them we learned that there is always a strength remaining somewhere, strengths unexpected that come from the most unexpected places [within ourselves]. I learned this, too, how enormously strong we become as we become weak."

The location of the Uruguayan plane that crashed in the Andes in October 1972

INGENIOUS INVENTORS

Without emergency gear, the Andes crash survivors showed amazing resourcefulness.

The survivors lacked footwear and clothing appropriate for the brutal subzero cold. They had no medical supplies and little food. But they were able to cobble together some of the gear they needed to live:

→ **Sunglasses:** To prevent snow blindness, Eduardo Strauch, 25, cut lenses from the cockpit sun visors and connected them with wire.

→ **Snowshoes:** Eduardo's cousin, Fito Strauch, 24, suggested attaching the plane's seat cushions to the soles of their shoes with seatbelts.

→ **Bedding:** Roberto Francois, 20, thought to use the plane's seat covers as blankets. The group also stitched together quilted insulation to form a sleeping bag for the trio who went to get help.

→ **Fuel:** The survivors had cigarette lighters, but almost no wood for fires. They burned $7,500 worth of paper money.

→ **Antiseptic:** They used cologne to clean wounds.

Destiny's Child

AUSTIN HATCH SURVIVED NOT ONE BUT TWO PLANE CRASHES, LOSING HIS ENTIRE FAMILY. HE PURSUED A LIFE TO HONOR THEIR MEMORY.

Austin Hatch shoots during a high school regional basketball tournament.

"I think God has his hand on me and that there is a plan for my life," said Austin Hatch, reflecting on the circumstances of his cataclysmic life. In August 2014, the former high school basketball star played his first game for the University of Michigan basketball team in a preseason tournament in Rome, Italy. For 19-year-old Austin, who had survived not one but two plane crashes that together claimed the lives of five members of his family, it represented the realization of an important goal—and a moment that neither he nor his doctors ever dreamed he would see.

Double Jeopardy

Austin was just eight years old in September 2003 when his father, an anesthesiologist, was piloting a plane from northern Michigan to Indiana. The plane ran out of fuel, hit a utility pole, and crashed. Dr. Hatch and Austin survived, but Austin's mother, Julie, 38; sister, Lindsay, 11; and brother, Ian, five, all perished. In the aftermath, the boy and his father developed a powerful bond. "I'm what kept [my father] going, and he's definitely what kept me going. He was my best friend, my basketball coach, my mentor—everything," Austin said.

Unspeakably, in June 2011, tragedy struck again. Sixteen-year-old Austin was a passenger once again as his father flew a single-engine plane along the very same route. It went down, and this time his father was killed, along with Austin's stepmother, Kim. "They're all gone," said Austin's basketball coach at Canterbury High School in Fort Wayne, Indiana. "He's the only one left. What's the chance of that happening? A million to one, if that. It's just unbelievable."

An Uncommon Man

Austin's injuries in the second crash included a broken collarbone, a punctured lung, and brain trauma. He spent eight weeks in a medically induced coma and in the two years that followed, had to learn how to walk, talk, and eat again. He was thrilled when the University of Michigan signed him to a full scholarship in November 2013, honoring a verbal commitment made just nine days before the plane crash. Though Hatch played just three minutes for the Wolverines during that preseason game in Rome, he received a standing ovation from the Michigan fans in the crowd.

In August 2014, when an interviewer on the *Today* show asked Austin if he ever

A single-engine plane carrying Austin Hatch and his family crashed into a garage in a neighborhood in northwestern Michigan.

questioned his ability to get through all the tragedy—if he ever considered giving up his dream of playing basketball for Michigan—he answered, "No. I can hear their voices in my head when I face a difficult situation. I can hear my dad guiding me. That's really all I strive to do, is just to honor him with my life." He added, "My dad and mom raised me to be an uncommon man."

FLY AWAY

Statistics show that private airplanes and helicopters are involved in more crashes than commercial airliners.

Small, private airplanes and helicopters are popular with wealthy business executives and celebrities. But they can also be risky. In 2013, there were 1,199 crashes in the U.S. involving private planes and helicopters; 347 people were killed and 571 were injured. By contrast, not a single U.S. domestic commercial flight crashed that year. In most of the cases, manufacturers and investigating agencies blamed operator failure. Defective plane parts could also have created risk, according to a 2014 investigation by *USA Today*. The newspaper highlighted these flaws:

Airplane exhaust systems that leak gas, causing fires in the engines

Helicopter fuel tanks that ignite easily, causing fire-related deaths and injury

Pilot seats that suddenly slide backward, causing planes to nose-dive when pilots lose their grip

Flawed ice-protection systems

Carburetors that flood or starve engines

Tsutomu Yamaguchi survived two atomic bombs.

WHEN FORTUNE FROWNS

There is no explanation for some coincidences.

→ **On August 6, 1945,** Tsutomu Yamaguchi was in Hiroshima on a business trip when the American B-29 bomber *Enola Gay* dropped an atomic bomb on the city, killing some 140,000 people. Yamaguchi survived, only to be in Nagasaki on August 9, when a second U.S. atomic bomb was detonated. He was the only known, officially recognized survivor of both bombings.

→ **In July 1975,** 17-year-old Erskine Ebbin was riding his moped in Hamilton, Bermuda, when a taxi hit and killed him. The previous July, the same taxi—with the same driver, carrying the same passenger, on the same road—had killed his brother, Neville, also 17 at the time.

→ **English couple Jenny and Jason Cairns-Lawrence** were vacationing in New York City in September 2001 when the attacks on the World Trade Center occurred. They were also visiting London for a few days in July 2005, when a bus and Tube trains were bombed by terrorists; and were on holiday in Mumbai, India, in November 2008, when Pakistani terrorists bombed the city's landmark buildings.

Whole in Spirit

LUCK, QUICK THINKING, AND A STRONG WILL SAVED A MAN SEVERED AT THE WAIST BY A RAIL CAR.

"I think I am cut in two," Truman Duncan told the 911 operator. He sounded out of breath but remarkably calm, considering what had just happened to him.

In June 2006, Duncan, a railroad worker, was connecting two moving cars at the Gunderson Southwest rail yard in Cleburne, Texas, when he fell. For nearly half a minute he clung desperately to one of the moving cars, running backward to avoid being dragged underneath. But he couldn't hold it back. "It was like a monster pulling me in," he said later. The 20,000-pound car overtook him, dragging him 75 feet before severing his body in two.

WHO KNEW?
The fatal injury rate for railroad workers is more than double that for workers as a whole, according to U.S. Department of Labor statistics.

Pinned under the steel wheels, the 36-year-old father of three remained conscious and, astonishingly, dialed for help with the cell phone that was still attached to his belt. Then, in the 45 minutes it took rescuers to free him, he placed calls to his family as well.

Soon it would become clear how very much Duncan had lost. The accident took most of his right leg and his entire left leg, kidney and pelvis. He was bleeding profusely and was in critical condition. To this day, doctors remain mystified as to how Duncan survived, but they hypothesize that the weight of the train must have

"I NEED HELP NOW."

Despite the railroad car on top of him, Truman Duncan managed to make a coherent call to 911.

911 Operator: Cleburne 911. State your emergency.
Truman Duncan: I'm at Gunderson Southwest. I got ran over by a rail car... I think I am cut in two. I need help now....
Operator: Someone got run over by a rail car?
Duncan: Yes, ma'am, and I'm about to pass out.
Operator: You got run over?
Duncan: Yes.... You've got to hurry.
Operator: ...Stay on the line with me....
Duncan: I think I am about to pass out. I guess I am going into shock. Hurry up.
Operator: Tell me your name, sir?
Duncan: Truman Duncan
Operator: Tim?
Duncan: OK, hurry up, ma'am, because I am about to pass out.
Operator: Can you stay on the line for me, please?
Duncan: I can't stay awake much longer.
Operator: Stay with me. Stay on the line.
Line goes dead.

Firefighters work to free Truman Duncan from the train.

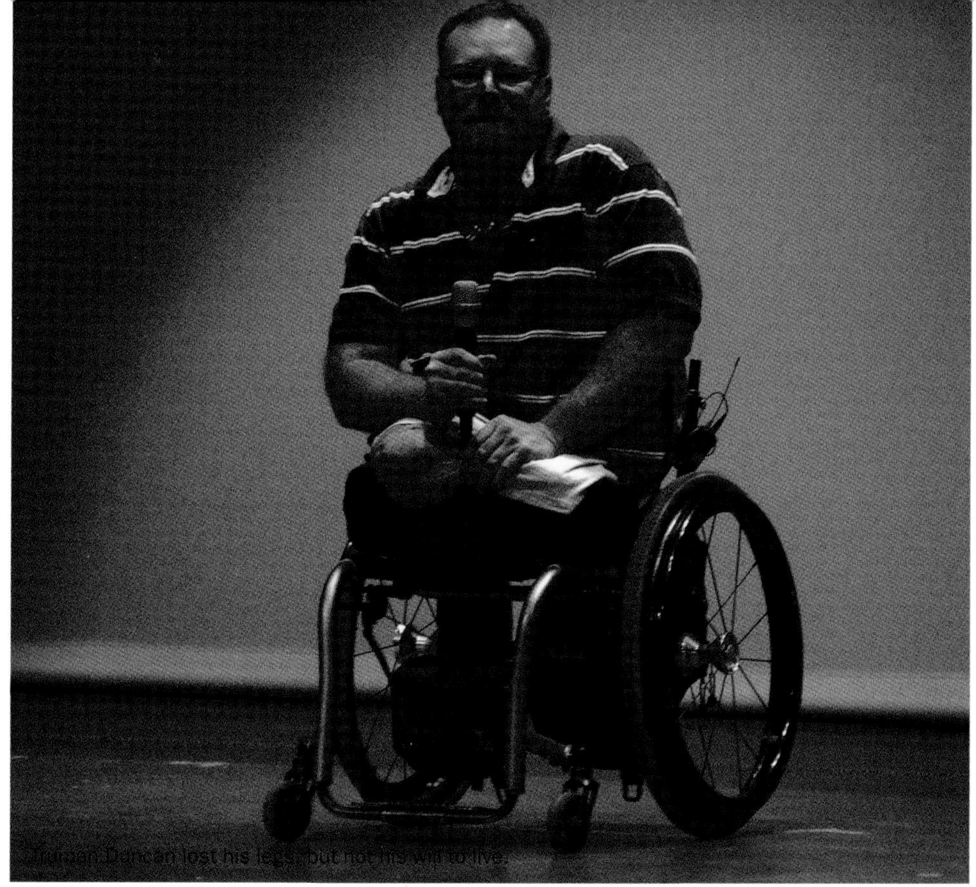

Truman Duncan lost his legs, but not his will to live.

kept sufficient pressure on his arteries to prevent him from bleeding out.

Duncan's own theory is a bit more spiritual: He had the will to live. "I wanted to see my babies grow up, just like everybody else," he told *Today* in 2008.

A Second Chance

Duncan spent three weeks in a coma and endured 23 surgeries over the next four months before finally leaving the hospital. Throughout the ordeal Duncan remained upbeat—and continued to do so after. He eventually returned to work at his company, repairing and refurbishing rail cars. Two years after the accident, he was driving himself around in a car equipped with hand controls and leading a productive life that included many of the things he did before, such as throwing a football with his kids.

"Life is good," Duncan said. "Life goes on."

Case Study:
Phineas Gage

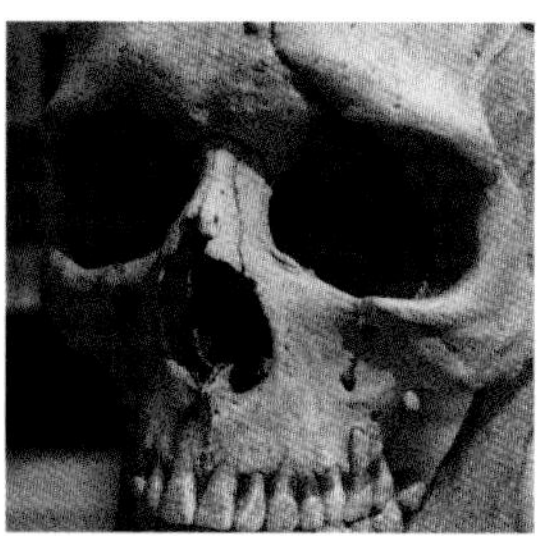

In 1848, a railroad construction foreman named Phineas Gage was blasting rock in Vermont when a charge went off early and drove a large iron rod through his head, destroying much of his brain's left frontal lobe. Gage somehow survived, and the accident's effect on his personality was marked: He became rude, odd, irritable, and unpredictable. His case became one of the most famous and studied instances of brain damage in the early years of neuroscience and psychology.

LEFT: Phineas Gage's skull is displayed at the Warren Anatomical Museum at the Countway Library of Medicine.

Robert Evans survived two separate accidents in one night.

TWO STRIKES

In 2008, a man was hit by two different vehicles within six hours and still pulled through.

At 10 PM on September 24, 2008, Robert Evans was riding his bicycle in Boulder, Colorado, when a hit-and-run driver struck him and sped away. An ambulance took Evans, a 46-year-old homeless man, to a hospital, where he was treated for injuries to his knee and arm and released at about 3 AM.

As he walked his bicycle the five miles back to the campsite where he slept, Evans came to a narrow 50-foot railroad bridge. Though he saw a train approaching in the distance, he thought he could beat it across the bridge. He was wrong: The train sideswiped him, knocking him into a creek 10 feet below. Evans was taken to the hospital a second time and treated again for only minor injuries. He did, however, receive a ticket for trespassing on the bridge.

Sole Survivors

ONLY A HANDFUL OF PEOPLE SHARE THE MIRACLE—AND THE BURDEN—OF BEING THE ONLY ONE TO LIVE THROUGH A DEADLY AIRPLANE CRASH.

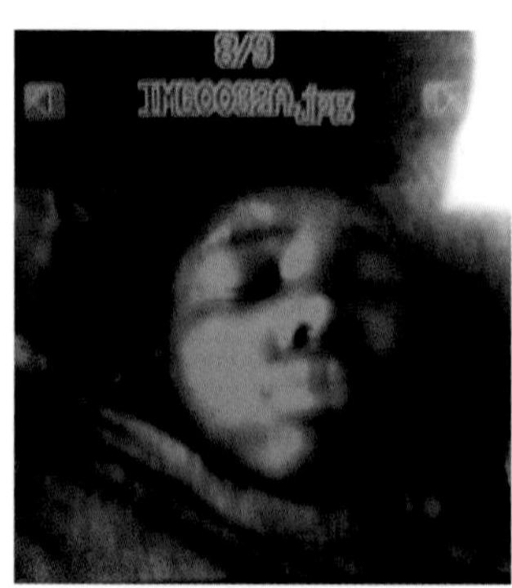

Bahia Bakari, a 13-year-old French girl and the only known survivor of the Yemenia airline flight 626 crash, after her rescue

It is an incredible scenario: A plane plummets from the sky and crashes to the ground, killing all aboard—with the exception of a lone passenger or crew member. But it is not unheard of. Since 1970, there have been 15 such survivors. Here are some of their stories.

Adrift in the Indian Ocean

"I couldn't bear it any longer. I couldn't move any more. It was the end. I closed my eyes." It was June 2009, and 13-year-old Bahia Bakari was clinging to a piece of metal, part of the fuselage of Yemenia flight 626, amid the choppy waters of the Indian Ocean. She, along with her mother and 151 others, had been on the aircraft en route from Paris to Comoros, an island off the coast of Mozambique. Now, Bakari was adrift alone in the dark sea.

When the young girl first regained consciousness, she thought she had fallen out of the plane from pressing her forehead too hard against a window. But soon she "began to understand the atrocious reality. I was not the only one to fall from the plane. All of the passengers, the pilot, the crew, had fallen from the plane," Bakari wrote later. It would be 13 hours before she would be rescued.

The French teen, who could barely swim and wasn't wearing a life vest, was the sole survivor of Flight 626.

EXCESS BAGGAGE

For crew members, survivor's guilt can be particularly acute.

About 20 percent of sole survivors have been pilots or other crew members, yet for the airline workers who live through such ordeals, the guilt can be almost too much to bear.

"I wouldn't wish this on my worst enemy," said Jim Polehinke, the copilot and lone survivor of Comair flight 5191, which went down seconds after takeoff in Lexington, Kentucky, in 2006, killing the other 49 people aboard. "I've cried harder than any man has ever cried, or any man should be able to cry," Polehinke, now a paraplegic, told the filmmakers of the documentary *Sole Survivor.* His wife, Ida, added, "He would have given anything to have gone with all of them rather than be sitting here today, doing this."

When Comair Flight 5191 crashed at Blue Grass Airport in Lexington, Kentucky, in 2006, 49 people aboard were killed and one survived.

America's Orphan

The paramedics who discovered four-year-old Cecelia Cichan amid the wreckage of Northwest Flight 255, moaning quietly beneath a dead woman, were sure she must have been on the ground when the plane crashed on August 16, 1987. They couldn't imagine that a passenger had survived. But Cichan, who suffered broken bones and burns, was indeed on that flight, which went down shortly after takeoff near Detroit, claiming the lives of 156 people, including Cichan's parents and her brother.

Dubbed "America's orphan" by the media, Cichan spoke publicly about the deadly collision for the first time in 2013. "I think about the accident every day. It's kind of hard not to.... When I look in the mirror, I have visual scars," she said in the CNN documentary *Sole Survivor*. "When I realized I was the only person to survive that plane crash, I was maybe in middle school, high school... I remember feeling angry—and survivor's guilt. Why didn't my brother survive? Why didn't anybody survive? Why me?"

Thrown to Safety

George Lamson was 17 years old in 1985 when Galaxy Airlines Flight 203 plummeted to the ground just a mile and a half from the Reno airport runway. While the crash killed the other 70 passengers aboard, including Lamson's father, the teen was thrown to safety on a nearby highway, still strapped into his seat. "I thought I was dead. I got up... the plane blew up and knocked me down. I ran as fast as I could and got out of there," Lamson recounted later. He has said he has been haunted by many of the same questions as Cichan over the years. In CNN's *Sole Survivor*, Lamson was philosophical: "You think really deep about what you're doing with your life and all the people involved with this accident that may have done more with their life, and you feel guilty that you're not using your life to do something better."

HOW TO WALK AWAY FROM A PLANE CRASH

These five tips are from Ben Sherwood, author of *The Survivors Club: The Secrets and Science That Could Save Your Life.*

→ **Take comfort in statistics.** Contrary to popular belief, 95.7 percent of passengers involved in airplane crashes survive. Tell yourself, "If a plane crashes it's very likely that I'm going to survive it, and if I do the right thing, if I pay attention, if I have a plan, if I act, the chances are even better," says Sherwood.

→ **Sit within two rows of an exit.** Analysis by aviation-safety professional Ed Galea shows that the people who are most likely to survive a crash are either sitting right next to the exit or a row away.

→ **Sit in an aisle seat.** "Aisle seats are marginally safer because they afford more mobility and choices," notes Sherwood.

→ **Wear lace-up shoes, and keep them on.** "In the event of an impact, people's shoes have been known to fly off them, particularly flip-flops," says Sherwood.

→ **Skip the alcohol and the headphones,** and stay especially alert during takeoff and landing. "Research has shown that the first three minutes of a plane flight and the last eight... are when about 80 percent of airplane accidents take place," says Sherwood.

Track Attack

WHEN RUN OVER BY A SUBWAY OR THROWN AGAINST A MOVING FREIGHT CAR, IT'S A RARE PERSON WHO CAN EMERGE ALIVE.

Graphic from a New York City subway poster

STAND BACK!

The New York Metropolitan Transportation Authority doesn't believe in miracles; it prefers safety measures. In 2012, the MTA launched a major campaign warning riders not to get too close to the edge of train platforms. Posters plastered in subway cars and stations warned in multiple languages of the dangers.

When Mary Downey lost her balance and accidentally fell onto the New York City subway tracks in 2014, she thought her life was over. She had injured her shoulder in the early morning spill and was unable to pull herself to safety. As a train bore down on Downey, she had the presence of mind to hunker down into the channel between the tracks, and barely avoided being crushed. "It just wasn't her time," an amazed but helpless onlooker who arrived on a later train said.

After the first train thundered over the 22-year-old, Downey was safe, but still stuck on the tracks. She flattened herself into the track bed again as yet another train operator unknowingly drove over her. By the time the driver of the third approaching train noticed Downey's hand waving for help, she'd been under a total of 24 subway cars.

Like Downey, both the rescue medic and the firefighter who responded to the 911 call to help her were Irish. They kept her spirits up by joking that they were having an "Irish reunion." Downey, who was conscious through most of her terrifying ordeal, was taken to a hospital essentially unharmed, and released just hours later with her arm in a sling.

Downey's experience was unusual, but not unheard of. In 2013, when 4.3 million riders a day took the subway in New York City, 151 were struck by trains. Of those, 53 were killed and 98 escaped with their lives.

And although about 500 people die in the United States each year from being hit while walking on train tracks, somehow Darryle See, 22, managed to avoid becoming one of them. In 2013, the Michigan City, Indiana, man survived after he was hit by an Amtrak train traveling at 110 miles per hour.

See was wearing headphones and walking down the middle of the tracks. Although the conductor of the train barreling up behind him sounded the horn several times before desperately applying the emergency brakes, See went flying. He suffered cracked vertebrae, fractures to his pelvis, a broken arm, and neck injuries—but he was alive. His grandmother commented, "I would definitely call it a miracle."

Attacked and Thrown

Briton Robert Evans's train horror story unfolded at the hands of another passenger. Evans, 23, was waiting at a Shrews-

WHO KNEW?
There is less than two feet of clearance between a New York City subway track and the underside of the train.

In New York City, as many as 4.3 million passengers a day ride the subway.

bury, England, railway station in 2012 when he saw a drunk man making lewd comments to a group of women. After Evans asked him to stop, the thug grabbed him, spun him 180 degrees, and threw him at a freight train rolling through the station. A local police sergeant called the incident "a deliberate, violent, and totally reckless act which resulted in the victim being inches from death."

But in a tremendous bout of luck, Evans bounced off the side of the train and landed back on the platform. He escaped with cuts and back injuries, but alive. Nevertheless, six months later, he still refused to travel on trains.

Foolish Behavior

Then there are those who deliberately venture onto the tracks. At a station in Sydney, Australia, in 2011, a 12-year-old boy jumped onto the tracks and found himself caught between the edge of the platform and an oncoming train. Video footage shows him vanishing from sight as the train rushes past. Then, incredibly, the boy pulls himself up from the tracks and back onto the platform, alive and well except for a broken leg and elbow and numerous bruises. The New South Wales Department of Transport later released the frightening video to deter any potential future daredevils.

A subway conductor in New York City checks on riders.

TRAUMA CONDUCTED

A train accident doesn't just affect the victim.

Many engineers and conductors suffer from post-traumatic stress disorder (PTSD) after accidental collisions, even if not at fault. "I hear that 'clong,' that girl is in front of my train, and I'm screaming," William Smith, an engineer in New Jersey, said in 2011. He was recalling the sound of a train on which he'd been working five years earlier as a conductor. The train hit a young woman who had deliberately stepped onto the tracks. "She probably has friends and family who don't think about her as much as I do," he said.

An estimated 12 percent of U.S. rail transit operators who have been involved in what is called a "critical incident" experience symptoms of PTSD, including these:

- Health problems
- Acute stress
- Disturbed sleep
- Nightmares
- Tremors
- Restlessness
- Intrusive thoughts of the accident
- Flashbacks

Snakes are among the creatures most feared by humans, but they're not always the victors in a contest between the two.

CHAPTER 16

The Animal Kingdom

Attacked by a snake. Saved by a pig. Amazing tales of human meeting animal.

Stung to Life

THE IMPACT OF THE SKYDIVER'S FALL SHOULD HAVE BEEN FATAL. HER SAVIORS WERE SMALLER THAN A THUMBNAIL.

HEALING VENOM

A bark scorpion bite can kill, but it cured one man's debilitating spinal arthritis.

In 2011, a doctor vacationing with his family in Guerrero, Mexico, was swimming when he felt a sudden burning pain in his thigh. He reached down and trapped the tiny yellowish-brown creature responsible for it—a bark scorpion—and stashed it in a container. The doctor was rushed to the local Red Cross center, where medics injected him with an antidote to counteract symptoms such as numbness, electric-shock sensations, and even death.

Over the next few days, the physician noticed something surprising. For years, he'd suffered from ankylosing spondylitis, a chronic skeletal disease that causes painful and deforming inflammatory spinal arthritis. But just days after the scorpion attack, the doctor, who has never allowed himself to be identified, found that his back pain had disappeared. Two years later, he remained pain-free.

A faulty parachute is a skydiver's worst nightmare. One very fortunate woman lived through it—and, thanks to some angry insects, survived to tell the story.

In September 1999, Joan Murray, a 47-year-old bank executive and experienced recreational skydiver, was flying over Charlotte, North Carolina, preparing for another exhilarating jump. She exited the plane at 14,500 feet, planning to enjoy her bird's-eye view, but something went terribly wrong. Unable to deploy her parachute, Murray plummeted earthward. At the precarious height of 700 feet she managed to get her backup chute open, but because she was spinning frantically out of control, the chute lost most of its air volume and quickly deflated.

Joan Murray after her accident

Lucky Landing

Murray slammed into the ground at 80 miles per hour—so hard that the fillings shot out of her teeth. She broke most of the bones in her right side and lost consciousness. Then came a blessing in disguise. Murray had landed on a swarming mound of fire ants.

One to five millimeters long and known for the severity of their sting, these creatures build semipermanent mound-shaped nests with open-air craters. This particular colony was not happy with its uninvited guest. The angry ants stung the severely injured skydiver more than 200 times before emergency paramedics arrived at the scene.

Patient Stuns Her Doctors

The ants might seem to have added insult to injury, but Murray's doctors at Carolinas Medical Center in Charlotte believed the painful stings may have shocked her body into an adrenaline-fueled state that kept her heart beating. One incredulous doctor even scrawled "miracle" on her chart.

Murray's usually trim 115-pound body swelled from her injuries. It was two weeks before she regained consciousness and several more before doctors allowed her to go home to her husband and 19-year-old twin daughters. After more than 20 reconstructive surgeries, including the implanting of a metal rod in her right leg and five stabilizing spikes in her pelvis, plus 17 blood transfusions and countless physical therapy sessions, Murray returned to work in June 2001. And, believe it or not, a year later she was back in a plane, preparing to jump. "Sometimes we take life for granted," Murray said in a 2002 *Today* interview. "I truly have fun putting my shoes on in the morning."

There are more than 280 types of red ants around the world; one species is credited with saving the life of skydiver Joan Murray.

POISONOUS ENEMIES—OR FRIENDS?

Venom that protects animals from predators can sometimes help heal humans.

More than 100,000 animals produce venom. The various combinations of toxic proteins and peptides can be deadly killers, attacking the human nervous system and causing paralysis, cell and tissue collapse, and other deadly symptoms. But the very qualities that make venom so lethal give some medical researchers hope for its use in treating autoimmune diseases, cancer, and chronic pain. Many venom toxins and enzymes target the same molecules that doctors try to pinpoint to treat diseases. Medicines for diabetes and heart disease have already been developed from natural poisons.

LUCKY TO BE ALIVE

Skydiving is one of our riskier pastimes, but these lucky individuals survived horrific falls.

Craig Stapleton, an experienced skydiver from Lodi, California, was performing a complex partner flag stunt in March 2013 when his parachute jammed. The 51-year-old's backup chute got tangled, too, and he fell 8,000 feet, at a speed of 30 miles an hour, into patch of soft soil. Stapleton's incredulous partner found him on the ground, talking and untangling his gear, with only a few bruises and a dislocated shoulder.

In December 2013, **Victor Bryie**, 27, of Winter Haven, Florida, spiraled 9,000 feet to the ground when his chute became tangled in a friend's during an aerial stunt. While the friend, Shaun Phillips, was able to free himself and deploy his chute at 3,000 feet, Bryie spun horizontally, then hit the ground with a half-open chute. He suffered multiple broken bones and head trauma. He was airlifted to a nearby hospital in serious but stable condition.

Makenzie Wethington, 16, of Joshua, Texas, survived a 3,500-foot fall into an Oklahoma cow pasture after her parachute jammed during a January 2014 birthday-gift skydive. Wethington broke her back, fractured ribs and hips, and suffered liver and mild brain damage. Three weeks later, she walked 150 feet with assistance, and doctors expected her to make a full recovery. "I don't know if I can explain it," her physician Seema Sikka said.

Jaws of Death

ANIMAL HANDLER AND ENTERTAINER ROY HORN RECOVERED AFTER ONE OF HIS TIGERS TURNED ON HIM. BUT THE TRUE MIRACLE, HORN SAID, WAS THE BOND HE AND THE BIG CAT SHARED.

Siegfried Fischbacher with his sister Schwester Dolore and the tiger Montecore

Ten years after a white tiger nearly killed Roy Horn in front of a packed Las Vegas audience, Horn and his performing partner, Siegfried Fischbacher—better known as the legendary illusionist duo Siegfried & Roy—wanted to make one thing clear. Despite what news reports said at the time, the tiger had not deliberately mauled his trainer. "He never attacked me," Horn told the *Las Vegas Weekly* in 2013. "If a tiger attacks you, you are finished."

Horn certainly seemed done for on October 3, 2003, when things went awry at a sold-out performance of Siegfried & Roy's long-running show at the Mirage Hotel. The artists were famous not only for their spectacular feats of illusion but also for incorporating beautiful white lions and white tigers into their act. On that night, Horn was working with Montecore, a 380-pound, seven-year-old male he had known since birth. Horn had actually saved the struggling cub's life, giving the newborn Montecore mouth-to-muzzle resuscitation and warming him inside his shirt.

Eye of the Tiger

Horn and Fischbacher believe that on the night of the injury, Montecore was actually being protective. As the tiger and Horn went through their paces, Horn stumbled and lost his balance. The tiger clamped his teeth around Horn's neck and pulled him offstage, a gesture the men insist was meant to be benevolent.

The result, however, was catastrophic. Several days after the accident, Horn, 59, lay in critical condition at the University Medical Center in Las Vegas, having suffered not only severe injuries but also, doctors discovered, a stroke—possibly the cause of his onstage stumble. He went into cardiac arrest three times during the first night. He'd lost significant blood; doctors had removed part of his skull to relieve pressure on his brain; and even when he was out of critical condition, he remained paralyzed on one side and unable to speak or eat. He was told he would never walk again. Siegfried & Roy's show closed for good.

But by December 2003, Horn had improved enough to return home, and over the next several years he worked to overcome his brain injuries and much of his physical trauma. He learned to walk again and by 2013 was living a relatively full life, still fighting bouts of pain but happy to be alive. "I am very grateful every day," he said, "for every breath I am taking."

Siegfried Fischbacher (left) and Roy Horn (right) with their tigers.

WHAT HAPPENED TO MONTECORE?

The tiger responsible for Roy Horn's injuries got a reprieve, thanks to the owners who loved him.

"Make sure no harm comes to Montecore," Roy Horn insisted as he was transported to the hospital the night of his accident, and he meant it. The tiger was quarantined for 10 days and checked out for any signs of illness or other problems. When he passed all of the tests, he was returned to Siegfried & Roy's Secret Garden and Dolphin Habitat, a permanent zoo exhibit at the Mirage Hotel & Casino in Las Vegas. For the next decade, Montecore divided his time between the Secret Garden and his owners' 100-acre Vegas estate, Little Bavaria, along with their menagerie of other big cats. In March 2014, Montecore died at age 17.

"The flags at Little Bavaria are flying at half-mast," Horn wrote on Siegfried & Roy's Facebook page. "Farewell my dear friend . . . know that your image is forever burned into my heart."

The entrance to Siegfried & Roy's Secret Garden and Dolphin Habitat, the Mirage Hotel, Las Vegas, Nevada

Antoine Yates raised a tiger in a New York City apartment.

NEXT TIME, CONSIDER A GOLDFISH

Note of caution: keeping any kind of wild animal can be dangerous and is often illegal.

→ **Ming the tiger.** When New Yorker Antoine Yates showed up at a hospital in 2003 with a very large bite on his leg, officials were suspicious and sent police to Yates's apartment to investigate. There they not only found Ming—a two-year-old tiger Yates had bottle-raised from infancy—but also a full-grown alligator named Al. The animals were relocated to sanctuaries, and Yates served six months in prison for keeping dangerous animals in the city.

→ **The animals of Zanesville, Ohio.** In October 2011, a suicidal man released most of the 56 exotic animals that he and his estranged wife had kept on their property, including lions, leopards, wolves, and bears. A few were caught and sent to the Columbus Zoo, but police had to hunt down and kill 48, while the rest perished in traffic and other accidents.

Man Bites Snake

IN A STRUGGLE WITH A MARAUDING PREDATOR, SOMETIMES THE ONLY ALTERNATIVE IS TO USE YOUR TEETH.

Pythons aren't any fonder of people than most people are of them. The powerful constrictors, who kill their prey by squeezing, tend not to attack humans unless provoked.

That's exactly what Ben Nyaumbe did—accidentally—one evening in 2009. "I stepped on a spongy thing on the ground," the manager of a farm in the Malindi district of Kenya later told the BBC. The object turned out to be a 13-foot snake on the hunt for livestock. Angry at being disturbed, the constrictor coiled itself around Nyaumbe's leg, then worked its way up to his left arm and twisted around it, too. With all of the farm workers gone for the day, Nyaumbe had no one to call for help. Instead, he grabbed for the trunk of a nearby tree and hung on. Then, struggling, with one hand entangled by the snake and one holding the tree, he fought with the only weapon he had: His teeth. As the snake "waggled its ragged and scary tail on my mouth," he said, "I had to bite it."

The python kept its grip, and Nyaumbe continued to hold on to the tree trunk for about an hour, until he lost his strength and let go. After the snake dragged the farm manager up another tree, it rested for a moment, allowing Nyaumbe to retrieve his cell phone from his pocket and call his boss, who soon arrived with two police officers.

Rescuers With a Rope

But even then, the fight wasn't over. The police couldn't shoot the snake because they were afraid they'd hit Nyaumbe. Instead, Nyaumbe was able to tear off his shirt and cover the python's head with it. The rescuers then tossed him a rope, which he tied around the snake's body. As the men on the ground tugged, the snake wound itself around the branch, finally releasing Nyaumbe, who fell to the ground, followed, at last, by the enormous snake.

The officers were able to wrangle the reptile into the back of a pickup and drive it to a nearby animal sanctuary. The following day, the python was gone. Police spent two days searching for the wily snake, to no avail.

"How does a snake escape from a closed room?" Nyaumbe asked later. "How did it remove the rope from around its neck and my shirt which I had wrapped around its head?" That may be the real miracle.

WHO KNEW?

The world's longest snake in captivity is a reticulated python named Medusa who is 25 feet 2 inches long, according to the *Guinness Book of World Records*.

Many pythons live near the equator, where they can stay warm.

PREYING ON PETS

Humans aren't the only ones who have suffered predator attacks and made it through.

PREDATOR	VICTIM	THE ATTACK	THE RESULT
White monocled cobra, Thousand Oaks, California, 2014	Teko, a whippet	The venomous cobra, thought to have escaped from an exotic-pet owner, bit Teko, then slithered away.	Teko was rushed to the vet and survived. After days on the loose in the suburban neighborhood, the snake was captured.
Seven-foot alligator, Lake County, Florida, 2012	Bounce, a West Highland Terrier	As Bounce neared a pond by his owner's yard, the gator grabbed his collar and dragged him into the water.	Bounce's owner, a retired grandfather, leapt onto the gator's back and safely freed the dog. Both man and dog were fine.
Pack of wolves, Fort Richardson, Alaska, 2007	Buddy, a bulldog	About eight wolves descended on a group of women and dogs during a morning jog; one bit Buddy as he tried to fight off the pack.	Buddy's owner repelled the wolf with pepper spray while the other women yelled. They kept the pack at bay for almost a mile. Buddy got stitches and survived.

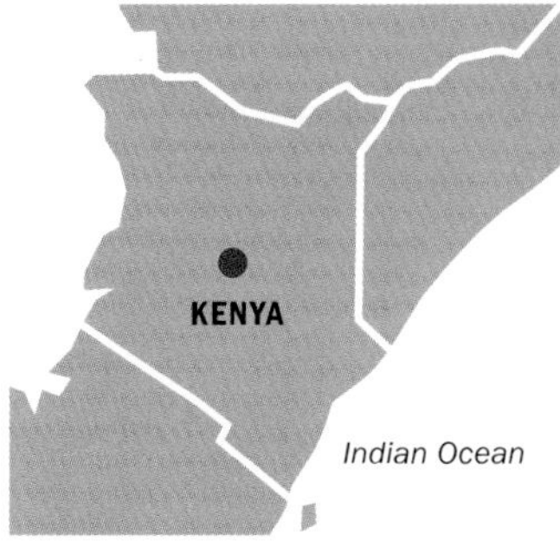

SNAKES OF KENYA

Kenya is home to at least a half dozen species of deadly snakes. Ben Nyaumbe was fortunate that he was not attacked by one of the venomous species.

→ **African rock python** This deadly serpent is the largest snake in Africa and third largest in the world but is not venomous.

→ **Puff adder** This snake causes the highest number of snakebite deaths in Kenya.

→ **Black mamba** The longest snake in Africa is also the fastest and most venomous land snake in the world. It is highly aggressive when cornered.

→ **Cobra** Kenya is home to four species of cobra, the black-nest spitting cobra, the red spitting cobra, the forest cobra, and the Egyptian cobra.

→ **Boomslang** The venom of this shy and nonaggressive tree snake contains a deadly hemotoxin that prevents blood from clotting.

→ **Green mamba** The highly poisonous venom of this tree snake is a neurotoxin affecting the brain and nervous system.

Doctor Dog

A GROWING BODY OF RESEARCH SUGGESTS THAT DOGS CAN DETECT LIFE-THREATENING CANCERS IN HUMANS.

WHO KNEW?
Dog noses have hundreds of millions of odor-receptor cells; human noses have a relatively paltry five million.

Claire Guest believes that a Labrador retriever named Daisy saved her life. In 2009, Guest, an animal behavioral psychologist who trains medical-assistance and cancer-detecting dogs in the United Kingdom, was taking her own pets out for an evening walk. When Daisy kept bumping up against Guest and pawing aggressively at her chest, Guest suspected something was wrong: The spot was sore, and she could feel something underneath.

A mammogram revealed that the lump was benign. But it also showed something else: a small, very deep malignancy that Guest, 46, likely would not have been able to detect herself so soon. "The specialist told me that by the time a lump had become noticeable, this cancer would already have spread and my prognosis could have been very different," Guest said in 2014. Since then, her savior, Daisy, has participated in studies of dogs' ability to detect cancer, successfully identifying more than 550 instances of malignancies by sniffing 6,000 urine samples.

PLEASE DON'T PET

Who wouldn't want to cuddle and praise a stranger's service dog? Here's why it's important to resist the urge.

Americans love dogs—particularly the super-intelligent, noble, and meticulously trained ones who assist people with disabilities. Service animals can perform such impressive duties as pulling a wheelchair, bringing medicine or other items to their owners, or detecting diabetic conditions or allergens. It's only natural to want to pet these dogs, feed them treats, and otherwise love them. But it's kinder to the dog—and more respectful to the owner—not to. Although a service dog is trained to ignore distractions, he's still a dog, after all. If something else commands his attention, he may not perform his job properly. So, before interacting in any way with a service dog, ask his human for permission, and never be offended if the owner declines: It's nothing personal.

Doggedly Determined

Dogs have long been known for their health care talents. They assist people with physical, mental, and emotional disabilities and are a common sight in many hospitals, where specially trained therapy canines make the rounds comforting patients. But in the early 2000s, researchers began to suspect that man's best friend had the potential to diagnose various diseases. Dogs, they realized, can sniff out particular

Claire Guest (right) poses with a policewoman and Copper, a nine-week-old cocker spaniel who was being trained to detect cancer in humans.

odors in the human body that indicate the presence of certain malignancies.

In 2014, researchers in Italy trained two female German shepherds—both former bomb-sniffing dogs—to recognize compounds present in the urine of men with prostate cancer. Once trained, one of the shepherds was able to detect the presence of the compound in new samples more than 98 percent of the time. The other was 100 percent accurate. In a study conducted at the University of Florida in 2004, canines were trained to accurately sniff for melanoma and even detect precancerous conditions. In yet another study, dogs learned to accurately detect the presence of lung cancer by sniffing the breath of patients.

Daisy the Labrador has reached a diagnostic accuracy of 93 percent.

Though shepherds and retrievers are unlikely to replace cancer-screening technologies wholesale, they could be used to supplement more traditional and invasive diagnostic tools. At times, the dogs have even proved smarter than their human handlers. In one study of urine samples, a dog's insistent response to a supposedly healthy control patient led to a surprise early diagnosis of liver cancer.

Oscar the cat was featured in the *New England Journal of Medicine*.

KITTY CORNER

Canines aren't the only ones with amazing powers of detection and communication.

→ A stray cat named Oscar, adopted by the Steere House Nursing and Rehabilitation Center in Providence, Rhode Island, starred in a 2007 article in the *New England Journal of Medicine*. When a resident was dying, Oscar seemed to know; he would curl up next to the patient or keep vigil at his or her doorway.

→ Wendy Humphreys of Wroughton, England, found it odd that her newly adopted kitten, Fidge, sat on her right breast every night as she lay on the couch. A scan revealed what Fidge seemed to have suspected: Humphreys had breast cancer. "She saved my life, definitely," Humphreys said in 2012.

→ In 2014, a sleeping Australian man awoke to his tabby, Sally, behaving badly. "She jumped on my head and was screaming at me," Craig Jeeves, 49, told a local television station. For good reason: Jeeves's house was on fire. Man and cat both escaped safely.

Go Get Them

IN THE AFTERMATH OF A SNOWMOBILE ACCIDENT, A FAITHFUL GOLDEN RETRIEVER SAVES HER SEVERELY INJURED MASTER.

On March 2, 2014, 52-year-old Otis Orth was driving his snowmobile along an icy road from Trapper Creek, Alaska, to buy supplies in town. Riding along was his 15-month-old golden retriever, Amber.

Suddenly, the vehicle hit a hollow snowdrift and both Orth and Amber went flying over the handlebars. Orth slid for about 40 feet. "Amber came running over to me. I couldn't move, but I could talk to her, and she was licking my face," he later said. His face was bleeding, he was unable to move his arms or legs, and his shoulders had dislocated. As it grew dark, the dog lay by Orth's side with her head across his stomach, her warmth helping the snowmobiler survive through the night as temperatures dipped well below freezing. When Orth woke up still unable to move, he feared both wildlife and the cold and wondered how long he would make it. Ravens hovered above, kept at bay only by Amber's barking. After a few more agonizing hours, Orth was relieved to hear snowmobiles approaching. "I told her, 'Go get them,'" Orth said.

Barking for Help

Tom Taylor, 68, of Trapper Creek, and his brother Maynard were snowmobiling in the area after a weekend trip to their nearby cabin. When they passed Orth's vehicle, just off the main trail, they figured its driver was somewhere nearby. That's when Amber appeared, barking. When the Taylors sped up, Amber ran faster

ROAD HOG

When one woman needed life-saving assistance, her pet pig waddled into action.

On August 4, 1998, JoAnn Altsman was vacationing in a mobile home in the woods of Presque Isle, Pennsylvania, with her dog, Bear, and Lulu, a housebroken 150-pound Vietnamese pot-bellied pig.

Suddenly, Altsman collapsed. She was having a heart attack. The 61-year-old tried desperately to alert someone by breaking a window. Bear began barking agitatedly as Altsman yelled for help. But it was Lulu who saved the day. The pig, who had never before ventured beyond the yard unleashed, barreled through the mobile home's pet door. She pushed the gate open and headed toward a nearby highway.

Shocked witnesses said the pig lumbered calmly onto the road and lay down in the path of approaching vehicles. Rattled drivers began swerving and beeping. The determined pig kept trying to get someone's attention, periodically trudging back to check on Altsman, then returning to the highway. After about 45 minutes, a young motorist stopped and followed Lulu to the mobile home, where Altsman lay in pain.

When the ambulance arrived, Lulu tried to climb into the back with Altsman and the paramedics. Other than cutting her large belly on the edge of the pet door, the pig was uninjured. For saving her life, Altsman gave Lulu her favorite treat: a jelly doughnut.

JoAnn Altsman and her heroic pig, Lulu

Amber, the golden retriever who saved her master Otis Orth, poses with Alaska state trooper Lucas Hegg.

and kept barking. When Tom looked back, he saw that Amber had returned to the snowmobile. Sensing something amiss, the brothers followed Amber and discovered a severely frostbitten Orth.

The Taylors helped keep Orth warm until a medical helicopter arrived. When one of the brothers tried to move the now-leashed Amber away from the chopper's landing area, the dog refused to be separated from Orth, who was soon airlifted to an Anchorage hospital. Later in the week, lying in his hospital bed with his neck in a brace, Orth waited for spinal surgery. "[Amber] never left me for more than 20 yards that whole time," the snowmobiler told reporters.

LIFESAVERS WITH TRUNKS, TAILS, AND FINS

In dangerous situations, all manner of creatures have been known to come to the rescue.

Phuket Beach, Thailand, was crowded with vacationers when a deadly tsunami rolled ashore in December 2004.

Dolphins saved Todd Endris from a shark attack.

➔ **Amber Mason**, eight, of Milton Keynes, Buckinghamshire, England, was vacationing with her family in Phuket, Thailand, on December 26, 2004. As she rode Ningnong, a four-year-old elephant, a deadly tsunami wave swept through the island. Amid the rushing waters, Ningnong lumbered toward higher ground, carrying Amber to safety. The grateful family now contributes to Ningnong's upkeep.

➔ **Fiona Boyd** of Castle Douglas, Scotland, was pushing a bellowing stray calf into a shed on her farm in 2007 when the calf's mother attacked her and knocked her down. Boyd, 40, rolled into a ball, terrified that other cows would join the stampede. But Kerry, her 15-year-old horse, took control, charging at the cow and scaring her away.

➔ **Todd Endris** was surfing with friends near Monterey, California, in 2007 when a great white shark attacked, mauling his right leg and tearing the skin off his back. A nearby pod of bottlenose dolphins swam over to the 24-year-old, encircling him protectively and blocking the shark long enough for Endris to ride a wave to shore.

➔ In July 2009, diver **Yang Yun**, 26, was in a competition at Polar Land, an amusement park in Harbin, China. The object was to stay submerged as long as possible, without breathing equipment, amid beluga whales in a 20-foot-deep arctic pool. Suddenly crippled by leg cramps, Yun began to drown, when "I felt this incredible force under me," she later said. Mila, a beluga, had taken Yun's ankle gently in her mouth and lifted her to the surface, saving her life.

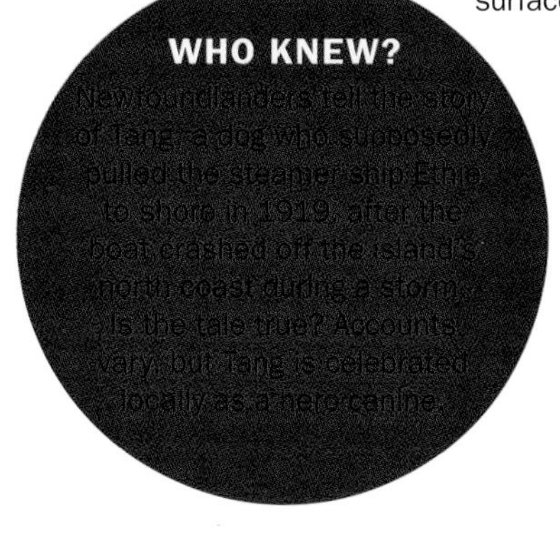

index

Page numbers in *italic* refer to photos or illustrations.

C

E

F

G

H

I

J

K

L

N

O

P

photo credits

front cover, (cover), © luckypig/ Alamy
front cover, (far left inset), iStockphotos.com
front cover, (2nd from left inset), Mondadori Portfolio/Getty images
front cover, (middle inset), © Scott Stulberg/Corbis
front cover, (far right inset), © George Atsametakis / Alamy
1, (inside front cover), Derek R. Audette/Shutterstock
2, TOC, (top left), © Corbis
2, TOC, (top, 2nd from left), Bridgeman Art Library/Getty Images
2, TOC, (top, 3rd from left), DeAgostini/Getty Images
2, TOC, (2nd row, far left), Fine Art Images/Heritage Images/Getty Images
2, TOC, (2nd row, 2nd from left), © Alinari Archives/CORBIS
2, TOC, (2nd row, 3rd from left), Lonely Planet Images/Getty Images
2, TOC, (3rd row, far left), Library of Congress
2, TOC, (3rd row, 2nd from left), istockphoto.com
2, TOC, (3rd row, 3rd from left), istockphoto.com
2, TOC, (4th row, far left), © Uwe Moser Moser / Alamy
2, TOC, (4th row, 2nd from left), AP Photo/Harry Koundakjian
2, TOC, (4th row, 3rd from left), © Neil Emmerson/Robert Harding World Imagery/Corbis
3, TOC, (top, far right), © Corbis
3, TOC, (2nd row, far right), © BOBBY YIP/Reuters/Corbis
3, TOC, (3rd row, far right), © Scott Stulberg/Corbis
3, TOC, (4th row, far right), © David A. Northcott/Corbis
4, (left), Mauro Cociglio/Getty Images
6-7, De Agostini Picture Library/ Getty images
8-9, © Corbis
10-11, © The Gallery Collection/ Corbis
12, (top), © The Gallery Collection/ Corbis
13, (bottom), © Chronicle / Alamy
13, (top right), Getty Images
14-15, © Stefano Bianchetti/Corbis
16, (middle), © Corbis
17, (middle), © Mary Evans Picture Library / Alamy
17, (top right), © PRISMA ARCHIVO / Alamy
19, (left), Bridgeman Art Library/ Getty Images
19, (top right), © Bettmann/ CORBIS
20-21, Getty Images
22-23, (middle), Hulton Archive/ Getty Images
24-25, (top), © Fine Art Photographic Library/CORBIS
25, (top right), Andrey Nekrasov/ Getty Images
25, (bottom), © Lebrecht Music and Arts Photo Library / Alamy
26-27, Musee des Beaux-Arts, Nimes, France/Getty Images
27, (right), © Alinari Archives/ CORBIS
29, (middle), © World History Archive / Alamy
29, (top right), © B.A.E. Inc. / Alamy
30, (bottom), © Historical Picture Archive/CORBIS
31, (middle), DEA / G. DAGLI ORTI / Contributor/Getty Images
31, (top right), © Stapleton Collection/Corbis
32, (left), istockphoto.com
33, (middle), Ann Ronan Pictures/ Print Collector/Getty Images
34, (bottom), © Burstein Collection/CORBIS
35, (middle), Louis Hersent/Getty Images
35, (top right), © World History Archive / Alamy
36, (left), © Eddie Gerald / Alamy
37, (middle), © Mary Evans Picture Library / Alamy
37, (top right), © Judith Collins / Alamy
38-39, DeAgostini/Getty Images
40, (left), © Reproduced by permission of The State Hermitage Museum, St. Petersburg, Russia/CORBIS
41, (left), Godong/Universal Images Group via Getty Images
41, (top right), Ann Ronan Pictures/ Print Collector/Getty Images
42, (left), © Reynold Mainse/ Design Pics/Corbis
43, (top), SuperStock/Getty Images
45, (left), © Chronicle / Alamy
45, (top right), istockphoto.com
46, (left), © Brooklyn Museum/ Corbis
47, (left), Prisma/UIG via Getty Images
47, (top right), Fine Art Images/ Heritage Images/Getty Images
48-49, © Corbis
50-51, © jozef sedmak / Alamy
52, © jozef sedmak / Alamy
53, (bottom), Sergio Anelli/Electa/ Mondadori Portfolio via Getty Images
53, (top right), Mondadori Portfolio/ Getty Images
54, (left), © Godong / Alamy
55, (left), © Stan Pritchard / Alamy
55, (top right), Getty Images
57, Bridgeman Art Library/Getty Images
58-59, (left), © PRISMA ARCHIVO / Alamy
59, (top right), © Thomas Nebbia/ National Geographic Society/ Corbis
60, (left), Arkady Mazor/ Shutterstock.com
61, Leemage/UIG via Getty Images
62, (left), © North Carolina Museum of Art/CORBIS
62, (lower right), © Mary Evans Picture Library / Alamy
63, (top), SuperStock/Getty Images
63, (bottom), Ann Ronan Pictures/ Print Collector/Getty Images
64, (bottom), Hulton Archive/Getty Images
65, DeAgostini/Getty Images
66-67, © The Print Collector / Alamy
68, (top left), © Bettmann/CORBIS
68, (right), © PAINTING / Alamy
69, © jozef sedmak / Alamy
70-71, Fine Art Images/Heritage Images/Getty Images
73, © jozef sedmak / Alamy
74, (top left), Susana Gonzalez/ Getty Images
74, (bottom right), LUIS ACOSTA/ AFP/Getty Images
75, Independent Picture Service/ UIG via Getty Images)
76, Robert Harding World Imagery/ Getty Images
77, Wikipedia, Creative Commons Share-Alike
78, Three Lions/Getty Images
79, © INTERFOTO / Alamy
81, Wikipedia, Creative Commons Share-Alike
82, (bottom), myLoupe/Universal Images Group via Getty Images
83, Keystone-France/Gamma-Keystone via Getty Images
85, © ILYA NAYMUSHIN/Reuters/ Corbis
87, (left), AP Photo/George Constantinou
87, (top right), Ap Photo/Gianpiero Sposito
88-89, © Alinari Archives/CORBIS
90-91, Imagno/Getty Images
92, DeAgostini/Getty Images)
93, (left), AP Photo/Massimo Sambucetti
93, (top right), © Eddie Gerald / Alamy
94, (left), © age fotostock Spain, S.L. / Alamy
95, (left), © Art Directors & TRIP / Alamy
95, (top right), © Ted Foxx / Alamy
96, © Beth Wald/National Geographic Society/Corbis
97, (left), © Brian Overcast / Alamy
97, (top right), © Ted Soqui/Ted Soqui Photography/Corbis
98, (far left), © Mary Evans Picture Library / Alamy
98, (top), © Niday Picture Library / Alamy

98, (middle), Renata Sedmakova/ Shutterstock.com
98, (bottom, middle), © INTERFOTO / Alamy
98, (top, right), Hulton Archive/ Getty Images
98, (bottom right), © imageBRO-KER / Alamy
99, (top left), Fine Art Images/ Heritage Images/Getty Images
99, (bottom left), © Holmes Garden Photos / Alamy
99, (top middle), istockphoto.com
99, (middle), © Peter Horree / Alamy
99, (bottom, middle), © Art Directors & TRIP / Alamy
99, (top right), © PRISMA ARCHIVO / Alamy
99, (bottom right), © Hemis / Alamy
100, MPI/Getty Images
101, (left), © LUCAS JACKSON/ Reuters/Corbis
101, (top right), © Richard Maschmeyer/Robert Harding World Imagery/Corbis
102, (left), William Thomas Cain/ Newsmakers/Getty Images
103, (left), AP Photo
103, (bottom), © Vittoriano Rastelli/CORBIS
103, (top, right), © Folio / Alamy
103, (middle), AP photo/Sisters of St. Francis of the Neumann Communities
103, (bottom), © Bettmann/ CORBIS
104, Paolo Da Re/Electa/ Mondadori Portfolio via Getty Images
105, (top left), Mondadori Portfolio via Getty Images
105, (middle left), Ann Ronan Pictures/Print Collector/Getty Images
105, (bottom left), Prisma/UIG via Getty Images
105, (top right), DeAgostini/Getty Images
105, (middle right), Leemage/UIG via Getty Images
105, (bottom right), © Historic Collection / Alamy
106, Universal History Archive/UIG via Getty images
106-07, (left), © Bettmann/CORBIS
107, (bottom), © CORBIS
107, (top right), © Bettmann/ CORBIS
108, Courtesy of the Eastern American and New York Diocese of the Russian Orthodox Church
110, Creative Commons Share-Alike
111, (bottom), John Saniidopoulos
111, (top right), PETER PARKS/AFP/ Getty Images
112-13, Lonely Planet Images/ Getty Images
114-15, © BRIAN HARRIS / Alamy
117, (left), GraphicaArtis/Getty Images
117, (top right), Lonely Planet Images/Getty Images
118, © Everett Collection / Alamy
119, AP Photo
120, Leonard McCombe/The LIFE Picture Collection/Getty Images
121, (left), © Science Photo Library/Corbis
121, (top right), © Bettmann/ CORBIS
123, (left), Courtesy of Bruce Leininger
123, (bottom), National Archives and Record Administration
123, (top right), Courtesy of University of Virginia Public Affairs
124, (bottom), Joe Nickell, Ghost Adeventures Press Photos
124-25, (top), Courtesy of The Travel Channel
126-27, © BOBBY YIP/Reuters/ Corbis
128, Ann Ronan Pictures/Print Collector/Getty Images
129, (left), © Tim Draper/SOPA RF/4Corners Images/SOPA/ Corbis
129, (top right), © Godong/Robert Harding World Imagery/Corbis
130, Dayna Smith for the Washington Post/Getty Images
131, (top right), Godong/Universal Images Group via Getty Images
131, (left), © Money Sharma/epa/ Corbis
132, Sonu Mehta/Hindustan Times via Getty Images
133, © Atlantide Phototravel/ Corbis
134-35, Library of Congress
136, Library of Congress
137, (left), © Everett Collection Historical / Alamy
137, (top right), © Everett Collection Inc / Alamy
138, © Kirn Vintage Stock/Corbis
139, (top), Walter Bellamy/ Express/Getty Images
139, (bottom), Library of Congress
140, APIC/Getty Images
141, (top), © Everett Collection Historical / Alamy
141, (bottom), AP Photo
141, (top right), AP Photo/Jacques Brinon
142-43, © Design Pics Inc. / Alamy
144-45, iStockphotos.com
146, iStockphotos.com
148, (left), © Louie Psihoyos/ CORBIS
148, (right), © Paul Liebhardt/ Corbis
149, Hung Chung Chih/ Shutterstock
150, (left), iStockphoto.com
150, (middle), iStockphoto.com
150, (right), Shutterstock.com
151, AP Photo/Albany Democrat-Herald, Jesse Skoubo
152, (top left), Courtesy of Kelly Turner
152, (top), © D. Chan /Demotix/ Demotix/Corbis
152, (middle), © Frank Trapper/ Corbis
152, (bottom), Kevin Winter/Getty Images
153, (left), iStockphotos.com
153, (top right), Richard Cummins/ Lonely Planet/Getty Images
154-55, (middle), Amy T. Zielinski/ Redferns via Getty Images
155, (top right), © Blue Jean Images/Corbis
157, (left), © STEFANO RELLANDINI/Reuters/Corbis
157, (top right), © RADEK PIETRUSZKA/epa/Corbis
158, University of South Carolina
159, (top left), © Roger Ressmeyer/ CORBIS
159, (top right), Scisetti Alfio / Shutterstock.com
159, (middle), draconus / Shutterstock.com
159, (bottom), Elena Elisseeva / Shutterstock.com
160, © John Spellman/Retna Ltd./ Corbis
161, (left), © Aaron Rapoport/ Corbis
161, (top right), © Bloomsbury Photo inc. / Alamy
163, (bottom), © James Leynse/ Corbis
163, (top right), Worldwide Features / Barcroft Media / Getty Images
163, (left), istockphoto.com
165, (left), Drew Hinshaw, Wall Street Journal
165, (top right), Jessica McGowan/ Getty Images
165, (bottom), © CORBIS
166-67, istockphoto.com
168, (left), © Angela Hampton Picture Library / Alamy
169, (top), Derek R. Audette/ Shutterstock.com
169, (top right), Petrenko Andriy/ Shutterstock.com
170, Mitch Bear/Newspix/Getty Images
171, (left), © Ted Horowitz/Corbis
171, (top right), Keystone-France/ Gamma-Keystone via Getty Images
173, (top left), The 700 Club, Christian Broadcast Network
173, (bottom), istockphoto.com
173, (top right), AP Photo/Loyola University Health System, HO
174-75, © Scott Stulberg/Corbis
176, AP Photo/National Science Foundation, File
178, (top left), Library of Congress
178, (bottom), AP Photo/NOAA, Joel Michalski
179, AP Photo/USAF
179, (bottom), AP Photo/Denver Police
180, Adam du Plooy
181, (left), Stone/Getty Images
181, (top right), AP Photo/The Deseret News,Sam Penrod
182, AFP/Getty Images
183, (left), Samuel D. Barricklow/ Getty Images
183, (top right), istockphoto.com
184-85, © Uwe Moser Moser / Alamy
186, Library of Congress
187, © Bettmann/CORBIS
188, (left), Wikipedia, Creative Commons Share-Alike
188, (right), Library of Congress
189, (top), © Underwood & Underwood/CORBIS
190, Merchant Navy Archives
191, (top left), AP Photo
191, (bottom), AP Photo
191, (top right), istockphoto.com
192, istockphoto.com
193, (top), Planet Observer/ Universal Images Group via Getty Images
193, (top right), © TWO ARTS LTD / Ronald Grant Archive / Alamy
193, (bottom), © Photos 12 / Alamy
194, istockphoto.com
194-95, (top), © Steele/ A-Frame/ ZUMAPRESS. Com
195, (top right), iStockphoto.com
195, (bottom), © ZUMA Press, Inc. / Alamy
197, (top), GIFF JOHNSON/AFP/ Getty Images
197, (bottom), STR/AFP/Getty Images
198, (left), © Lekan Oyekanmi/AP/ Corbis
199, (top), © Logan Mock-Bunting/ Corbis
199, (left), Heather Barnes
199, (middle), Brett Archibald
199, (bottom), AP Photo/Richard Drew
200-01, (top left), AP Photo/US Coast Guard, Ross Ruddell
201, (bottom), © Frank Eltman/ / AP/Corbis
201, (bottom), AP Photo/Daytona Beach News-Journal, Peter Bauer
202-03, AP Photo/Harry Koundakjian
204, Courtesy of The Columbian
205, (top), © Steve Terrill/Corbis
205, (top left), Alex Fortier, The State Press
207, (left), Photo Researchers/ Getty Images

207, (top right), Craig F. Walker/The Denver Post via Getty Images
208, © JIM BOURG/Reuters/Corbis
209, BOB DAEMMERICH/AFP/Getty Images)
210, (left), AP Photo/The Oklahoman, Bill Waugh
210, (right), AP Photo/The Oklahoman, Steve Sisney
211, (bottom), Steve Liss/The LIFE Images Collection/Getty Images
211, (top right), AP Photo/J. Pat Carter
212, Spencer Platt/Getty Images
213, Todd Plitt
214, (top left), Todd Maisel/NY Daily News via Getty Images
214, (bottom), Creative Commons Share-Alike
216, (left), © HOTLI SIMANJUNTAK/epa/Corbis
216-17, (middle), © BEAWIHARTA/Reuters/Corbis
218, (top left), Carol Guzy/The Washington Post via Getty Images
218, (bottom), Alison Wright/National Geographic/Getty Images
219, (top left), Chip Somodevilla/Getty Images
219, (bottom), © Lannis Waters/ZUMA Press/Corbis
219, (top right), AP Photo/Ramon Espinosa
220-21, MARTIN BERNETTI/AFP/Getty Images
222, Mariana Eliano/Getty Images
223, (left), HUGO INFANTE/AFP/Getty Images
223, (top right), © Bettmann/CORBIS
224, © Rick Westhead/ZUMA Press/Corbis
225, (top left), AP/Photo courtesy of the Land, Infrastructure, Transport and Tourism Ministry's Tohoku Regional Bureau
225, (top right), TORU YAMANAKA/AFP/Getty Images
226, © Zakir Hossain Chowdhury/NurPhoto/NurPhoto/Corbis
227, © Zakir Hossain Chowdhury/NurPhoto/NurPhoto/Corbis
228, © /AP/Corbis
230-31, © Neil Emmerson/Robert Harding World Imagery/Corbis
232, Hallie Ephron
233, (top left), AP Photo
233, (top right), Alison Wright/Getty Images
234, Photo by Franziska Krug/Getty Images
235, (left), AP Photo
235, (top right), © United Archives GmbH / Alamy
236, AP Photo
237, (left), AP Photo
237, (top right), AP Photo
238, AP Photo/The Journal-Gazette, Michelle Davies
239, (left), AP Photo/Petoskey News-Review, Heather Lockwood
239, (right), Kyodo via AP Images
240, Cleburne Times-Review
241, (left), Cleburne Times-Review
241, (top right), Boulder Police Department
241, (bottom), John Blanding/The Boston Globe via Getty Images
242, AP Photo/Sayyid Azim
243, AP Photo/Ed Reinke, File
244, New York Metropolitan Transit Authority
245, (left), © Louis K. Meisel Gallery, Inc./CORBIS
245, (top right), © Paul Matzner / Alamy
246-47, © David A. Northcott/Corbis
248, Famous Things, People and Events
249, (top), Gallo Images/Getty Images
249, (bottom left), Craig Stapleton
249, (middle), Victor Bryie
249, (right), AP Photo/LM Otero
250, Peter Bischoff/Getty Images
251, (top left), Boris Roessler/picture-alliance/dpa/AP Images
251, (bottom left), © Kumar Sriskandan / Alamy
251, (top right), John Roca/NY Daily News Via Getty Images
252-53, © Anup Shah/Corbis
255, (top left), Andrew Milligan/PA Wire URN:7489452/Press Association via AP Images
255, (bottom), © MedicalDetectionDogs/Splash/Splash News/Corbis
255, (top right), AP Photo/Stew Milne
256, Creative Commons Share-Alike
257, (left), AP Photo/Alaska State Troopers
257, (middle), AP Photo / APTN
257, (right), © Monterey County Herald/ ZUMA Press/Alamy
back cover, (top), AP Photo/ Francisco Seco
back cover, (middle), MARTIN BERNETTI/AFP/Getty Images
back cover, (bottom), © Steele/A-Frame/ ZUMAPRESS.com/Alamy

Publisher Margot Schupf
Vice President, Finance Vandana Patel
Executive Director, Marketing Services Carol Pittard
Executive Director, Business Development Suzanne Albert
Executive Director, Marketing Susan Hettleman
Publishing Director Megan Pearlman
Associate Director of Publicity Courtney Greenhalgh
Assistant General Counsel Simone Procas
Assistant Director, Special Sales Ilene Schreider
Assistant Director, Finance Christine Font
Senior Manager, Sales Marketing Danielle Costa
Senior Manager, Category Marketing Bryan Christian
Associate Production Manager Kimberly Marshall
Associate Prepress Manager Alex Voznesenskiy
Associate Project Manager Stephanie Braga

Editorial Director Stephen Koepp
Art Director Gary Stewart
Senior Editors Roe D'Angelo, Alyssa Smith
Managing Editor Matt DeMazza
Project Editor Eileen Daspin
Copy Chief Rina Bander
Design Manager Anne-Michelle Gallero
Assistant Managing Editor Gina Scauzillo
Editorial Assistant Courtney Mifsud

Special thanks: Allyson Angle, Katherine Barnet, Brad Beatson, Jeremy Biloon, John Champlin, Ian Chin, Susan Chodakiewicz, Rose Cirrincione, Assu Etsubneh, Mariana Evans, Alison Foster, David Kahn, Jean Kennedy, Hillary Leary, Amanda Lipnick, Samantha Long, Amy Mangus, Robert Martells, Nina Mistry, Melissa Presti, Danielle Prielipp, Kate Roncinske, Babette Ross, Dave Rozzelle, Matthew Ryan, Ricardo Santiago, Divyam Shrivastava

Published by Time Home Entertainment Inc.
1271 Avenue of the Americas, 6th floor
New York, NY 10020

ISBN 10: 1-61893-366-3
ISBN 13: 978-1-61893-366-9

We welcome your comments and suggestions about Time-Life Books. Please write to us at:

Time Home Entertainment Books, Attention:
Book Editors, P.O. Box 11016, Des Moines, IA 50336-1016

If you would like to order any of our hardcover Collector's Edition books, please call us at 800-327-6388, Monday through Friday, 7 a.m.–8 p.m., or Saturday, 7 a.m.–6 p.m., Central Time.

Produced by The Stonesong Press, LLC
Project Director Ellen Scordato
Project Editorial Director Laura Ross
Writers Kerry Acker, Walter Bonner, Bree Burns, Jennifer Foley, Tom Gavin, Constance Jones, Lauren Lipton, Nancy Ellen Shore, Jon Sterngass
Photo Researchers Eric Harvey Brown, Aaron Clendening
Designed by Vertigo Design NYC
Art Director Alison Lew
Designers Gary Philo, Lisa Story